No Freedom Shrieker

No Freedom

THE CIVIL WAR LETTERS

OF UNION SOLDIER

CHARLES FREEMAN BIDDLECOM

147TH REGIMENT NEW YORK STATE
VOLUNTEER INFANTRY

TRANSCRIBED AND EDITED BY

Katherine M. Aldridge

Paramount Market Publishing, Inc.

Shrieker

Paramount Market Publishing, Inc.
950 Danby Road, Suite 136
Ithaca, NY 14850
www.paramountbooks.com
Voice: 607-275-8100; 888-787-8100
Fax: 607-275-8101

Publisher: James Madden
Editorial Director: Doris Walsh

Cover: Wounded New York volunteers being tended in the field after the Battle of Chancellorsville, May 2, 1863.
Maps: Hal Jespersen
Family photos: The Nebraska Historical Society

Library of Congress Catalog Number available
Cataloging in Publication Data available
ISBN 10: 0-9830436-7-1 | ISBN 13: 978-0-9830436-7-6 *paperback*
ISBN 10: 0-9830436-9-8 | ISBN 13: 978-0-9830436-9-0 *cloth*

For Charlie

CONTENTS

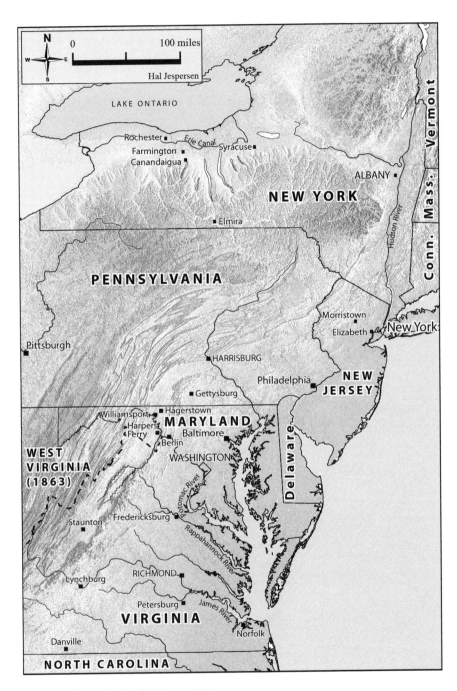

The Northeast United States, 1861

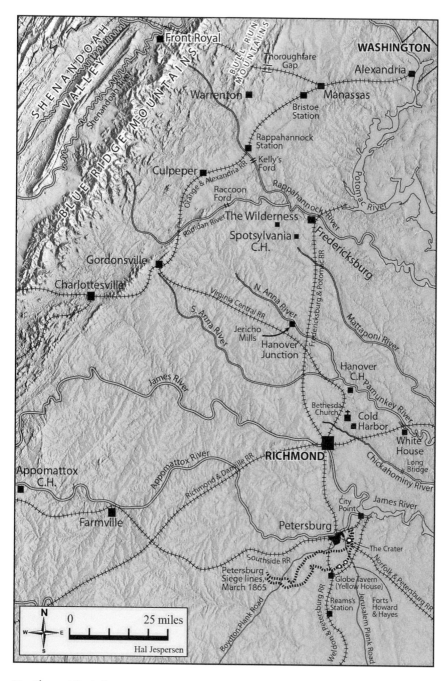

Northern Virginia

BIDDLECOM — LAPHAM FAMILY HISTORY

The following details about Biddlecom and Lapham ancestry were obtained from hand-written records saved by family members. Dates and names were confirmed and relevant details added through various credible sources. The information has been formatted in a fashion similar to the original handwritten records kept by the family for over 100 years.

BIDDLECOM[1]
NON OMNIS MORIAM (I SHALL NOT FULLY DIE)

Thomas Biddlecom 1673–1735. Immigrated to Warwick Neck, Rhode Island, from Devonshire, England. Married Martha Sheldon Matthewson.

Thomas Biddlecom (II) Born in Rhode Island in 1726. First married to Sarah Burlingame (b. 1736 Cranston, R.I.) until her death (1756) and then married her sister, Mary Burlingame (1738–1835). According to a list of men who commenced service during the Revolutionary War dated January 9, 1777, Thomas was a private in Captain Thomas Rice's company of Colonel John Waterman's regiment, and Captain Millard's company and Captain William Clark's company of Colonel Benjamin Symond's regiment. Thomas was captured and held prisoner on an English prison ship at Halifax, Nova Scotia. After the war, Thomas moved from Rhode Island to Adams (Hoosac), Massachusetts. In 1786 Thomas sold 25 acres of land in Hoosac, Massachusetts, and moved to Deerfield, Oneida County, New York. He died in 1813 and was buried in the Old Whitney Cemetery, Utica, New York.

Thomas Biddlecom (III) Born in 1769. Married in 1793 to Sarah Read

(1770–1837). Sarah was the daughter of Daniel Read and Eleanor Southwick. Eleanor was the daughter of Daniel and Ruth Shove. Daniel was the son of Lawrence and Cassandra Southwick who have been memorialized in American history as committed Quakers who were fined, tortured, and imprisoned, their children almost sold into slavery, in Salem, Massachusetts, in 1658 for not adopting the Puritan religious standards. (Read Whittier's poem, *Cassandra Southwick*.) According to the 1790 Census, Thomas lived in Adams, Berkshire, Massachusetts, with his wife and three children (they had nine children in all). In 1786, Thomas sold his 25 acres in Massachusetts and traveled west toward Macedon, New York, in a series of moves across Western New York. He was buried in the Macedon Village Cemetery.

Children: **Joab Stafford**, Otis, Susan, David, Daniel

Joab Stafford Biddlecom Born 1803. Married in 1833 **Olivia Matthewson**

(1808–1885) a descendant of Bostonian (Lincolnshire) immigrants who came in the ship *Lyon* to Boston in 1631. Joab owned a farm in Phelps, New York, with his father and brother before moving to Macedon, New York. There he held the position of Macedon Town Supervisor, grocer, and mill owner. Joab holds an 1870 United States

Patent No.102,649 for an Improvement in a Clapboard Gauge. Died in 1897 and was buried in the Macedon Village Cemetery.

Children: **Charles Freeman,** Sarah (born 1835) married Addison Gates, and **Laura** (born May 15, 1841) married Stephen Bosworth Pound, mother of Roscoe Pound, world famous legal historian and dean of Harvard Law School.

Charles Freeman Biddlecom Born February 5, 1832, in Phelps, New York. Married Esther Aldrich Lapham in 1854. Educated at the Macedon Academy and Clinton Liberal Institute.

Children: Bayard Thomas (1855–1922), Stafford (1856–1872), Isabel (Belle, 1860–1861), Emma B. Sweet (1862–1923) a women's rights activist.

None of Charles and Esther Biddlecom's children bore any descendants, thus leaving this book Charlie's sole legacy.

LAPHAM[2]
AMOR, HONOR ET JUSTITIA

John Lapham Born about 1610 in Tenterden, Kent County, England. Twenty-five years later he is found in Scituate, Massachusetts, married to Mary, daughter of Nathanial Tilden.

John Lapham Born 1635 in North Molton, Devonshire, England. Settled in Providence, Rhode Island. Married Mary Mann (1640–1710). In Rhode Island John was admitted and served as a Freeman, Deputy to the General Court, and Constable. In 1676, after his house was burned by Indians during King Philip's War, John fled to Newport, Rhode Island, and then to Dartmouth, Massachusetts, where he participated in building the town's first Friends Meetinghouse and lived until his death in 1710.

John Lapham Born 1677 in Providence, Rhode Island. In 1700 he married Mary Russell (b. 1683) and moved to Dartmouth, Massachusetts where he died in 1734. Fourteen children.

Joshua Lapham (1722–1799) Married (Hannah) Mary Sherman (February 3, 1747).

Children: Ruth Jinks, Lydia Rogers, **Abraham**, Nathan (Vermont Laphams), Nehemiah (swallowed a watermelon seed and died at four years old), Hannah, (b. 1773) married Humphrey Anthony. Hannah and her husband acquired her father's homestead, the historic site in Adams, Massachusetts, called "The Hive." Their son, Daniel Anthony, was the father of Woman's Suffrage activist Susan B. Anthony.

Abraham Lapham (1755–1836) Born in Smithfield, Rhode Island. With his first wife, Esther Aldrich (1756–1822), moved to East Hoosac, Massachusetts, and finally settled in Macedon, New York, in 1789. Abraham's brother Asa married Esther's sister, Hannah Aldrich. Later, Asa and Esther both died and Abraham married Hannah, his sister-in-law. Consequently, he was turned out of the Farmington Quaker meeting.

Children: Deborah, Ira, David, Abraham, **Daniel**, Stephen, Lydia, John, Esther, William Savery.

Daniel Lapham (1784–1842) married Martha Jane Gage. Dismissed from the Society of Friends, i.e., the Quaker Congregation, in 1775 by Thomas Lapham and George Comstock of East Hoosac because he did not marry of the same order.

Children: **Esther**, Cornelia Scott (1830–1874), Daniel (1832–a ripe old age) David Mortimer 1834–1867, Stephen (1839–1866), Mary Anne (1836–1855).

Esther Aldrich Lapham (1827–1904) Born in Farmington, New York. Educated at Macedon Academy and taught at that school for thirteen terms. Married in 1854 Charles Freeman Biddlecom.

Children: Bayard Thomas (1855–1922), Stafford (1856–1872), Isabel (Belle, 1860–1861), Emma B. Sweet (1862–1923) a women's rights activist.

NOTES

1. Biddlecom is a corruption of the English spelling Biddlecombe.

2. Lapham: "hearthstone" from *lapis* (stone) and *helm* (home).

CHAPTER I

WRITING CHARLIE

N EARLY a century and a half of accumulated clutter, dust, and debris was left behind in five historic barns—under piles of straw, behind stairwells, at the bottom of grain bins—when Wixom Farm was sold for the first time. Shortly before the deed was signed over to me, the owners held an auction and thinned out the collectables that had been acquired by the five generations of relatives who considered the farm partly their own. Distant cousins and neighbors arrived to snatch up the most valuable antiques and still-useful tools, but left behind most of the everyday items that had long been retired from duty. Among the disorder of unwanted knick-knacks, broken tools, scraps of wood, and critter nests that I inherited, I discovered a dusty, red, cardboard liquor box. On its lid, scrawled in crayon was written *Cousin Emma's Old Letters.* Working farms accrue fresh clutter as new projects begin, the parts and pieces of finished or failed projects are packed away, shoved into corners, and eventually forgotten. With its sheltered piles of debris tucked into almost every corner, my weathered old farm bore strong evidence of this long-standing reality. Curious about the letters, but too busy with the tasks required of a 130-acre farm and four kids, I put the box aside and set to work bringing order to the more obvious projects calling for attention around the property.

Once the farm was brought to an almost acceptable level of disorder, with the anticipation of discovering a lost treasure (and an uncanny knowing that opening the cardboard liquor box would be immensely time consuming), I peeled the crackling tape off of the musty smelling lid, opened its flaps, and uncovered a mess of papers, crammed and jumbled together.

Inside: newspaper clippings, daguerreotypes, calling cards, and dozens of documents that at some point in time were deemed too important to throw away, but not valuable enough to occupy precious space inside the house. Of the hundreds of fragile pieces of paper, a handful had been neatly folded, tucked securely back into their envelopes, and stacked. The rest were in a tangle. The ink and pencil had faded, but nothing appeared seriously damaged. Except for the small square cut from the corner of every envelope where its stamp had been removed, everything in the box appeared intact. Grabbing up a sheet from the top of the mess, I squinted to make out the sweeping script,

> June 22nd and a bright morning. Johnny Rebs are very much irritated this morning. The bullets are whistling over and around right merrily, whispering in our ears the admonition of, "Keep down heads, for death is in the air." Several bullets have struck our earthwork and two men of the 95th NY have mustered out of the government service and been taken home by the Father of mercies.

Immediately I felt the heavy burden of responsibility that I had just unwittingly taken on by recognizing that the humble, cardboard box contained numerous letters written by a Civil War soldier. So masterly did this writer express his mind that the Blue Ridge Mountains were clearly drawn into my view and his pains of hunger and illness were palpable. I gingerly lifted another page from the pile and spent the ensuing two years acquainting myself with its writer.

From records found inside the box, I learned that the soldier's name was Charles Freeman Biddlecom (hereafter referred to as Charlie) and that he was mustered in to the 28th Regiment New York State Volunteer Infantry, Company E, on May 22, 1861. As did tens of thousands of American Civil War soldiers, Charlie began writing letters home almost as soon as he walked out his door. Using any hard surface that would pass as stable enough—a hat bill, slab of wood, a knee—on whatever scrap of mostly clean, blank paper that they could find, with any mostly working pencil or pen which could be begged, borrowed, or stolen, Civil War soldiers wrote letters. Whether passing the slow moving time in a tent or "dog hut" in camp, waiting in the woods for a rotation on picket duty[1] or hunkered down in the mud at the bottom of a rifle pit, men poured their emotions onto paper. To the best of their ability they scratched out thoughts phonetically, drew sketches when words would not do, and painted images with words if they were unable to draw. Those who were illiterate often hired official letter writers or tent-mates to scribe their words. If conditions were rainy or frigid, the smoke in the tent too stifling, mosquitoes too bothersome, or when the bullets flying overhead caused too much of a distraction, there might be an apology for the shortness or sloppiness of a letter, but still that letter was written. An article printed in the *Boston Journal* in 1861 stated that the Washington Post Office processed forty-five thousand letters per day.[2]

So, what makes Charlie's letters so special?

The United States National Archive and Records Administration in Washington, D.C., preserves important documents, such as the Declaration of Independence, Bill of Rights, ancestry records, as well as the military service records for each individual soldier who served the United States government. Yet, however thorough these records may be, they offer only a shortsighted glimpse into the emotions and concerns, the whys and hows, of the individuals to whom they are connected. From records obtained through the National Archives, I learned that Charles F. Biddlecom was five feet six inches tall, though sometimes he was measured to be two inches taller than that. I have yet to discover a single photo of Charlie, but from his Military Service Record I learned that he had a dark complexion, black hair, black eyes, and weighed a buck-fifty.

Charlie was twenty-nine when he volunteered for service in the spring of 1861, older than the average volunteer, but in no other way a stand out. If reviewed strictly from the records, Charlie's military career merged inconspicuously with the tens of thousands of men who responded to Lincoln's call for volunteers. The National Archives list the facts and figures, but they paint a flat and colorless portrait of the lives and incidents recorded. During a lifetime each one of us becomes a number, part of a statistic in some way, but in the shadow of each fact and figure there is a story, one that usually goes untold. Each time Charlie was marked absent from roll call there is listed the explanation: *Absent due to illness.*

Data from the Muster Roll is confirmed in Charlie's letters and tells part of the story, but fails to give an account of the weeks of pain and fatigue he tolerated all the while still performing his work before finally seeking medical attention and being relieved from duty. Endured by all the troops, the days of near starvation, weeks of short rations, exposure to harsh elements, freezing temperatures, wind, rain, heat, sun, not to mention the ever gnawing homesickness and fear, are of no account in the official records of each soldier. The National Archives preserve and keep records of individual soldiers, but the facts and numbers alone fail to accurately reflect the son, brother, lover, or father to whom each set of data belongs.

Before reading Charlie's letters I thought of the Civil War Era with a general nostalgia, its rough edges polished down: cartoon-like images portraying serious, clean cut, (white) men wearing traditional blue uniforms with shiny, brass buttons, slinging rifles with sparkling (unused) bayonets attached. I imagined a soldier always to be valiant and his actions during war just. But, as I read Charlie's stories of duty, camp life, combat, and his feelings about society and politics, my image of a polished Civil War soldier changed. The battle re-enactments I watched as a kid now seem carnival-like by comparison. I recall being taught as a young student that North battled South and thus ended slavery; the causes and outcomes of the conflict were skimmed over. We studied the heroic military leaders made immortal for chaperoning soldiers into the most famous battles: Ulysses S. Grant, George Meade, Robert E. Lee, "Stonewall" Jackson,

Jeb Stuart; and visited cemeteries filled with row upon row of stark, white headstones marking the graves of soldiers who perished during our nation's horrific battle for human rights. Before reading Charlie's personal account, thoughts born in the midst of combat, it was easy to distance myself from the realities of war and even to dismiss a soldier's life or death as a dry statistic—merely one of the unavoidable costs of winning a necessary war and rarely delineating between the solder as a tool and the same as a person. Finding Charlie and reading his experience changed my view completely.

Since beginning this project I have met numerous passionate, hard-working, and deserving amateur and professional historians who all but drool when I relay my story of finding the letters. The decision to transcribe Charlie's letters was, for me, simple; every step has felt like an undeserved privilege. That I would preserve history and resurrect Charlie's voice was never a question. As Linda, the librarian at the Nebraska State Historical Society, said, "it would be almost criminal not to preserve them." However, the decision to publish, rather than archive and keep the letters private, was (still is) more complicated. In letter after letter Charlie admonished:

Don't show my letters to Ed Brown, or anyone else.

Give my kind regards to my family, but don't show my letters.

So, burn this up or put it away where no one will find it.

The letters that I write are not intended for publication and I do not wish the learned ladies of Macedon to find out what a poor grammarian I am, nor what a soft head I am.

. . . Charlie dislikes the plan of having his inferior productions published to any except the family.

You see my dilemma. I wonder sometimes if the letters were hidden in the barn at Charlie's behest. Charlie wrote boldly, as if he meant to impact an audience, but was at the same time humble enough to acknowledge his shortcomings—grammatical and emotional—and did not want his flaws broadcast. He was not the type to tout his opinions publicly, but wrote with such clarity and purpose that I suspect he must have known the power his words had to make an impression on more than the one person to whom he wrote. His reasons for insisting that his wife, Esther, keep certain letters private varied, but I argue against myself that none of those reasons exist today. Still, every time I come across his requests for privacy, my stomach lurches. Consolation comes only from perceiving that Charlie was a good-hearted fellow who would have been glad to know that so long after his flesh has turned to dust, his sentiments, as he stated on December 2, 1864, *"will interest you enough to pay for the paper and ink."*

After two and a half years enduring the eye-squinting tedium of organizing thousands of scraps of paper, unscrambling tangled lines of faded script, interpreting outdated word uses, decoding misspellings, and intuiting implied sentence breaks, Charlie's letters are finally preserved and his voice returned. The Spencerian script,[3] so full of tiny, graceful loops spelling out the 19th-century language, at first appeared to me as a foreign language, but now reads comfortably; I would recognize his handwriting anywhere. Charlie was fairly well educated, but still the original letters are akin to a 60,000-word run on sentence; Charlie did not use punctuation liberally. His spelling was inconsistent. There are a few unreadable words and lines where the pages have been folded, ripped, or soiled, a handful of mistakes, and a sentence here and there that simply does not make any sense. His script varied slightly depending on his mood or the circumstances—if he was sitting at a table or hunkered down in a dirt pit, but all the letters are of the same hand—Charlie wrote his own letters. Letters that have been penned by another person, a tent-mate or professional letter writer, typically begin with the clue, "I take my pen in hand."

I slightly edited the transcriptions to present the collection in a manner that makes them easier to follow and understand than are the originals. In editing, I retained all of Charlie's sentence structure and the order of his words, but changed spelling and punctuation to be modern and consistent.

I corrected the few blatant mistakes, such as repeated words, but left his grammatical style alone. The headings have all been reformatted to read in a uniform fashion, but the details contained therein, location and military unit, are just as Charlie wrote them. A handful of lines were obscured by folds and too worn or faded to make out. Incomplete thoughts or sentences, due to torn paper or missing pages, and words that were indecipherable, I simply left out. Throughout the process of transcribing and editing my utmost goal has been to return to Charlie his voice, as untainted as possible, while yet being digestible to modern readers.

NOTES

1. *Pickets:* guards posted around the outskirts of camps

2. In later American wars, the government censored soldiers' letters and diaries were prohibited to prevent an enemy from deriving any intelligence from them if captured. This is one of the reasons that the American Civil War has such a rich collection of primary sources.

3. The common handwriting style developed by Platt Rogers Spencer (1800–1864). Taught in most schools, the ornate script was held as the standard in the U.S. until replaced in the 1920s by typewriters and simpler methods.

CHAPTER 2

TRACING CHARLIE

AFTER the last of Charlie's letters had been transcribed, I downloaded the file onto a tiny USB flash drive, put it in my pocket, and drove to Kinkos. I expected to feel overjoyed. For months I had been anticipating the moment when I could sit back to read the printed letters in chronological order, minus the glare of the computer screen, the double and triple checking of each typed transcription against Charlie's letters, and the detailed sorting and filing. So much organizing, editing, and scrutinizing had gone into reassembling the collection that, though I knew the contents of each page, I had not yet read through the letters uninterrupted. Surprisingly, instead of feeling satisfied or even slightly relieved about reaching such a milestone, I (often accused of being stoic and overly pragmatic) cried, sniffled, hiccupped, and wept all the way to town. My unexpected tears gushed with the stark, and somehow new, realization that I would likely never discover another new anecdote of Charlie's again. In my attempt to revive his voice, in a way I had shared his anticipation, fear, boredom, and longing. It often felt like I was right there beside him witnessing his religion floundering, his character changing, and even his writing skill improving. On the way to the printer, I mourned the idea that our time together had ended. Every last word about his soldiering experience had been read; there was no more; it was over. I had listened to his thoughts and words, recorded his voice, and now all that he had left behind was situated on a small, cold peg of metal in the linty pocket of my blue jeans.

While working on Charlie's letters there were times that I was so drawn into his life that I began to think, write, and speak about him in the present tense. My husband (and occasional editor) has also fallen prey to these lapses in reality and overlooked obvious shifts in my writing from past to present tense. Even my children have been guilty, frequently walking through the door after school asking, "How is Charlie today?" in the same way they might ask about a friend or neighbor. Aware of the fine line between passion and insanity I will not admit the number of times that my emotions were caught off guard and I was shaken from Charlie's presence with the painful realization that my hopes for him in the specific circumstance of whatever letter I happened to be reading were futile. With a startle I would remember that he has long been gone; the battle is over. Charlie's first printing day was like one of those moments. What I did not yet realize on that teary drive to Kinkos was that I barely knew Charlie. Even though I had, indeed, read his last words, I had not come close to untangling their full meaning.

Freedom, Fairness, and Advocacy: The atmosphere in Farmington and Macedon, New York

On delicate paper bound with silk thread into a booklet titled *The Young Ladies Commission,* scripted by the young editress, Mary Anne Lapham, Esther's youngest sister, there is this description of their hometown in 1854, the year Charlie and Esther married:

> What a pleasant place Macedon is with the most splendid side-walks, elegant crossings, and beautiful bridges that you ever saw or heard of. It contains the most magnificent gardens imaginable. It really is a feast to look upon. The splendid vegetables arranged so tastily, with here and there a burdock standing out in bold relief, showing by their appearance that their owners do not join in that too common prejudice that flowers are useless, but intersperse

the useful with the ornamental. It is so pleasant. Let us take a walk where we cannot only converse on these beauties, but can also view them. We will first pass up Main Street. Do you see that lofty two story edifice? That is Macedon Academy, one of the finest institutions in the world. How finely it is situated on that commanding eminence and how beautifully the grounds are laid out . . .

All but a few of the letters that I found in the cardboard box were directed to Esther and mailed to the post offices in Farmington or Macedon, neighboring towns in Western New York. During the time it took me to sort, scan, and transcribe his letters I became as familiar with Charlie's language and well-worn phrases (my family refers to them as Charlie-isms) as I am with each snag of my favorite wool sweater, but had gained only a limited comprehension of the place and period in which they were written. Throughout the process of transcribing Charlie's letters my goal has been to revive and share his voice as genuinely as possible. So, to prevent tainting his expressions, or my perception of them, with post-war opinion, I did not venture outside of the box to gather more information until after I had finished transcribing each letter. I avoided reading the well known Civil War memoirs, novels, and history books suggested and even given to me by well meaning friends, because I wanted to first hear Charlie's version of the story. Consequently, my understanding of Charlie and of the time and places about which his letters were written was somewhat vague and, obviously, one-sided.

At the same time that I began my first read through the printed transcriptions, I dug into Charlie's family history, as well as a study of the Civil War. I combed through the letters and genealogical records that had been stashed in the cardboard box and searched elsewhere to learn more about Charlie's extended family and the region where he and Esther had spent their childhoods, met, married, worked, and raised their children. I Googled, joined Ancestry.com, studied census records, and read old, local history books that contained details about both Charlie and Esther's ancestors and the places where they had lived. As I uncovered bits of Charlie's past and learned more about the intricacies of the war, I began to see that I had overlooked entire words and missed the meanings of full sentences and phrases. That is, I had not clearly or fully heard all Charlie had to say. Rereading the letters with these new insights gave me a sense of how his opinions had been formed, what compelled him to enlist, and what ghosts from his past may have driven him to serve and to write about it in the way that he did. By not initially connecting the letters to the people, places, and events that surrounded them, my comprehension had, indeed, been limited. Because of the religious beliefs of their forefathers, the political environment of their communities, and the value they placed on education, Charlie and Esther communicated a unique perspective of their time period. Thus, equipped with a deeper awareness of the history that surrounded their lives, Charlie's voice took on a new tone and dimension.

Religion — The Quaker Influence

The roots of Charlie and Esther's characters run deep and a look back through their American ancestry will trace their sources. In 1788 when approximately six million acres of Western New York land was purchased from the Commonwealth of Massachusetts by land speculators, Oliver Phelps and Nathaniel Gorham, settlers began moving across Western New York. By way of dubious negotiations, the land company connived leases from the Native American inhabitants and the following year sold the first parcels of New York land. After selling their land in Hoosac, Massachusetts, Charlie's grandfather Thomas, his uncle, and his father, Joab, slowly made their way west, stopping in Clifton Springs and Phelps before putting down roots in Macedon. Around the same time as the Biddlecoms, Abraham Lapham left Hoosac with a group of ardent Quakers and settled directly in Geneseo County (later divided into various towns). For leaving their

Berkshire County community without approval, the Quaker group was formally disowned by the Society of Friends. Nevertheless, the settlers promptly built a Meeting House, a log cabin to be used solely for worship, and continued their religious customs just as before.

Charlie was not a member of the Quaker Society, but he was the fourth generation of Biddlecom men to make his home and conduct business in a predominately Quaker community and to marry a birthright Quaker woman. A cousin's letter written in 1854 critically describes Quakers as,

> . . . an ignorant, bigoted, disagreeable set of people who go to church, sit, and look down. Rise up with a jerk and quake incorrectly some passage of Scripture. Tell you they are saved, go to shaking hands, then go off visiting and carousing the remainder of the day.

Despite whatever truth the accusation may hold, the Quaker religion has more often been characterized by its fair and equal treatment of all people, especially protecting the rights of women, prisoners, invalids, and the mentally ill, regardless of race or religion, in all aspects of social and political life. Though he shared some of his cousin's disdain toward Quakers, Charlie's life carried an aura of the industrious, honest, and humble society.

Letters and newspaper clippings indicate that the Biddlecom family associated themselves with Universalist and Baptist churches, and, at times, boasted no religious affiliation at all. Two of Charlie's uncles were Universalist ministers and more letters imply a bent toward that denomination. Similarly, Universalism and Quakerism are founded on the premise of being creedless religions with commitments to social justice, and it is not uncommon to see the two denominations working side by side to support human equality and security. Quaker meetings were not exclusive and community folks were often permitted to attend worship regardless of membership to the Society. While Charlie and Esther were growing up, the nation's population was exploding (growing over 35 percent between

1840 and 1850) and expanding westward spreading new ideologies, but it was members of the Quaker Society, leading by principles of fairness and equality, who strongly dominated the political and social activity in Farmington and the adjoining village of Macedon.

A History of Advocacy in Farmington and Macedon

From its foundation, the strong Quaker influences on the social environment of Farmington and Macedon were reflected in peaceful, but powerful political involvement in reform movements, especially vying for the civil rights of Native Americans, slaves, and women. Powerful rumblings of activity in support of Native Americans, people of color, and women resonated out of Farmington's earliest residents. Through consistently exercising a policy of fairness and pacifism, the Farmington Quaker community maintained friendly and trusting relations with their indigenous neighbors, the Haudensaunee, and several times mediated on their behalf during land negotiations with government officials, land companies, and settlers. During the autumn of 1794, Farmington Quakers led by Esther's grandfather, Abraham Lapham, worked alongside prominent Quakers from Philadelphia, led by William Savery, to ensure the fair treatment of the Six Nations of the Iroquois Confederacy (Seneca, Cayuga, Oneida, Onondaga, Tuscarora, and Mohawk) during treaty negotiations between United States officials and the Six Nations. The seminal 1794 Treaty of Canandaigua, also known as Treaty with the Six Nations, clarified the promise of peace and friendship between the United States and Iroquois Nation and officially recognized the sovereignty of the Six Nations to establish laws as individual nations.

The oldest letter from Emma's cardboard box is dated April 1, 1795. Written to Esther's grandfather and signed by William Savery, a well-known Philadelphian Quaker, preacher, writer, political activist, and abolitionist, the letter confirms the friendship and Savery's visit with the Laphams. In his published journal about his trip to Canandaigua, William

Savery noted, *"seeing some persons in the garb of Friends, they informed us they lived about five miles beyond this, and, being glad to see us, invited us to their homes."* It was shortly after the Laphams' hospitality to Savery in 1794 that the reputation of those disowned Quakers of Farmington was restored and their Meeting House officially recognized as a "base preparative meeting" under the care of the Easton Meeting in Saratoga County. In 1804, after fire destroyed the log cabin that had been used as a sanctuary and schoolhouse since 1796, Farmington Quakers built a wood framed meetinghouse measuring 44 by 32 feet. By 1810, the well-respected Farmington congregation had increased in number and authority to the extent that it was named Farmington Quarterly meeting, collectively conducting the business of all of the monthly meetings in Western New York. In 1816 a new meetinghouse was built to accommodate the growth and provide space for worship and business.[1]

In 1838, Seneca Nation leaders implored the aid of Farmington Friends to defend themselves against the Ogden Land Company concerning the fraudulent Treaty of Buffalo Creek. Taking swift but non-violent action, members of the Farmington Quaker community published the illegitimate claims of the land company and successfully effected steps toward a compromise, thus allowing the Seneca to retain their Allegany and Cattaraugus homelands known as the Tonawanda Reservation. Thanks to the responsive action of the Farmington community, the ensuing Compromise Treaty of 1842, ratified at the Farmington Quaker Meetinghouse, prevented a Trail of Tears similar to the deadly marches that were occurring in other parts of the nation.

Again, the Farmington community of Quakers extended their hand toward civil rights advocacy when the Fugitive Slave Act was passed in 1850, making it illegal to aid, or to fail to return, anyone suspected of being an escaped slave. In response to the law, the Farmington Quarterly Meeting declared that, "any acknowledgement of obligations to such laws is a violation of our testimony against slavery." The Western New York region was a known haven for African Americans. William Wells Brown, an escaped slave turned abolitionist lecturer and writer, wrote his biography while living in Farmington between 1844 and 1846. Escaped slaves, Mary and Emily Edmondson, lived with families in Farmington before being ushered off to Oberlin College by Harriet Beecher Stowe. Quaker minister and author Joseph John Gurney in his book *A Journey in North America* wrote,

> I know of no district in America in which the anti-slavery cause, as well as that of total abstinence, are more vigorously maintained by the bulk of the population, than in the parts which I was now visiting (Farmington). Great was the zeal of the young people, both amongst Friends and others, in the pursuit of these objects.

Imagine being raised in a community where the core leaders of the anti-slavery society regularly mingled.

Anti-slavery activism often went hand in hand with the women's rights movement, and the women of Farmington were often found standing in disproportionate numbers at the forefront of the activity. The anti-slavery political party called the Liberty League held a meeting in June of 1847 at the Macedon Locks (the town center shared by Farmington and Macedon). That meeting boasted the first recorded instance in our nation's history that a political party included female voters at its national convention and the first known time in American history in which females received votes for president. Lucretia Mott (a Quaker) and Lydia Maria Child (Universalist) both received one vote as a candidate for president of the league. The Western New York Anti-Slavery Society was comprised of several religious denominations, but at its center were the Quaker women from the Farmington Quarterly Meeting. According to the seventh annual report of the Anti-Slavery Society, thirty-two bold women hailing from Farmington independently formed their own female sect of the organization. In yet another example of the progressive culture of Charlie and Esther's hometown, twenty out of the sixty-eight women who signed the Declaration of Sentiments at the first women's rights convention in Seneca Falls, New York, in July of 1848, were from the Farmington Quarterly Meeting.

Long before men were compelled (by fancy or by force) to risk their lives fighting for equality, Farmington families had been waging war against discriminatory laws by working intimately with major political activists such as Susan B. Anthony (also know as Aunt Susie), William Chaplin, Frederick Douglass, William Lloyd Garrison, Joseph C. Hathaway, Elias Hicks, Lucretia Mott, Amy Post, Elizabeth Cady Stanton, and Austin Steward. So many prominent reformers came from, lived in, or visited, the towns of Farmington and Macedon that an entire book could be written to draw a complete picture of what it must have been like to be raised and educated in an environment so geared toward ensuring individual civil rights. Though I have found very little of Esther's writing, based on Charlie's letters I assume that her questions were in no small way the provocateur of her husband's perspicacious responses. Seeped in an atmosphere of progressive political activity and efficacious Quaker principles, it is not hard to imagine why Charlie volunteered for duty.

Education

Following similar timelines the Biddlecoms and Laphams traveled almost identical paths, immigrating from Devonshire, England, to Rhode Island, then from Rhode Island to Hoosac, Massachusetts, both gradually moving westward before settling in Western New York. Outside of tracking similar routes across sea and land, I found no recorded connection between the Lapham and Biddlecom families before the union of their children by marriage in 1854, even though their families had been near neighbors for generations. The Biddlecoms sometimes rented their homes, labored in industry, and established a mill and a grocery, while the Laphams, who had been relatively wealthy landowners since before the Revolutionary War, supported the fledgling educational systems and mingled in the politics of their communities.

After losing both of her parents at age fifteen, Esther continued to study at the Macedon Academy and worked as a teacher to support the education of her five younger siblings (Daniel, David, Stephen, Cornelia, and Mary Anne) who had all been taken in by various relatives after their parents' death. School records indicate that Esther studied at the academy, considered an intermediary school between high school and college, for only three terms, but taught thirteen terms. In a letter written in 1852 to her little sister, Esther writes,

> I like old Macedon about as well as any place. . . . However, I must say something about school affairs. First, I have no notion of graduating. I mean to have a good education, though. Whether I go to school, or not, it will not interfere with yours and Mary's arrangement. I wish you could commence next spring, if possible, but I hardly want you should go to Lima . . . LeRoy Seminary is as good a school as there is in the state. If I can see you and Mary go through, I shall feel satisfied.

That her sisters would be well educated through college, and that she would be the one to make the sacrifices needed to support them, never seemed to be a question. As could be surmised by looking at their extended family, cousin Susan B. Anthony in particular, education was considered a high priority to the Lapham women.

It is likely that Charlie's first brush with Esther was while she was a teacher and he and his sister, Laura, were students at the Macedon Academy. Charlie attended the Academy in 1851 and 1852 before going on to receive a degree in Mechanics at the Clinton Liberal Institute. Burned to the ground in 1900, few records remain of the Clinton Liberal Institute's earliest students. However, accounts of several prominent members of American society who attended the academy reveal the possibility

that Charlie brushed shoulders with the likes of Simon Lake, inventor
of the first modern submarine; Grover Cleveland, twice president of the
United States; Clara Barton, educator, humanitarian, Civil War nurse,
women's rights advocate, and founder of the American Red Cross; and
Leland Stanford, one of the four major investors in the West, Republican
Governor of California, credited for initiating the transcontinental railroad, and founder of Stanford University.

By gathering the parts and pieces left behind by the Biddlecom and
Lapham families, studying census data, Quaker records, and the documentation of other historians, and by then stringing those accumulated
impressions together, I began to see how their religious, political, and
social environment had shaped the lens through which the Biddlecoms
viewed the world and consequently influenced their actions and writing.
Charlie's cultural surroundings point toward an environment supportive of
the abolitionist cause, though that point does not always shout out from
his letters. I imagine that his strong civic-minded heritage strengthened
a resolve to serve and his solid education and exposure to politics ignited
the purpose felt in his letters.

Following The Army of the Potomac

Once acquiring an understanding of who Charlie was within his family
and community, I attempted to trace Charlie as a soldier by studying the
Civil War—logically, starting at the beginning of the war. It did not take
long for me to realize that the war had been simmering for decades and
was much more complicated than the few chapters allotted to the subject
in high school textbooks. Trying to avoid biased and varnished versions
of history, I attempted to use primary sources as much as possible for my
study, a process that proved to be hugely time-consuming. Following long
and varied rabbit trails seemed to be the only way to really understand the
war era. So much, almost too much, material is readily available: countless
books, encyclopedias, detailed maps, educational websites, old newspapers,

even letters like Charlie's, are easily accessible in public libraries, town halls, and historical society museums. Finding information about the Civil War was really too easy; determining what information was accurate, and then what was relevant, was not. I began to narrow my study to follow only Charlie's experience through the war: names, locations, battles, and vocabulary—details about the Army of the Potomac and even more specifically, the Fifth Corps. I began to assemble a timeline of battles and attempted to draft my own maps. This is when I discovered the Civil War maps and battle summaries of historian and cartographer Hal Jespersen.

Hal calls himself an amateur, but by what unreachable measure one could become more professional than he, I cannot imagine. After deflecting only two of my desperate pleas for help, he agreed to review my work. With the speed of an elite marathoner, Hal nitpicked his way through Charlie's letters and applied his knowledge of the strategy and operational aspects of battles and of the generals who fought them by correcting my mistaken assumptions, fixing blatant mistakes, and adding enough detail to the annotations to turn Charlie's letters into a stand-alone study of the military aspect of the Civil War. Because of Hal's knowledge and drive to understand the logistics and intricacies of combat, he easily recognized the locations and battles that Charlie wrote about (whereas I had only a vague idea) and infused accurate tidbits of information to help better explain specific engagements. An understanding of the military actions and politics helps to define who Charlie was as a soldier and explain where he stood politically.

As interesting and informative as the information added to Charlie's letters might be, this book is not meant to be a complete textbook, nor is it meant to be an academic analysis of any aspect of the war. Rather, the endnotes are intended as a starting point and, hopefully, an inspiration to learn more and to acknowledge the lives of individuals who gave of themselves for future generations.

A historian like Hal might use a collection of letters like Charlie's to pinpoint the army's movements or to confirm who was in charge at a specific time. Military men will read first-hand reports and attempt to conclude how a specific strategy worked to gain an advantage in a particular battlefield, or why ground was lost. They may make guesses about what might have happened if an individual had done something differently.

Students of the Civil War might compare these letters against the Official Records[2] to further confirm or refute data and reports contained therein. Those who are interested in the psychology of soldiers will look for clues about the soldier's emotional status—perceptions about the progress or failure of a campaign, reasons for enlisting—and try to make assessments of a soldier's mental state before, during, and after combat. Without doubt, studying those aspects are important and soldiers' letters are useful for gaining a better understanding of the Civil War, or any war for that matter. However, battlefields and generals and the politics and strategies behind them little represent the lives of the three million average Joes who were engaged in the war. When I read Charlie's letters I do not see blue or gray or feel a connection to a piece of my own genetic make-up (remember, Charlie is no relation to me). I envision a common man whose naiveté was ripped from him, his faith broken and remade, and how his character endured relentless, daily pounding of war against one's countrymen, against brothers and friends. I think of Esther anxiously anticipating, reading, and answering her husband and wonder if it was not her writing that dimmed for Charlie the thunder of battle, smoothed over the frustration of politics, and shored him up enough to keep out of the line of fire.

CLINTON, ILLINOIS
MARCH 24, 1853

Dear Esther,

Thursday has come again, but it did not bring a letter from the one I love, from you, my dearest. I presume you did not get my last in time to answer so that I would get it today. I was disappointed when the mail came in this morning and did not bring a letter from you, or from home. I had thought that this would be my last day in Clinton, but it seems I shall have to pass one more Sabbath here. Perhaps, I may get away by Saturday. I know I shall get your letter before you will get this, yet it does not keep me from writing to you the same as if I had your anticipated letter to answer.

I have but little to busy myself with, with the exception of writing letters. Dear Esther, you must know whom I like to write to the best. I shall probably be at home next week, what day I cannot tell. I shall see you as soon after my arrival as circumstances will admit. I will then answer your anticipated letter in person, if you have no serious objection, and I know you have none. For I am, as yet, your very own Charles, and will ever strive to be worthy of the confidence you place in me. So dearest, have patience. I shall see you before many of these sunny, spring days have passed, and, dear Esther, you will see me calmer than I was when we parted the morning of the ninth of January. For my mind is at ease on one or two points that kept me in a continual boil. One of those points you know better than I can tell you. The other is this, I now know what is to be my course next summer, which I did not know the last time you saw me. I shall go to school, but where I do not know. Perhaps at the Locks. I can bear the thought of going there now that I know I am not hated or despised by thee. You love me now, aye, I know you do. If not for your love, there would be a feeling in my heart that would ruin me for study. My feelings are too sensitive, I know, but I cannot help it. So I am and ever shall be.

Esther, I believe this letter is the best written, as far as the writing is concerned, of any you have had from me. I have got a first rate pen this time, which accounts for it. As for length, it is quite a respectable letter, is it not?

> *Good Afternoon. I am as ever thy servant,*
> *Charles Freeman Biddlecom*

—•—

NOTES

1. The 1816 Farmington Quaker Meeting House has been restored and still stands today, preserved as a Historic National Center for Women's Rights, Native American Rights, African American Rights, and the Underground Railroad thanks to the support of numerous private, state, and national contributors.

2. *War of the Rebellion: Compilation of the Official Records of the Union and Confederate Armies,* also known as the Official Records, are compiled into 128 volumes of official documents and reports of all Civil War operations.

CHAPTER 3

THE BRINK OF AN IMMINENT CRISIS

L ETTERS written the decade before the war intimately detail the lives of the Biddlecom and Lapham families: business in the western territories, education, farming, hired hands, housework, marriage, babies, illnesses, and death fill hundreds of pages. Even though both the Biddlecoms and Laphams express astuteness about community happenings, barely do any of the dozens of pre-war letters note the imminent political crisis. Dozens of sappy love letters draw a picture of Charlie and Esther's early years as a couple. Charlie returned to Macedon from his uncle's farm in Illinois, but not to attend the Academy as he intended. Instead, he returned only briefly, married his *dearest* on August 31, 1854, and took his newlywed wife back to Clinton (where at the same place and time Abraham Lincoln happened to be practicing law and contemplating a senatorial bid). The couple did not stay away from their hometown for long and before the end of two growing seasons returned to Farmington, leaving personal letters as the only evidence of their short adventure in the near-west.

At the brink of the war, Charlie's father, Joab, farmed, while his mother, Olivia, cared for the house and the elderly Grandfather Thomas Biddlecom. His sister Sarah taught at a common school and Laura attended Lombard University[1] in Galesburg, Illinois, one of the first coeducational colleges in the country. Esther's siblings maintained frequent contact with each other through letters after they were dispersed among relatives between New York and Michigan following their parents' death in 1842. Despite an oath to live out her life as an independent old maid, Cornelia Lapham shelved her degree from Mount Holyoke Female Seminary and submitted to a position as the second wife of Hiram Wheeler (also known as "Mr. W."), a former principal of Macedon Academy, prominent businessman, a pioneer in Iowa and Illinois, and a Democrat. From Pipestone, Michigan, Daniel Lapham relayed stories about his successful farming venture and growing family in letters scripted by his wife, Mary. Ignoring the distressed admonitions of his family, David Lapham joined the Spiritualist movement, abandoned his wife for a mistress, and filled various teaching positions in and near Round Prairie, Illinois. Stephen Lapham wrote to his sister from Michigan, where he farmed with his wife, Olive, until he enlisted in the 25th Michigan Infantry Regiment. The youngest and dearly loved Lapham sibling, Mary Anne, attended various boarding schools around New England and sadly died in the first year of an unhappy marriage. In the years before the war, this educated, hard-working Northern family's letters reflect their evolving opinions about religion, the hardships of Western expansion, and the challenges of women's education, but barely skim over the hot issues of human or states' rights boiling around them.

———

DAVENPORT, IOWA
SUNDAY SEPTEMBER 2, 1860

My dear sister Es,

I am thinking and thinking about you today. How are you feeling with your dear little girl baby, now two weeks old today? How I would like to just throw on my sunbonnet and run over to your house. I will make an air castle for our imagination . . .

And here I am. Knock-knock.

"Come in," you answer. And I bounce in. How aren't you surprised? Not a bit of it, you expected me and are up and dressed and sitting in a chair by the cradle where baby lies, all dressed to fits, so very clean and pure and spotless, quite an angel of innocence. Bayard is outdoors this morning, giving little Stafford a ride in his wagon. Margaret, I suppose she is your girl yet, has all her work done, the house in complete order, and herself, too. Perhaps she is fixing to go to meeting while I stay with you.

How soon do you expect Mr. B. back from shooting that nice, fat squirrel, or one dozen of them, that he has promised you for your dinner? I hope he will come before I have to go home, for I want to see whether he has changed one bit. And, also, the pride he feels for that bundle in the crib. Oh, yes, I know you are proud, Es, whether he is, or not, no need to tell me. No.

You are not changed one bit, Es, unless it is to grow younger. I see that it can't be otherwise than this—a happy mother in a happy home never grows old.

I like it here, better than the Payne place where you lived when I visited you before. If I can't have you for neighbors over here in Iowa, I hope you will stay there. It seems so very comfortable and home-like. It is near to your Father B. and near some good friends of both yourself and Mr. B.

"Why didn't Mr. W. come with me?" you ask. First, he is no hand to visit. Secondly, he is in a furious hurry to finish the bins in the corn house to have them ready for the grain when it is threshed. His work altogether drives him very much. I expect there will be a falling out shortly, for he works almost as much Sunday as any other day. And, you know, too great a familiarity with any one thing breeds contempt. I anticipate daily the sight of industry taking French leave.[2]

Mr. W. has never said a word about your baby except to plague me into crying in spite of myself; how it was that you did not let me know it was expected and continues to say that he knows I am mad about it. tc. tc. It is no such thing. Mr. W. is as great a hector, as is Mr. B. I sometimes think worse. I am mad at myself because I am plagued by his teasing. Does Charlie like to tease as well as ever? Do you ever cry about it?

Mr. W. is going to town just now. I will have to send my letter unfinished. I will say goodbye promising to write very soon again. Ever your loving sister, Cornelia

LOMBARD UNIVERSITY
GALESBURG, ILLINOIS
FEBRUARY 22, 1861

My dear sister, Es,

Having a little leisure tonight I think I will take advantage of it and write
what little I am able to you and some to Charlie, too, if I have time. Today
being the anniversary of Washington's birth, the seniors in our college
petitioned the faculty for a Holy Day. Not wishing to be too generous or
too selfish, they compromised the matter by giving us a half Holy Day and
the privilege of having a sociable in the evening at the University.

SUNDAY, FEBRUARY 24, 1861

I had written so far Friday evening when I was called for by a senior to
attend said sociable. Consequently, I was obliged to put by writing and as
I have some three or four letters besides this to write today, I have come
to the conclusion that my time is too precious to waste it by beginning
another and will continue this. Today is one of the first days that is like
some of our April days. The sky is clean and bluer than any I ever before
saw. The wind that generally blows from the four corners of the heavens as
if it will carry everything before it, for a wonder, is quiet today. I can hardly
believe it is February and that you are having cold, blustering weather at
home, though our mud isn't to be underestimated.

Tonight our Pastor, Mr. Hibbard, preaches a sermon on the imminent
crisis.[3] As he is a very fine speaker and always writes fine sermons, I think
I shall enjoy it exceedingly well. His sermon this morning was very interesting, his best. From Psalm 9:17 "The wicked shall be cast into Hell, and
all the Nations that forget God." He was formerly a Presbyterian minister
and in his sermon quoted some parts from an old sermon of his preached
from that text. Trying to prove endless misery from it, the contrast was
very marked.

How are Bayard, Stafford, and baby? Is Belle as pretty as ever? Does
Stafford's health get any better? Is Bayard learning to read as fast as he

ought? Don't let him shirk out of reading, Esther, but stick him to it. We will get him another book when he needs it.

Do not think when you are seeing this that because I have written a short letter you must do the same, but take the will for the deed and think that if I had the time I would write more and measure yours accordingly. Hoping you will excuse all marks of haste.

> *I remain as ever your affectionate sister,*
> *Laura J. Biddlecom*

———·———

> BOX 1009 DAVENPORT, IOWA
> SUNDAY EVENING
> MARCH 5, 1861

Ever dear sister Es,

Yours of February eleventh came to hand in due time and you may be sure I was glad to get it. I now intend to redeem my broken promise of writing every two weeks. Your letters do me so much good, Es. It is the next (only since I cannot see you) the best thing for my health. Is that selfish?

First, and foremost, I have good help now and the good prospect that she will remain through spring, if not all summer. She is a widow with an eighteen month old child for whom she hires board in town while she is out at work. She has to pay one dollar per week for the child's board. We pay her a dollar-fifty per week. So, you see, she only clears fifty cents per week, barely enough to clothe her child. She is good and faithful help, I think the best we have ever had. As soon as the traveling will admit it, she plans to go into town to bring little Michael out to visit with her for a week. If I find that we can get along comfortably with the baby here and still get the work done, we shall propose to pay her the fifty cents and keep the baby. If she continues to do well, we shall then increase her wages to seventy-five cents or perhaps a dollar. But, if he is so trouble-some (as she anticipates) as to prevent her from working while he is here, when the week's visit is up he will have to be carried back to his boarding place. Poor little fellow!

My aching bones and lameness have well neigh disappeared since my release from the hard work by Sarah's coming (my present help), although, I can't lift anything without feeling it. If I have good help all this summer I expect to gain better health than I have had for a year past.

Tomorrow Abraham Lincoln is inaugurated President of the United States.[4] We only take the *New York Herald*[5] now. I suppose it gives a somewhat one sided view of things, but it admits that if Lincoln does thus and so, that the Union will continue, and more of a Union than ever, and then prosperous times are coming to all. But, the unsettled state of the country makes every kind of business dull. A great many banks are breaking. Men are failing, losing everything, while others lose by them. I hope Charles and his Father will get their pay off Bancroft. Mr. Wheeler thinks he will lose some money, perhaps not a great deal, by the recent failure of a bank here.

Ever your loving sister, *Cornelia*

DAVENPORT, IOWA
MAY 18, 1861

Ever Dear Sister;

Yours stating that Charles had enlisted for the Army is just received and as Mr. W. is going to Davenport today in an hour from now, I have only time to scribble a very little.[6] I don't mean to worry about you, only I can't help it. Nobody who is acquainted with Charles can call him a coward. I had thought it quite probable, but as you did not mention it, I would not put it into your mind. I mean that, I thought it quite probable he would enlist. Now that he has done so . . . I tell you, I hope he can have the honor of bringing Jeff Davis[7] within hanging distance. But Mr. Wheeler says perhaps the sober second thought may, or the entreaties of his friends will, prevail upon him to hire a substitute.[8] It is often done, a common thing, and in his case, a man with a family could easily do so. Two years is not very long, my darling, Es. He may not be in a single engagement. If he should be, you must think how many there are who return to their homes with honor—and not of those who die with honor on the battle-field. I can't help praising you for your plucky spirit—I think you are full as "Plucky" as Abe Lincoln's wife.[9]

Keep up good courage, Es. I suppose Charles has gone by this time. I am afraid you will see some lonely house with all your good courage. Your blessed little children, Es, they will be real company. Mr. W. thinks it quite probable that he will have a call in the Navy in a few months. If he does I think he will go, though opposed to the war. If such a thing should come to pass, I shall come to visit you and we will be "grass widows together," Mr. Wheeler says. Goodbye, my darling girl. I will write again very soon. Do write very soon to me and let me hear how you get along. My hand trembles so I can hardly write.

> *Ever yours,*
> *Cornelia S. Wheeler*

———

Less than a year before Abraham Lincoln's call upon the general popula-tion of the northern states and western territories to form a militia and halt the secession of southern states, Charles Freeman Biddlecom owned 47 acres of land in Monroe County New York, a modest farm with a recorded value of $1,410. At the time of the 1860 United States Federal Census, Charlie's wife was expecting their third child and managed their house and two sons with the help of a twenty-four year old Irish girl named Margaret Clancey. Before the idea of soldiering gained a foothold in his mind, Charlie's barn boarded two horses, four milk cows, five pigs, and a flock of fifteen sheep from which he sheared 150 pounds of wool. By his measure, the homestead produced 150 bushels of wheat and 300 bushels each of oats and Indian corn, all of which he worked with about $100 worth of equipment. Work, farm, and family filled his days until on May 18, 1861, Charlie was mustered in to Company E 28th Regiment New York State Volunteer Infantry.

NOTES

1. Lombard University was founded on Universalist principles in 1837 by a group of social reformers. Co-educational from its founding, it did not combine men and women in classes until after the start of the Civil War when enrollment of men declined dramatically. The school population strongly opposed slavery and actively supported Lincoln.

2. *French leave*: absent without permission or leave; absent without announcing one's departure.

3. Lincoln's election in November 1860 further strained relations between the regions caused by issues of State's Rights and slavery. By February 1861, seven states had formed the Confederate States of America and elected Jefferson Davis as president. Newspapers both North and South were fueling rumors of war and justifying its purpose and cause.

4. Lincoln was actually inaugurated on March 4, 1861. Cornelia often wrote letters over a period of days and may have started this letter on the fourth and dated it on the fifth.

5. The *New York Herald* founded and edited by James G. Bennett, Sr., was a partisan Democratic newspaper that supported the Union during the war, but not necessarily Lincoln.

6. Lincoln's stated reasons for calling out a militia: To execute the laws of the Union, suppress insurrections, and to repel invasions. According to *Harper's Weekly*, April 27, 1861, Jeff Davis called up a militia *"in response to President Lincoln's proclamation announcing his intention to invade the confederacy with an armed force for the purpose of capturing its fortresses, subverting its independence, and subjecting the free people thereof to the dominion of a foreign power, to repel the threatened invasion, and defend the rights and liberties of the people by all means."* In a nutshell, the South mustered to resist aggression. On April 15, 1861, in response to the Confederate attack on Fort Sumter, Lincoln called on Northern states to enable their militia to serve a term of 90 days, the maximum allowed by statute (Congress was not in session at the time to change this). On May 3, he called for 42,000 three-year volunteers, 18,000 for the Navy, and an enlargement of the Regular Army to 23,000. (He cited his authority as Commander in Chief, assuming that Congress would back him up retroactively; they did.) On July 22, Congress passed a law authorizing one million three-year volunteers. In the meantime, some of the states had begun recruiting two-year regiments, about 30,000 men, which the War Department reluctantly accepted.

7. Davis, Jefferson, F. (1808–1889) Elected President of the Confederacy on February 18, 1861. Declared January 21, 1861, the day he resigned his U.S.

Senate seat to follow his native state of Mississippi out of the Union, "the saddest day of my life."

8. If a person could afford it, a replacement could be hired to stand in for military service. At 18 years of age and being nearly a "perfect man physically and morally as could be found," J. Summerfield Staples of Stroudsburg, Pennsylvania, was selected by President Abraham Lincoln to represent (substitute) himself for military service.

9. Lincoln, Mary Todd (1818–1882) was the daughter of a wealthy slave owner. Her siblings actively supported the Southern cause despite their sister's position. The First Lady's mental instability and eccentricities since her youth (her "pluck" as Cornelia puts it) had been a source of public scrutiny.

CHAPTER 4

28TH REGIMENT NEW YORK STATE VOLUNTEER INFANTRY AND AN HONORABLE DISCHARGE

CANANDAIGUA, NEW YORK[1]

JUNE 1861

Dear Wife,

We have news that we leave tonight at 7 o'clock. I would like very much to come home once more before leaving for good, but I suppose it is out of the question. Take good care of the children and do not let them forget that they have a father and in case I should meet with an untimely death learn them to know for what I died.

> *With much love I remain,*
>
> *Charles*

CAMP MORGAN

ALBANY, NEW YORK

TUESDAY, JUNE 1861

Dear Wife,

Yours of the 30th came to hand in due time last Saturday morning. I intended to answer it on Sunday, but was called on to do guard duty about 12 o'clock and did not get discharged until Monday noon. It rained all night and I got soaking wet, but as good fortune would have it, I did not catch cold. I shall not be called on again for about one week. You will see by the heading of this that we have left Albany. We left Saturday morning at 8 A.M. and came here to camp. The camp is situated in the town of

Bethlehem (3 or 4 miles south and west of Albany) on a nice, level plot of meadowland. To the south and west of us distant (I should say some 25 or 30 miles) are the first mountains I ever saw. I think I should like to take a ramble over them. Our camp is only 3/4 mile from the river, yet it must be some 300 feet or more above the water in the river. Taking everything in consideration, I think it would be hard to find a more pleasant location than this.

There are two regiments encamped here. The 16th and 28th. The 16th is made up of companies from the northern parts of New York: Ogdensburg, Potsdam, Plattsburg, Gouverneur, DePeyster, Stockholm, Malone, West Chazy, and Mooers. The 28th are all from west of Canandaigua: Lockport, Medina, Batavia, Albion, Niagara Falls, and one company from Monticello in Sullivan County. Both regiments are riflemen.

Now I will give you a little idea of a camp by making a picture of this one. This is a representation of the east half of our regiment and is the center, right center, and right flank of the regiment. The front is towards

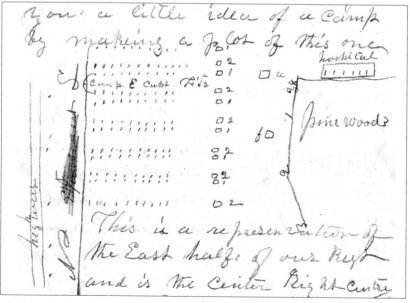

Charlie's sketch, Camp Morgan

the road. The little marks are made to represent the tents of the privates and noncommissioned officers. The little squares numbered *1* and *2* are the Captain and lieutenant's tents. The letters *a* and *b* are the tents of the Sergeant Major. So you see, the privates take the front, the company officers next and the regimental officers next. I have represented six companies on this plot. Our Company E has next to the most honorable position in the regiment, the right flank being considered the best of all. The other four companies are located on the line to the south of us. The 16th Regiment is in the field south of us distant forty or fifty rods.[2]

Colonel Davy[3] is the commandant of this camp and he is a mean old cuss, so say the boys. I don't know anything about him, good or bad. All I know is that his men run the guard and take pains not to come in again, if such a thing is possible.

> *Believe me your loving husband,*
> *Chas. F. Biddlecom*

                                                    CAMP MORGAN, NEW YORK
Dear Es,   1861

. . . This victuals[4] arrangement here makes me think that this war will not amount to much. If the northern troops get up bread and meat riots, what are the poor southern pups to do that have very little of either? Good or bad, men won't fight in a bad cause without being well fed, clothed, and paid in money besides. For this reason, I think the war cannot amount to anything, nor can it be possible for it to last more than two or three months at the longest. The time may have been with some people when they would fight and starve, but they do not now inhabit the south. They will not fight and starve when by yielding they can have peace and plenty. With plenty of money and food, they might fight a while, but without either, they won't.

Yesterday I went to a creek about a mile north of here and washed my under shirts and some stockings. They look clean and nice and if I had a flat iron I should try a fine shirt just to see what kind of a looking thing I could make of it.

I have not got the money to come home with now, and I may not be able to get it. If I get a leave of absence for the last of this week or the first of next, I shall write to Father for money. That is, if they don't pay us off soon. I have written to sister Sarah and must write to some of our folks in a day or two. I don't want Father to feel bad because I wrote to Hunter, for I thought he would be at our house most of the time and would see all of my letters to you and, consequently, would know all about how I was getting along. I promised to write to Hunter almost the last thing I done. I don't want any of you to harbor the least ill feeling towards me, for I may never see you again on Earth. I do believe there is a final resting place where we shall all of us meet again. I wish to be at peace and good will with all my own family. Let others do and say what they may.

Ed Brown's[5] cousin is lieutenant colonel of our regiment and a real fine man he seems to be. I think of you and the children almost all the time and sometimes I feel very lonesome. If I were free, I would enlist on any account. I presume I should tell Margaret that I want her to stay with you 'til I come home. I do not think I would move to Father's this winter if I were you, for you will not get along with them on account of the children. You must do as you please.

Send my white linen pants and my best pair of light shoes; one of them wants the heel straightened up before sending. I spoke to Isaac[6] about getting my trunk full of victuals cakes and bringing it down when he came. I could send my things home in it and it would cost less than this box.

Esther, dear, dear, Esther, I do so long to see you again before we go south that it almost makes me sick. I cannot write any more. Kiss my little darlings for me.

> *Your Affectionate,*
> *Chas. F. Biddlecom*

CAMP MORGAN
JUNE 7, 1861

Dear Esther,

I write again today for fear that I shall have to be on guard again next Sunday. Isaac and I have been fixing our bed today so as to have it up out of the mud. It rained last night and drowned us out. After digging ditches for about an hour to try and dry out our quarters, the colonel came along and ordered us over to the barn to sleep. If there had not been from thirty to forty sick in one end of the barn, which had been fixed up for a hospital, I should have slept first rate, for it was the first soft spot I have found since I left home. I done some pretty fast sleeping towards morning light. I have fashioned a pole bottom to our bed and covered it with hemlock bows and straw. It looks quite decent and I think it will do first rate. I presume there will be some hard spots in it, but that we don't mind, for I believe any of us could make out first rate on any decently cleaned floor as though it were white oak. Nothing like getting used to a thing, you know. We eat victuals here and call them good that we would hardly look at were we at home. We have got so that hairs and dirt don't scare us a bit. In fact, we hardly notice them.

Three of our boys have gone home, two to Canandaigua and one to Victor. I would like to come home and probably shall before we leave here, but not just yet. For I should want to come again before I leave here and it would be impossible. We all think that we have made fools of ourselves by enlisting at all and are quite confident that the fuss (we don't see fit to dignify it with the name of war) will be finished before we will be wanted or before the government will be able to arm and equip us. Well, if so, I can't help it, but I would like to sight a good rifle at the southern whelps a few times just to see if I could hit one. If nothing more, blast their skins home. They do need a good flogging.

I suppose the old Quakers have quite a good deal to say to you about thy husband. Well, let them talk. What do I care for them? Doubtless as much as they do for me. William Chilson[7] wrote to Ike and in his letter let slip what one of them said about me. I could hardly make out what it was, but I found out enough to know that they meant to insult me. That is nothing strange for them. They always did hate me for some cause. What it is I don't know and don't give a d—n cent.

How do Hiram's folks get along? Say, keep clear of them. Ask no favors of them and grant none and then you will get along first rate and have no trouble with them. When you write again, tell me how Steve's folks get along and the folks over at the mill. Say, tell me about all the folks generally and yourself in particular. I received a letter from Laura yesterday. She said she was going to write to you the same day she wrote to me.

I think I shall come home in about two weeks if everything is nice. How it will be though, I can't tell. The old colonel is pretty hard in the mouth, so the boys say. I have no experiential knowledge, however. If it is so, I don't know, but the boys hate the colonel in command. I should not wonder if an unlucky shot hit him one of the dark nights, for his men are hard set, sure as you live.

Our meals are brought on to the campground for us now so that it saves a wade in the mud three times a day. I think we shall get along first rate after a few days, as soon as we get things regulated. There is but two things that bother us much now a days. They are lack of water and the want of clean clothes. We could get our clothes washed if we had more or we could wash them ourselves if we had the conveniences to do so. The fact is, we are a most abominable, dilly set and there is no way as I see to avoid being so. The State is in our debt, but won't pay up. Consequently, we shall be dirty until they furnish us with a change of clothes and find us the time and place to wash our clothes.

Send the things I mentioned in my last letter when Hook's folks send Isaac's package. Tell Steve to catch you once in a while a mess of fish and charge the same to me and I will be his uncle 'til I find it convenient to do my own fishing.

Kiss the babies for father and don't let them forget me.

With much love I remain your husband,

C.F. Biddlecom

———

LOMBARD UNIVERSITY
GALESBURG, ILLINOIS
JUNE 18, 1861

My Brother,

Having just finished a letter to our sister Sarah, it seemed hardly fair not to write to you, too. Though, you are still owing me a letter, I have made up my mind to write to you. It has been excessively warm here for the past few weeks. Like a new June day, everything is fresh and green, yet drooping by the too ardent ways of the sun. While the gentlest of breezes bring in the perfume of Hannah's roses blossoming beneath my window, fleecy white clouds fly around the horizon in that deep blue sky only found here.

I did not go to church according to my custom this morning, but stayed home to write, thinking it quite as profitable as boring myself in a reverie in the midst of a sermon and not waking from it 'til the *Amen* is said. I find it most impossible to confine myself to the sermon. While I am aware of the sermon, music, text, and all, in my mind I am back home in the old Baptist Church led by the minister, Elder Hall, and surrounded by the villagers, the girl beside me, our sister, Sarah. I go back farther yet and we three who are so far apart now, are children again, romping together as we used to before Father Time made men and women of us. I cannot help sighing when I think of Sarah, toiling away in that little district school, and your enduring hardships of a soldier's life, while I am leading so happy a life here. But, as we cannot always be together or always enjoy ourselves, I expect to receive sometime trouble enough to counterbalance all happiness.

I have seen in the newspaper that our Governor Morgan[8] takes excellent care of his soldiers and looks after their wants in a fatherly manner.

I have tried to comfort myself thinking that perhaps you are faring well enough. In any rate, Charlie, though they may starve you, keep up your courage and be faithful to the end. Do not talk as some of the soldiers have of desertion, but remember that it is brave and honorable to die for one's country and that whether you fall gloriously as Colonel Ellsworth,[9] or starve for your country's sake, it will be one and the same in the eyes of our Heavenly Father.

Every day I watch the newspapers to see if any more New York regiments have been ordered on, but have not yet seen yours mentioned. Whenever you go, remember to write to me for very anxiously I wait for your letters. Do Sarah or Mother ever write to you, or Father? They ought, if they do not. For the sake of having them write to you, I will be willing to forego some of my letters.

I am enjoying myself better here than in any other place that I have attended school. They are not here as at Macedon Center, continually watching for fear of breaking some regulation, but are willing the students shall enjoy themselves and as a course, a better behaved class of students cannot be found. I like the people here very much, they being nearly all from the East.

I am almost at the bottom of my sheet and as I have not time to fill another, I will condense what I have to say and put it in half.

> *Yours with a brave heart,*
> *Laura*

DAVENPORT, IOWA
JULY 28, 1861

Dear Es,

I have not had the last war news—shall today. The last I read was about the fight at Bull's Run and General Patterson's division was not in the engagement.[10, 11] So, Charles was safe then. I suppose you have heard from Charles since I last heard from you. Do send a line as you have time. I wish to know if he is safe. Love to the children, blessed ones, and all inquiring Friends. Write when you get this, if you can conveniently. In a greater haste than I ever wrote before,

Your loving sister, Cornelia

———

BERLIN, FREDERICK COUNTY
MARYLAND
AUGUST 7, 1861

Dear Wife,

I write to you this morning, I hope, for the last time, for I am coming home just as soon as the proper papers can be made out. I have been sick ever since I wrote you from Hagerstown Hospital.[12] When I left there to join the regiment at Harper's Ferry, I felt quite well, with the exception of feeling very severe cold. I have since had an attack of rheumatism and at the same time, my throat has become affected so that the Potomac fogs almost choke me to death nights. Pretty much all of the sleep I get is in a sitting posture and from that cause; my back has become very weak. But, I can tell you all about it when I come home. You may commence cooking for me as soon as you receive this for I shall not be far behind it, i.e. if I get no worse.

I am your own,
Charlie

———

Charlie Freeman Biddlecom
Honorably Discharged for Disability, August 22, 1861

Records show Charlie spent time at a regimental hospital and at the Hagerstown hospital. He is marked absent from duty July 14 – 20 due to diarrhea and disabled by rheumatism while in Martinsburg, West Virginia. After being discharged for disability from Washington, D.C., on August 22, 1861, due to rheumatism, he returned home.

———

From the death notices listed in the *Christian Ambassador* printed in Auburn, New York:

November 9, 1861:

In Macedon on 16 Sep, Thomas Biddlecom, age 92. Formerly of Oneida Co., where he raised a large family. Two sons became Universalist ministers: David Biddlecom, who died in 1846, and Daniel R. Biddlecom of Galesburg, Il. A son and a daughter took care of him during his final illness.

February 22, 1862:

Macedon on 1 Nov 1861, Bell Biddlecom, age 1 year and 2 months. Daughter of Charles Biddlecom.

ROCHESTER, NY
NOVEMBER 11, 1861

Friend Charlie and wife,

I learned this morning of your bereavement and kindly offer my letter of sympathy and condolence. 'Tis hard, very hard, for you so young to be brought to bear an early affliction (aye, your earliest loss) in your own family. Although little Belle was a morning and evening joy to you just now, and would have been your idol in long years to come, yet believe that aside from this our common lamentations nothing unhappy will come of her going so early. She was the Bell of your leisure times and you know how sweet it was to see her little hands well freighted with her favorite toys; yet near to these sweetest recollections run damped with joyless tears for Bell is not forgotten, lost, sad, or unhappy, but has her hands as full of new plucked buds as ever.

Kindly Yours,
Addison Gates [13]

NOTES

1. The 28th Regiment was mustered in at Canandaigua, New York, on May 22, 1861, and trained at Camp Morgan outside of Albany.

2. A rod = 16.5 feet: "forty or fifty rods" is 660 – 825 feet or 220 – 275 yards.

3. Davies, Thomas A. (1809–1899) Enrolled May 15, 1861, in Albany, N.Y., age 52 and recently retired from military and civil careers. Mustered in as colonel to serve two years; promoted to brigadier general, March 7, 1862, by the President of the United States for gallant conduct at the battle of Blackburn Ford, July 18, 1861.

4. *Victuals:* food

5. Brown, Edwin F., from Medina, N.Y.; Lt. Col. of 28th Regiment, lost an arm and was captured at the Battle of Cedar Mountain in 1862; promoted to colonel, August 16, 1862; discharged June 2, 1863. After the war he served as Governor and Inspector General of National Homes for Disabled Volunteer Soldiers.

6. Wilson, Isaac S., (*a.k.a.* Ike) age 31. Enlisted May 14, 1861, Canandaigua, N.Y., to serve two years as private, 28th Regiment NY Company E; accidentally wounded in action; discharged September 3, 1861, Darnestown, Maryland. Continued as a Quaker speaker and minister throughout his life.

7. Chilson, William H., age 34. Enlisted July 30, 1862, Farmington, N.Y., to serve three years; mustered in as sergeant 126th Regiment NY Company H, on August 22, 1862; surrendered September 15, 1862; paroled September 16, 1862, at Harper's Ferry; wounded in action May 6, 1864, at the Wilderness, Virginia; transferred to 7th Regiment Company I Veteran Reserve Corps on August 29, 1864; 22nd Regiment Company I Veteran Reserve Corps, sergeant October 17, 1864; mustered out with detachment July 3, 1865, Camp Cleveland, Ohio.

8. Morgan, Edwin D. (1811–1883) Union Army major general commissioned in 1861 while governor, to allow him to exert military authority as the commander of the Department of New York; he never served in the field. Applied his common sense view of business successfully to political matters. 21st Governor of New York State (1859–1862); United States Senator (1863–1869); Chairman of the Republican National Committee.

9. Ellsworth, Elmer Ephraim (1837–1861) Lawyer, soldier, and a friend of Abe Lincoln. While removing a Confederate flag from an Alexandria, Virginia, hotel within view of the White House, he was shot by the hotel's owner. He is considered the first officer killed in the Civil War.

10. The First Battle of Bull Run, also known as First Manassas, was fought on July

21, 1861. Thinking it would bring a quick end to the war, the Northern public pushed for a march against the Confederate capital of Richmond, Virginia. Succumbing to the political pressure, Brigadier General Irvin McDowell advanced his unseasoned Union troops, the 90 days men, across Bull Run Creek against an equally unprepared Confederate Army under Brigadier General P.G.T. Beauregard near Manassas Junction. Neither the new recruits, nor the excited citizens, who hiked their picnic baskets up to the hills to watch the "show," had anticipated what was to come. Initially finding themselves at a disadvantage from a surprise flank attack, the withering Confederate troops were rescued by reinforcements under the command of Brigadier General Joseph E. Johnston. A brigade from Virginia under Thomas J. Jackson held their ground long enough to launch a counterattack and in so doing gave "Stonewall Jackson" his nickname. The Confederates' counterattack sent Union troops fleeing toward Washington, D.C. Heavy losses on both sides sobered and erased any idea of a quick end of the war.

11. Patterson, Robert (1792–1881) Major general assigned to advance against Brigadier General Joseph E. Johnston's Confederate army in the Shenandoah Valley, keeping it occupied so that it could not reinforce P.G.T. Beauregard's army at Manassas. Patterson was so unthreatening, however, that Johnston was able to pass him by and transport his army by railroad to Manassas, where they made a crucial contribution to the Union defeat at First Bull Run. Patterson was relieved from duty and mustered out on July 2, 1861.

12. Of the 620,000 soldiers' lives lost during the Civil War, nearly two-thirds of these deaths were due to disease. Farm boys who had not built up immunities to germs outside of their hometowns were suddenly thrust into unsanitary camps crowded with thousands of men. Dysentery, typhoid fever, smallpox, and other diseases took more lives than did bullets.

13. This letter was scripted on traditional mourning paper: heavy white paper with a thick black border.

CHAPTER 5

DRAFTED
"KISS THE CHILDREN FOR ME"

T HE Regimental Descriptive Book states that Charles F. Biddlecom, age 39, though, he was actually only 29, enlisted for service on October 1, 1863, in Canandaigua, New York. Only a portion of those drafted actually served. The rest were excused for various reasons: medical, only son, owning property, affording a substitute. Some simply failed to report for duty. The Conscription Act[1] of March 1863 required all able-bodied males between twenty and forty-five years of age to serve a three-year term in the military. In advance of his service Charlie was paid a bounty of $25, with an additional bounty due to him of $75, and was mustered into the 147th Infantry Regiment Company A New York State Volunteers.[2] His date of his enrollment was later altered from October to July 28, 1863, in accordance with the Company Muster Rolls of January and February 1864, which lines up with the account given in his letters. Whether by error or a change of heart, records also indicate that Charlie enlisted in First Cavalry Regiment Company I on September 5, 1863, at Camp Sherrill, Geneva, New York. Even though he was with the 147th Regiment at the time, his name was published in the Palmyra Courier as a deserter from the First Cavalry, a misunderstanding cleared up, at least to some extent, by his sister, Laura.

The 147th Regiment New York Infantry was organized in Oswego by Colonel Andrew S. Warner and mustered into service September 22, 1862. Before Charlie joined them, the regiment had suffered fewer than ten casualties in engagements at Pollock's Mill Creek[3] and Chancellorsville,[4] but had been severely crushed at the Battle of Gettysburg. There, marching straight into a superior force of the enemy, the 147th was surrounded in an unfortunate position at the bottom of an unfinished railroad bed. Trapped between two steep slopes, the troops did not receive an order of retreat because their commander, Lieutenant Colonel Miller,[5] had been wounded just after hearing it. The battered regiment held their position under Major G. Harney[6] until finally receiving the order of retreat from Captain Ellsworth. Union Brigadier General Lysander Cutler reported that 79 percent of their total had been killed, wounded, captured, or missing "within a half an hour." Of the 380 men who were engaged during the three sultry days of battle in Gettysburg, only 79 were left to stack muskets. On October 10, 1863, to replace the tragic losses, 222 conscripts, one of whom was Charlie, joined the weakened 147th Regiment.

———

FARMINGTON, NEW YORK
SEPTEMBER 13, 1863

MR. AND MRS. J. S. BIDDLECOM
NOT TO BE OPENED UNTIL AFTER MY DEATH

To my dear Father and Mother,

I write this, my only request, in case that I never return from the Army. I will you to take my children and bring them up (or provide for their bringing up) so that they will be able to provide for themselves when they arrive at a suitable age. I wish you to take the entire control of them if I die before I am discharged from the service or before I return.[7]

Chas. F. Biddlecom

———

[The letter below is from David M. Lapham, Esther's brother.]

SPRINGFIELD, ILLINOIS
SEPTEMBER 14, 1863

Dear Sister,

I had a letter from Cornelia the other day in which she informs me that Charles is drafter. I hope he will not go. I should not, if I was drafted.

In their Convention here on this issue, the Republicans and Abolitionists made no bones about saying the war should be carried on for abolition, not for the restoration of the Old Union. I believe the masses of the slaves are much better off in slavery than out of it, especially in the manner the abolitionists would take them out, if they could.

It was not convenient for me to make Cornelia a visit this fall. I shall be apt to take another school soon. McVeigh asked me if I would take their school the other day. He is to see me Monday about it. The last I saw of folks on Round Prairie they were all well. Smith has gone to Missouri this summer. I don't hear any thing from our brother Stephen. Do you know where he is? Write soon.

> *Your affectionate brother,*
> *David*

———

ELMIRA, NEW YORK
OCTOBER 4, 1863

Dear Esther,

We poor forsaken conscripts arrived here about 11 o'clock today and, of course, we as yet know nothing of our fate or where we are to go. If we can all keep together, i.e. Peckham,[8] Crocker,[9] and myself, we shall be well pleased, but it looks rather uncertain whether it will be so or not. I rather think we shall not have the privilege of choosing, but will be drawn by lot. If that is the case we shall stand a pretty good chance of being separated. We do not find any officers here from our part of the country. We shall try to get into the 136th Regiment, but if we fail in that I do not know what else we shall do. How long we shall be here I do not have the least idea, maybe a week and maybe not two days. At any rate it will not be long. Whether you had better write or not is more than I know, but if you do, direct to Elmira 3rd Barracks.

With much love to you and the babies, I am your husband,

> *Chas. F. Biddlecom*

———

ELMIRA, NEW YORK
OCTOBER 6, 1863

Dear Wife,

We are off this evening at 5 o'clock for some place. Probably we shall go direct to Alexandria. Peckham and Crocker are in the same batch. Say, I have the foundation of a discharge already laid in the shape of a bad cold and rheumatism. How long it will take to work up to a strong enough case for a discharge I do not know, but I think not long. We have had a pretty hard time since we have been here. The victuals have been just tolerable, that is all. Bread, beef, and pea coffee[9] for breakfast, soup and bread for dinner, mush and milk for supper, and freeze to death nights, hence a cold and rheumatism. Well, so it goes. Were I at home again, I think I should stay, but let her rip; I am not going to whine over spilled milk. Take good care of the children and put the flannel on them the first cold weather that comes. Do not feel bad for it will all come right in a little while. Do the best you can and we will make everything smooth some of these days. You had better not write until you hear from me again.

I am your husband,

Chas. F. Biddlecom

———

NEAR CULPEPER, VIRGINIA
OCTOBER 11, 1863

Dear Wife,

I left Elmira the evening of the 6th, to Baltimore the 7th, and the same night left for Alexandria, traveling the morning of the 8th, and the afternoon of the 9th we arrived here, or here abouts. Yesterday, the 10th, we took in sixty rounds of ammunition and started to hunt up the Rebs, but it looked last night like a retreat. Whether it was meant for one or not, I can't tell, neither do I care much. For it is all the same whether we fight or run, the war will drag its dreary length along 'til the toil passes out of sight, which, pray to God, may soon happen.

Whatever may be the feeling at home there as regards the crushing out of this rebellion, the opinion here is that there is too much money speculation among the officers to have the war pushed to a final conclusion before another year. There is considerable red tape circumlocution in every move that is made here.

Yesterday we filed in with knapsacks and stood about an hour waiting for the order to march. Finally we got orders to unpack and rest in position. We rested about five minutes and slung again, trampled about three miles down the Rapidan, and stayed there all day waiting an order to cross. Finally we were ordered to pitch tents. So, we put up our dog kennels and fixed our beds for a good sleep (which, by the way, I have not had since I left Canandaigua week ago last Saturday). Well, we stayed there 'til 10 or 11 o'clock p.m. During that time we struck tents, packed up, and fell in three or four times. Finally we got off and tramped about eight miles and stacked arms and bunked for the night, or so we supposed. But, in the course of an hour and a half we were routed up and ordered to fall in with knapsacks on. We stood about an hour waiting for the order to march, which never came. Finally, we fixed bayonets, stacked arms again, and dropped down to sleep again. We are here yet. 9 A.M. and no prospects of a move today as the pickets are going well out to the front and everything looks like a stay of a day or so. Still, we may have to dig out in ten minutes. The fact is I don't believe there is a man here that knows anything about what is to come of tomorrow or in an hour. Yet, I doubt there is much of chance for a fight for some time to come.

George Peckham is not in the same company with me. He is in Co. F and I am Co. A. Crocker is somewhere, I suppose. I wish you would find out and write to me where he is, as we would like to find him if he is in this army.

With the exception of having a hard cough and a snotty nose I am all right. My right leg is considerably swollen and pains me some, probably it would give out on a hard march, as it showed indications of failure last night. It showed some indications of rain last night. If I had, it would have been all up with me today so far as marching or fighting is concerned.

Write to me as soon as you get this.

Direct to:

> 147th Reg't NYS. Vols Co A
> Washington D.C.

Be sure and direct your letter plain so there can be no mistake. Kiss the children for me and keep your courage good. With much love I am your husband,

Chas. F. Biddlecom

Tell Ches's folks that George is well.

———

THOROUGHFARE GAP, VIRGINIA[11]
OCTOBER 21, 1863

Dear Wife,

We left Haymarket last night about five o'clock and marched through to this point west of the mountains and went into bivouac[12] about nine p.m. Where we shall go from here is yet a mystery. The pack up call has just sounded and we are off. I will finish this when we stop, which may be an hour, and may be in a week. When will I get a letter from home? Who knows? It does seem an age since I left home. We only moved about half a mile and went into camp on a side hill where it is impossible to sleep without rolling out of our tents. We have had pretty hard marching in the rain and through the mud, shoe mouth deep. Such sticky mud as this Virginia mud I never saw in my life, even in Illinois.

. . .

Well, we have moved again, and it rained, of course, back through the Gap and through Haymarket and Gainesville to Bristoe Station and one mile beyond, making a march of twenty or some miles in a heavy rain storm and in mud ankle deep. I was completely saturated. We built a good fire after we pitched our tents and by twisting and turning like a piece of meat on a turnspit, we managed to dry ourselves so as to sleep tolerably comfortable. If I had my breakfast I should feel pretty well, but I have not had a bit to eat since yesterday morning and as a consequence I feel like an empty corncrib.

. . .

It is now nine o'clock Sunday morning the twenty-fifth of October and a shiny day, but rather cool. Our wagons have come up and we shall soon have provisions in plenty. My health is first rate and my appetite is good, but I feel tired out and shall not stand such marching very long. As for fighting, I think there is not the most distant probability of any large battles in this department from the fact that General Lee[13] has not force enough to face us. It is so far from here to the Reb's strongholds that the Federal forces can't get at them without endangering our lines of communication and leaving us short of rations. Again, Meade's policy seems to be to try and fight the Rebels at an advantage, or else not fight at all.[14, 15] So, I think the most of the fighting will be done in some other department, as we shall hardly be able to find any Rebels this side of Gordonsville. Lee is too smart to be outgeneraled and compelled to fight an open field fight where he does not stand the ghost of a chance. If Lee outgenerals Meade and gets an advantageous position on our flank or in rear of us, then we will have to fight him. As for his fighting on even chances, Meade is not the man to do any such thing.

Now, about getting discharged: in the first place, I have got to get into the hospital. Then, if I am not able for service, I shall have an opportunity to apply for a discharge. But, if I am well I shall get along first rate and am not homesick, nor do I mean to be if I can help it. Sometimes I think of home and its comforts, but I do not repine at my lot. No, not in the least. The truth of the business is there is no use in making wry faces over what may happen here, for those that are responsible are too far from us to care for it. When or where this war will end is, as yet, among the things that are beyond human ken.

Now, I must tell you about our leaders and company. Well, the Captain is one first-rate fellow. He lives with his men, carries his own baggage, and takes things as they come. He is not stuck up in the least and the men all like him. His name is McKinlock.[16] He is from Oswego. The company is made up of every name and nation, trade and occupation under the sun. There is some first rate men and some so mean that the Gentleman in Black has long ago given them over and forsaken their company altogether. We have lost five men since I joined the company. Three taken prisoners and two have failed to return themselves after a march and have no doubt taken French lieve.[17] They will be shot if taken. There is in this regiment something like five hundred conscripts and substitutes and I do think them the best men for service I ever saw together.

Esther, do not get lonesome or desolate or melancholy or anything else of that nature, but keep yourself cheerful and be sure that I shall come home again in good time. For I do not believe I shall be killed. As for dying a natural death, why, I might die at home as well as here. Remember that I have not been in the service but two weeks yet, and I may not be in more than that much longer. For I know well enough when I shall fail and that will be as soon as the fall rains set in. Now, just as soon as I get sick it will be all over with me, for as for getting well of colds and rheumatism in camp, it is out of the question.

George Peckham is in the hospital with a carbuncle on his ankle. I saw Sampson Fry[18] today; he is in the First New York Sharpshooters. I mean to get transferred into that company if I can. Write as often as possible and let me know how you all get along and I will write as soon after this as I can. Do not wait to get a letter from me before you write, but write to me at least once every week and I will write every opportunity. Accept this as a homely, awkward letter written under very adverse circumstances by your husband,

Chas. F. Biddlecom

P.S. Accept my most heartfelt thanks for your letter of the twentieth.

I came long near forgetting mention having received one from you. I received one from you last night after I had laid down to get a little shivering, miserable sleep. Esther, be sure of one thing, you can't want to hear from me worse than I do from you.

> *Ever thine own,*
> *Charlie*

———

Dear Sister;

I got your letter informing me that M. Gage would wait a little before sending that forty dollars. Tell him I would like to have it as soon as possible as there is a way I can make advantageous use of it. I had a letter from Cornelia yesterday. She was in reasonable good health. I have not had a letter from our brother Daniel for a long time. Of course, none from Stephen.

I hope that Charles feels better now since he has let off his spleen in the calling of names and epithets applied to me in his last letter.

You might not have known it, but I have just engaged a school at forty-five dollars per month. I am in very good health. This has been written in a hurry, as you can see. I would like that forty in a couple of weeks. Write soon.

> *Your affectionate brother,*
> *David M. Lapham*

———

Dear Wife,

I received your very acceptable letter, it being the second from home since September the 30th. You may be sure I was glad to hear from home and to hear that you were all well. Which, by the by, I am not quite, but am not sick enough to be off duty. I hope I shall have the good fortune to keep in good health until this war is over. I presume I could play off and get discharged after a little, but I do not wish to come home in that kind of way.

We are in a good location and I hope we shall stay where we are until we are drilled sufficiently to take the field with a tolerable show of whipping the Rebels. We are living better at present than we have been to fore. We get soft bread, beans, dried apples, and fresh beef in plenty, with an occasional mess of potatoes, just enough of them to keep the taste in our mouths and a strong appetite for more. Apples are dearer here than lemons are in New York. Good sized, full Pippins will sell for eight to ten cents per apple. As for butter and cheese, it would cost a man of fair appetite about fifty cents a meal to get even a lick of butter or a crumb of cheese. Common quart cans of tomatoes or peaches sell at $0.75 per can; such are sutler's[19] prices. They may go to [——] with them and be [——] with them before I pay them any such prices.

I was sick the other day and got a can of tomatoes and ate them all for my dinner. Got up the next morning sound as a whistle so that I considered the money well invested. I hope I shall not be sick again, for it costs too much to diet up here and I fear that many feeds of tomatoes would create an appetite that the pocket could not resist. But, oh, if I had one dozen good, large apples how I could feast. But, at eight cents apiece, I am afraid of them. I am afraid they would stick in my throat as they went down.

So, Hunter is in the cider trade again this fall. Well, I am glad we have got rid of him and I hope Steve will get enough of him, for I am sure I have had quite a plenty. As for Steve being afraid that the other neighbors will be thought more of than he, I can tell him one way to save himself, and that is to tend strictly to his own business, then he will get along first rate. Another thing, his wife must quit telling everything she sees and hears and then they will get along first rate. I would be glad if you would not go to their house very often, for it is sure to hurt your reputation. Steve is one of those that in conversation with a certain class is not over scrupulous of what he says. So, just look out for him. Instead of his Esther checking him, she just thinks him smart and laughs when he casts a black guard slur on some woman's character for virtue. You may be sure that there is not a woman whose husband is away from home that does not come in for a share of his slander. Levi Allen is as bad as Steve. So, just stand clear of both of their families as much as decency will admit. I think more of Robert's folk and Lorenzo Hathaway than I do all the rest of the folks in the neighborhood. I consider Andrew Roberts one of the best men I ever knew and should be glad to know that you were on the most intimate terms with them. With this exception, do not trust them to keep anything secret.

I think it best for you to have a coal stove this winter. Get a good one, if ever you get one, so that you can have a low fire all night. It will be easier on you than wood fires to have the room warm nights, for you no doubt will have to be up with the children some cold nights and I shall not be there to make the fires for you. So, get coal and a coal stove. I will try to send you some money as soon as we are paid off. We were mustered for pay yesterday. I think we shall be paid by the middle of November and it may be sooner. If I get what is my just due I shall get $39.00, but how it will be I can't tell, as I do not know how the pay rolls are made out.

So, Andrew Roberts thinks it a shame to put such shoes upon the men. Well, perhaps, but I do not think so. Those shoes are considered by the men as being very best marching footgear there is in the world as they do not make the feet sore and that is of the utmost importance. I know of men trading first-rate boots costing $8.00 the pair for a pair of those shoes and giving money to make the exchange. So, you can see how the soldiers regard those government shoes. I will tell you how it is. In warm weather when on the march there will be no better shoe. Ten chances to one, wading any stream that crosses our path when on the march the water will be over the tops of boots, and if it is, what will be the difference? Socks will be wet just as soon. The shoes will quickly be dry, while the boots would be full of water and blister the feet. But, in the fall and winter boots are better for they keep out the mud and slush and feet stay warm and dry. But, for the summer use, shoes are the best.

Es, this is Sunday by the day of the week, but so far as business is concerned you would hardly know the difference, for all is noise and confusion. You cannot imagine the difference between a soldier's life and the life at home. At home the noise incident to butchering or threshing day would be peace and quietness in comparison to a Sunday in camp. I am glad to hear that you are getting along so well at home. You may eat some apples and morsels of all the good things you have and think of me at the same time and it will do me some good.

So, William Daylor wants to buy the farm. What do you think? Had Father better sell it or not? I will leave it all for you to say. I am afraid if the farm is sold you will not have as good a place to live through the winter. I think I shall be home in the spring. I do not know but we might get a worse place than that is, instead of a better one. Still, I think $80.00 an acre is more than the farm is worth to me. I will let you say all about what shall be done with trusting in your and Mother's judgment. I shall write you again in a few days. Until then I bid you goodbye.

Chas. F. Biddlecom

(Tell Roberts to write me a letter and I will tell him all about camp life and soldiering in general)

———

RAPPAHANNOCK STATION,
VIRGINIA
NOVEMBER 12, 1863

Dear Esther,

After one weeks marching and camping, packing up and marching again, some times a long march and a fast one at that, and again a short and slow march, we find ourselves at this point guarding the railroad. We left Bristoe Station last Thursday the fifth and after a night march 'til ten o'clock the regiment reached Catlett Station, distant about five and one half miles. So, you can see that the march was slow, yet it was the most tiresome march I ever experienced. So much so that I gave out while on the way and laid my weary limbs to rest in a thicket of pines, where I waited for the light of day, confident that at the rate the regiment was marching I could overtake them in the course of an hour or two in the daylight. And so it proved, for by nine o'clock I was rejoined up with the rest. I am sorry to say I was yet quite sick with dysentery (caused by carrying eight days provisions on my back).

We rested at Catlett's the next day and I got some better. Saturday morning dawned bright and frosty and with the rising sun we took up our line of march. Such marching would I think use me up if I were well, for off we went at a quick step. After marching about four and one half miles I was taken very sick and fell out, thinking to be better in a little time. But, instead of better, I got worse. At night after having gone some five miles further I gave completely out and had to drop down by the roadside for the night. I was something like five miles behind the regiment and there was six in company with me. Again did we take to the pines for safety and this time we loaded our rifles for fear of surprise by the guerrillas. I bought a quart of milk off an old secesh[20] cuss of a woman for which I gave a half pound of first rate coffee and a pound and a half of sugar, worth at home about forty cents. I boiled it and a tablespoonful of black pepper together, soaked my hardtack[21] in it, and had as good a supper as I ever ate in my life. I think I should have died during the night following if it had not been for the boiled milk, for during the day and night I had over thirty passages of the bowels and passed so much blood and mucus and become so weak that I could hardly stand alone.

The next morning we took the road again for Morrisville and Kelly's Ford and as may be supposed, I progressed but slowly, my bowels giving me much trouble. About noon I came across a tree full of persimmons and as they are said to be good for such complaints I ate a good feed of them, which helped me to a certain extent. About two o'clock we got inside our pickets and in company with others. We were taken charge of by a squad of cavalry styling themselves Provost Guards[22] (by what authority it was not clear). They kept us from 2 p.m. Sunday afternoon until Monday morning when they started us on the road for Kelly's Ford, which we crossed about noon. The Cavalry are first-rate fellows and they took pains to accommodate us as much as was possible. I got some medicine from the surgeon of their regiment and it helped me very much so that I was able to march on Monday at a good sound gait.

I reached our regiment about 5 p.m. on Monday. Within an hour they left their camp near Brandy Station for this side of the river where we now are doing guard duty along the road from Warrenton Junction toward the front so as to protect Meade's line of communication with the front.[23] The report is that we are relieved from duty in front and are detailed to guard the railroad from Washington towards Culpeper and the advance of the army, where ever that is. If it is so, we have got a safe thing of it and it does certainly look like it at this time. Should we stay here a week or two we shall then go into winter quarters. If then I get a stray ball in my gizzard it will be but an accident, as there will be no general engagement that we shall be in this fall and it is said that winter campaigns are not played out since Burnside's Mud March[24] last winter. We are in hopes that before another spring the Rebellion will be over and we will be on the route for home.

What this campaign will amount to is, of course, a matter of mere conjecture, but we hope the Johnny Rebs are to take a good whipping this time, such a one as will fix their game for them in a way as to finish the war. One thing is sure, a part of the Sixth Corps whipped them out of the fortifications here and took 1600 of them prisoners in a very few minutes last Saturday.[25] 1500 of our men done the whole job for them and they say (the Rebs say) that the war is about over. All but one of the prisoners refuse to fight us again. We hear that Grant has made a good move in Tennessee,[26] but as none of us have seen a paper since the 7th, of course, we do not know much about it. We were told the other day that

Gilmore had taken Fort Sumtor.[27] We hope it is so, but of course, know nothing of the facts in the case.

Now, a little more about my health. It is very poor and I have no appetite. Should I continue in this way a week I shall be in the hospital in Washington and then you may look out for me for I shall be discharged just as sure as shooting. It is time I got another letter from some of you. The farm sold. As far as I am concerned I should like some other business besides farming and I think I am better calculated for something other than farming. My health is not good enough to stand the hard labor necessary to carry on a farm.

> *With much love I am your,*
> *Charlie*

———

RAPPAHANNOCK STATION,
VIRGINIA
NOVEMBER 20, 1863

Dear Esther,

I must write you a few lines this morning to let you know how I am and what I have been doing since I wrote last. My health is better this week than it has been for some time and with the exception of rheumatism in my right hip joint, I feel first rate. My appetite is good and if I can keep from eating too much I think I shall keep my usual health.

For the last few days there has been Fatigue Parties detailed from our regiment to help build fortifications down at the railroad bridge crossing the Rappahannock River. Yesterday it fell to my lot to be one of the number detailed from Company A and I was not sorry, for I had got tired of this ever lasting drill, skirmish, drill and was quite willing to shovel dirt instead. We did not have to work very hard, only one hour on and one hour off. And not very constant digging at that, but I was very tired when we got back to camp. My back and hips ached all night. I suppose the walk has something to do with it as we went and came by the Division Headquarters, which made the distance about three miles further than it would have been had we taken the direct route to and from our work.

Things look as though this corps is going into winter quarters here from the fact that the orders have been issued that the men build huts with chimneys to them. Yesterday while I was gone my chums commenced operations and got our habitations started. Both of them have gone down to the forts this morning to work and as I have nobody to help me, the shanty will have to stand still today. I tell you what, Esther, if some of the folks in Farmington could see these log huts of ours I think they would never grumble again about not having house room enough. Our hut will be about four feet high and this little dog kennel will be the habitation for four men this winter. You see. It will be less than one fourth the size of our kitchen at home and only high enough for us to stand up in the center. As the roof will be cloth there will not be any danger of our hurting our heads with knocking them against the roof. The old log cabin of Illinois would be a palace in comparison with our dog kennels, but these are the best we can have here for we have not tools to make better ones with. All we have had so far has been a little hatchet which would compare with an ax about as Stafford's little hammer does to a common nail hammer, and I think the hatchet is about as well as we will be able to do. Our house will not be a very warm affair, I think, but we shall have to make the best of it. The next paragraph is not to be read aloud.

I do not mean to winter in one of these dog holes. Oh, no, no, not a bit of it. Just look here, I can play off enough to get out of this and I mean to do it. There have been some men discharged since I came here, some of them came with us and they were not a bit more disabled and I am. Now you see I am going in for getting out of this just as soon as is possible. It will do no harm to try going home even if I fail. Do not let anybody see this because if I am found out it will make a devil of a rumpus. So burn this up or put it away where no one will find it. Look for me home in the course of six or eight days, for to the hospital I mean to go and from there to Washington and from there home, if there is any such thing and I know there is. I am as patriotic as any man, but I do object to fooling away time here when this war could be ended in a month just as well as not. For if men can carry eight days rations on their backs when there is no need, they certainly can go to Richmond and end this war in that length of time. That is time enough to go there and do all the fighting that is necessary to use up Lee and his whole army.

If you want money, let me know and I will decide with you. I had a dream the other night. I dreamt that you said to me that you wanted ten yards of flannel to make underclothing for the children and went to Palmyra and bought it. I think of home a great deal and I think of you and the children almost all of the time. It makes me so homesick that I could cry any time. I know that I think of you oftener than I did when I was out here last time. Almost every time I get to sleep I can see everything in the house and see you all. It has a bad effect on my mind and makes me discontented. I mean to come home just as soon as I can and if the administration wants me to do any fighting for them they must let me do it this fall for I do not mean to be here in the spring. That is just all there is to that. Go home, I will, or else to the doctors.

This is a funny looking letter written with red ink, but I could not get any black and I have got tired of writing with a pencil. Has Father consulted with you about selling the farm? I wrote to Laura the other day and sent her some change to send me some letter stamps.

Yours, Charlie

(I wrote to Ben McVeigh the other day and have commenced a letter to the Roberts. I want to write Sarah as soon as I can, for I do not want to have her think she is slighted, but I should think she might write to me if I do not write to her first thing.)

———

KELLY'S FORD SOUTH SIDE RAPPAHANNOCK
SATURDAY DECEMBER 5, 1863

Well, Esther, you see we have moved again, but not far this time, though, we traveled a circuitous route to get here. Sometimes I think the generals are drunk from the way they maneuver this division. For as a general thing we march about five miles to get ahead three. Why it should be so unless the officers are drunk or crazy I do not know. The boys are fixing up quarters again in hopes that our stay here will pay for so doing, but I can't see it so. I think I shall not go to too much trouble yet a while.

What will be done here I can't tell, but I have lost confidence in Meade ever giving us a fight. His generalship seems to consist in keeping us on short allowance and marching us to death. When we advanced this last time we all thought to strike a good blow for the ending of this rebellion, but it did not seem to be Meade's policy to do so.[28] There is a rumor in camp that we are to have Hooker back again.[29] If we do, we shall have rations and fighting as much as we desire.

Well, it seems from your last letter that the farm is sold. Though, I have never received any positive information of the fact of it to be so. I received your last letter last night, with it came one from Laura and another from Sarah. Laura wrote to me about my being published as a deserter and sent me a slip cut from the Palmyra Courier containing the list of deserters from Captain H.J. Draime's[30] Company First Volunteer Calvary and a letter published which was written by sister Laura correcting the fact. I hope in the course of human events to meet this Dutch Knight of the Saddle on equal terms. Then, I think I will try and coax a settlement out of him in the shape that best becomes a soldier. 'Til then the lying curse must go undisturbed, for he out ranks me. Now, you know, it would not do to pick a fight with him. I shall write a short note to the editor of the Palmyra Courier setting forth the facts in the case and demand that he publish it as prominently as he has the accusation.

The farm is sold and with it will be sold all we have in the world, I suppose. Well, I hope Father is satisfied with it at last. But, but, but, but! I am not going to The Locks to live a little dog's life, following Father around the same as Mrs. Kelly's Frank used to. They need not think it. Rather than that I will stay here in the service of Uncle Sam until I either fill a grave or am discharged a pensioner on account of being too old and used up to serve any longer. Now mark my word and see if I do not predict the truth (happen what may whether I live or die here) all the stock will be sold, sheep, cattle, horses and everything else that your immediate necessities do not require, and then the grumbling will commence because I am not able to take care of you out of the paltry $13.00 a month I receive from the government. And should it so happen that I come home debilitated in health, what sympathy would I get do you think? Well, about the same as it was when I came home before sick nearly to death. Charlie will have to go to work to get a few shillings to keep him out of the poor house, whether he is able or not.

Now, Esther, you go to the Locks and try to put up with it and I will go to work and try to get a commission in the negro regiments[31] that are getting up and see if we can live independent of them. I shall send this to Macedon on purpose that they may get it and read it, for I want them to know that I am down here suffering that the black men may be free. They are not going to fix things up at home so as to make me a servant, not by a long site.

The weather is fine and I feel quite well and am glad to hear that you are getting along so well. If you can send me your pictures and the children's, do so and I will send you the money to pay for them. Laura writes just a fair letter, but Sarah's letter looks to me just as though she had done just enough to pass muster and that was all. I have read two *Tribunes* and one *Harper*[32] from Laura.

Accept this from your Husband,

Chas F. Biddlecom

KELLY'S FORD, VIRGINIA

DECEMBER 9, 1863

Dear Esther,

I will write to you today for I am lonesome and writing is the only relief I have. We are building winter quarters again and I presume that by the time we get fixed up nicely we shall have to move as we did before. When do you move to the Locke and what disposition has Father made of all the stock? Tell me all about it. Have you made any definite arrangements yet as to how you are to live with Father's folks? Will you go in all in common or will you have a room to yourself and be partially alone even if you eat at the same table. If it was so, you could be by yourself part of the time. I think then you would get along better and have fewer collisions with Laura about the children. That will be the only trouble and if you can avoid giving offense in that way you will get along first rate. Do try and have everything go on smoothly.

Do the neighbors ever ask about me and do you suppose they care what becomes of me? I must try and write some of them, but when I think of it, it seems wrong to write to them when I know that you wish to hear from me as often as I get an opportunity to write to anyone. So, I write to you and let the other folks go without. I wrote to Nehemiah the other day and the same day wrote to Geo Peckham. He is in the hospital yet and I think will not come out to the front this winter, if he ever does. I do not know as I can blame him for not coming, for I do not think he is strong enough to stand camp life. His lungs are weak. I wish I were at home again for this exposure will ruin my health. I have not the least doubt. My throat is so sore that I can't hardly swallow and I cough a great deal. How long it will last I am not sure. It is impossible to keep from taking cold here. I am as careful as I can be, but it is no use, I can't prevent getting them. How I do want to see you and the children. I am homesick, homesick, and there is no use trying to deny it. How long, Oh, God, must I stay away? I have been gone little over two months and it does seem as though it was as many years.

We have to eat beef, bread, and pork, and I have had one mess of potatoes since coming here. We hope to have better soon, but I do not know how we are to get it, for we have been hoping all this time and still there is no improvement in the rations.

Write just as often as you can and tell me everything just as it happens. The most trivial circumstance has an interest for me that you can hardly

conceive of. Write twice a week if you can. Does Father ever talk of me
and what does he say? I do wish there was a different feeling existing in
our family towards me, but I suppose Charlie will always be the black
sheep in the flock, just as he always has been. I am sorry I wrote to you
as I did the other day, but when a fellow has so much to torment him
there must be some excuse.

> *With much love I am,*
> *Your Charlie*

KELLY'S FORD, VIRGINIA
DECEMBER 14, 1863

Dear Esther,

Your last dated the 8th came last night and I write to you because today
and tomorrow I am off duty by the order of the doctor. I may have to
work, that is, if I am considered fit for duty, as there is lots of work to do
fixing up for the winter.

We are encamped in a miserable mud hole of a place with but one
thing to recommend it, and that is the wood is handy. But, before the
winter is half gone we shall have to pack wood a mile or more. You have
no idea how much timber it takes to build huts and cook a soldier's beef
and beans. Within a week this regiment has stripped at least fifteen acres
of heavy timber. The sound of the ax is heard from early dawn 'til late at
night. Such axes were never seen outside the army. Axes heavy and axes
light, from seven-eighths down to lathing hatchets, and they all of them,
look to me as if grindstones were very scarce and valuable as gold. It takes
three or four times the labor to chop down a tree than it would if the axes
were sharp. I never saw a house built before without any tools except a little
hatchet. The fact is some of our huts look like those fabulous mansions not
made with hands. With this exception, they are not eternal, either here,
or in the skies. In fact, some of our huts look just as if they grew, they
are so stunted and twisted out of shape. A comfortable hog pen, such as
you see in New York, by far surpasses them in beauty of design. As for

the workmanship, I have seen many a playhouse made by school children that beat them out of sight. Of course, there are exceptions, but they are few. Most of the men fail on the fireplace, but we have got a good one. One of my chums is a bricklayer and he has built ours this morning. It is a good one and draws well, which can't be said of one in a dozen from appearances. I think we are to have a comfortable shanty when we get it plastered up with Old Virginia mortar, which is everywhere abundant.

One thing is sure that this is a muddy country. Even the mud that has been before now our discomfort we make use of to stop out those cold chilly winds of December of which we have heard Mrs. Kelly warble so many times. What has become of her Buck? Did she say anything about him when she was out, or is she on the lookout for another man? I do wonder what she wanted to see me so very badly for. This having a woman hooked to me that has got a husband in the army is something I should not fancy, especially one that knew no more than she does. I heard of her in Canandaigua the afternoon that I got there. Young Crocker told me that he had seen her and that she was hunting after me. Well, she wore herself out in hunting I reckon, for I did not take any especial pains to see her. I tell you what it is—I should be terrible miserable jealous of such a woman as Mrs. K.

. . .

This December 15th morning I went to the doctor again and he told me he could do nothing for me. Well, then, I shall go to the hospital in a few days and from there to Washington and the end will be home or a transfer to the Invalid Corps.[33] Darn the luck. I am always sick when I least want to be and distressingly healthy when the rations are short. What will come of me is more than I can guess. Our orderly sergeant does everything he can to favor me and I have had it very easy in comparison were I a sound man. I have not slept four hours in as many days and nights. I have to stand up most of the time and my legs are so sore and lame that I limp as I go. The reason why I can't sleep is cramp and pain in my left side and chest. I can't draw a long breath without its nearly killing me. I shall write to the Surgeon General if they do not do something for me before long, for I don't mean to die here for lack of attention. My old papers will be of great use to me now for the surgeons can't say I am playing off to keep from doing duty. I am not very bad today and shall probably get along until the next storm comes and, of course, rheumatism will pry me back again.

You have moved by this time and this I will send to the Locks. Of course, I got the daily Harper last night. Have not read any in it yet. It sure is a pity to send them to me for I can only read them and then they are thrown away. Do not send me any more *Tribunes* for we have them here every day and those you send from home are very cold by the time they get here. I should like to have you send me some local newspaper like the Palmyra or Canandaigua paper, i.e. if there is anything in them that you think would interest me. We get the *Washington Chronicle* every day and in the Sunday morning issue I saw a rumor that A.H. Stephens and five others had been (or were) down at Fort Monroe asking to be received as Peace Commissioners from the Confederate States, but our Uncle Sam could only see them as private citizens of Southern States.[34] I think the Government at Washington was more nice than wise. But then, it will not do to compromise our dignity as a nation by receiving them in as an official capacity in the least sense. Better sacrifice a few more hundreds of thousand men and a thousand million dollars than to admit them as men empowered to talk over matters and make some kind of peace. Well, I suppose somebody will have to talk over matters and fix things up if we fight another year or two. Why they could not do it this winter, as well as any other time, I can't see. How much wheat and oat did you have? Has Father sold many of the sheep? Are the pigs fat?

I am your husband,
Chas. F. Biddlecom

KELLY'S FORD, VIRGINIA
DECEMBER 17, 1863

Dear Esther,

The socks came last night. I have got a pair of them on this morning and they feel nice and warm compared to what the others did. Accept my thanks for the darning needle and the yarn. I shall be able now to reinforce the toes of my socks.

The weather is very wet and cold. The ground is covered with water and as a general thing is about as uncomfortable as our worst enemies (the Rebs or our generals) could wish. Mud. Mud over the shoe, above the knee and still rain. Rain as if to start another Noah's Flood. I don't know but I should be frightened if I did not bring to mind the old saying that those "born to be hung, are." One thing, when it rains we do not have to drill, so a rainy day has its advantages. Yet, I should like to have it a little drier under foot.

Esther, why didn't you do up the socks as I told you? Then the postage would have been but six cents per pair. Next time you send anything of the kind to me just put a wrapper around it the same as you would around a newspaper, leaving both ends open, and they will come through just as safe and not cost more than six or eight cents per pair.

I want Father to have Sam Phelte make me a pair of boots. I want calf or light kip, lined with calfskin. Be sure that there is no split leather in them. I want them double soled and then two half soles nailed on the outside. Be sure and make them so they won't run out and have a good, heavy iron plate on the heels. Sam has got my measure. I want them made stout. Be sure and have first-rate leather in the backs as well as the fronts, for this Virginia mud beats all for working its way through leather. I want the legs as long as the long boots he made for me two years ago. When they are finished fill them full of tallow and express them to me just as you direct your letters and I will be sure to get them. Kiss the little ones for me.

Your husband,

Chas. F. Biddlecom

———

[Records state that Charlie was in the hospital with dysentery from December 19, 1863 to January 2, 1864.]

KELLY'S FORD, VIRGINIA
DECEMBER 23, 1863

A Merry Christmas to you my dear wife and a kiss for each of my children. Hoping this will get through in time for you to read it on Christmas Day. I write to you at this time, Esther, but how I wish I could be home to enjoy this Christmas with you. Such is not the will of fate and I will do the best I can to enjoy myself here. We are having easy times now. Not much duty to perform and hardly any drilling to do. I have been somewhat unwell for the last week and the doctor has excused me from duty and ordered me to keep my shanty until I get better. I have a severe cold. I took it while on picket week ago last Friday and Saturday. It rained very hard part of the time that we were out. We, all of us, got wet through to the skin and most of us are sick to pay for it. The first night we had a chance to sleep a little, but Saturday night it rained nearly all night. We (the reserve pickets) had a big fire and managed to warm and dry one side while the other was getting wet. As for sleep, it was out of the question, especially for we chaps lately from home. Some of the old veteran troops from Indiana and Wisconsin would sleep if they were covered with water, only let them have the end of their nose out so they can breathe and they will sleep well enough.

The Captain of pickets belonged to the 14th Brooklyn Regiment.[35,][36] They have been out ever since the war commenced and know how to adapt themselves for all kind of circumstances. Rain or shine is all the same to them. He slept right along and such a bed as he had is enough

 to drive all ideas of sleep out of the heads of anybody except it be an old soldier. His bed was made of two oak poles about five inches in diameter laid side by side.

Thus, with a space of four or five inches between them, he laid length-ways of the poles. His pillow was an oak log; said log was the back log of our fire. He roasted his brains while his feet were getting wet and cold. I asked him if he did not feel sore after his night. Oh, no, he was used to such sleeping and did not care much what kind of a bed he had so long as he did not freeze. Bully for him thought I, but 'tis a little too much bed for Charlie.

There are a great many sick in the regiment, full as many here and in the different hospitals as are fit for duty. At the present ration of sickness and death there will not be a quarter of a regiment left for duty in a month more. For if a man gets sick at this time and goes to the hospital, he will not be fit for duty before next April or May, and maybe not at all. I am trying to keep out of the hospital and I think I shall be able to do so unless I take more cold. There is a rumor in camp that we are going to move again. How much truth there is in it, time alone can decide, for we poor devils have ceased to think or care for such things. Hoping that we will not move I keep on writing and listen to nothing in the shape of rumor and shall not be disturbed until I hear the pack up call. Then, I shall pack up and be ready to fall in to go as far as I can again. I wish I could be well once more, especially when we are to go on a tramp.

Esther, tell Bayard to be a good boy and learn all he can, for no knowing when his father will be home. Perhaps, he will be a man before I see him again. For there is no knowing when this war will end or what laws Congress will pass to hold us poor devils, but as near as I can guess, the laws will be made to fit the case, that is, if we are wanted after our term of three years is up. That there will be a peace soon I have at last ceased to hope for. From the past I judge the future and by the past I can but conclude that the war will be of at least twenty years duration. If it is, I have not the least doubt that we will be held as long as we are of any service to the government, for this government has a wonderful, handy fashion of fixing up laws to fit special cases.

As for me, I wish the powers "that be" would fix up some kind of a peace, for almost anything in the shape of peace would be better for the country than this misconducted war is. And as for subjugating the Rebs, that is a forgone conclusion, for I am satisfied it never is to be done unless we have a little more earnest man at the head of things. Uncle Abe is a good, honest meaning man enough, but, oh, so slow that he is forever behind the people and waiting. Waiting yet a little while to see, I suppose, if something is not going to turn up. Sure enough, it does turn up and is "Jack" in the Johnny's handful of trumps. How I wish we had Frémont[37] for President at times. What is the use of always prattling about what Lincoln has done so long as we all know that he has been pushed along by public opinion ever since he took his seat? That the government has done much, I do not deny, but is it not very plain that they have, as yet, not done the right thing to end this war? Must we forever go on fruitless marches and endure hunger, thirst, and cold to the end that the government may find out who is a fool and not who is fit to command? Must we go out and find the Rebs for no other purpose than to find them too strong, or in too good a position, for us to attack them? It does seem as if the Devil owed us a grudge and was taking revenge upon us by making us build winter quarters only to go away and leave them just as we get comfortably fixed up.

. . .

Dec 24th We (five of us that are on the sick list from Company A) are on the road together. Where we are bound, we know not.

. . .

Dec 25th Bright and cold is the morning. This the thirtieth Christmas since I was born and a sad lonesome day to me. God grant that I see no more such, but rather let the grave close over me and with its dark portal shut out all earthly hopes and cares. We, that is, the three companies of the 147th, are guarding a hospital. The rest of the regiment are at the same kind of business two or three miles away. Our move did not prove to be very extensive so far as this regiment was concerned. What has become of the rest of the corps has not as yet made itself manifest to us. Where they are gone, or when we are to follow, has not yet developed itself to our wondering minds. Perhaps we are forever doomed to go "carelessly wandering" up and down this desolate land of sin and slavery, and to and fro and cross ways in this slough of despond (or mud pond, only it just now happens to be frozen up), the balance of our lives. (I will not say natural lives for we shall not live out half of that period in this army.) Thunder, how lonesome I am without one single soul to talk over old times with.

Here is a Merry, Merry Christmas to you all. Hoping on, ever hoping to see you all again and to pass very many days with you all under our roof, free, where we can eat our Christmas dinner in peace with no Conscription Act to fear. Big pay is $100 and $13 per month for all the discomforts so endured by us, say nothing of the risk to life and limb we poor soldiers run. I do not know as I blame any body for paying $300 to keep out of this army, but it is not fair to leave the old boys to endure it all. Others take their ease on beds of down, while soldiers rest on a couple of white oak poles, merrily as only can be an old Brooklyn Captain.

How I wish I could write a good cheerful letter once more, but when I try to be pleasant there will come up in my mind the hard times we have had and are yet to have ere this "Cruel War" is over. Then, I get downhearted and sometimes almost feel as if the ends sought were not worth the sacrifice. Patriotism says different, but the mind reasons quite differently. Enough, enough of this. Let me try and get up a merrier heart and write a few lines that shall have a little sunshine in them.

We Poor Fellows have our fun, such as it is, even here. One gray backed louse will make fun for a company sometimes. And while speaking of lice, let me say that I have a regular louse hunt every chance I get, sometimes every day, sometimes once a week, and I never fail of finding some of them. Sometimes the game is so plenty as to make the hunt quite interesting. It is no disgrace for a man to have a few of the gray backed gentry on his person, but if he is too lazy to skirmish them out every little while he soon becomes despised by the whole company. I often think of a little song or story Mother used to tell me when I was a little boy like Stafford. It was about Davie losing the little toothed comb and we are overrun with lice. I should not wonder if Jeff Davis had lost the little toothed comb of the Confederacy, for the Rebs are over run with the nasty vermin. We always get a good seeding down of them every time we cross one of their old camps. The old boys tell of seeing the ground alive with them in the summer time, and I do not doubt the story, for the men are nearly all alive with them now. Do what they will; they can't get rid of them. I guess they are one of the natural products of this southern country. Lice first, crows next, and buzzards third.

In point of numbers, crows, clouds of them, for hours together, fly over, squalling as they fly, from the juvenile crow up through crowhood to the old, black bugger that has cawed and pulled corn (in I presume every state in the Union to say nothing of Canada) in every year since America was discovered (and how much longer it is not safe to say, for who has ever found a crow that had died a natural death?). Hundreds, thousands, and I guess it is safe to say, millions fly from the north towards the south in the morning. In the afternoon they come streaming back in long lines, from two o'clock till dark there is just a cloud of them on the way back to the thick pines (north of us) to west. Wish I could go to roost like one of them and sleep as sound as I believe they do.

All day long hundreds of buzzards can be seen wheeling in circles over some canyon. Some horse or mule that has worn himself out in the country's service is now left to be eaten by loathsome buzzards, his bones to whiten in the weather. Esther, we read that man was created a little lower than the angels, but I think the time has come when it should be written in this way, "Man is made in the likeness of the Devil and but little above the Brute." For man is acting as a mule or a horse and thought less of than.

What have you got for dinner today? Chicken, I will bet. And, Sarah is at home and Gates is there, too, and you are all enjoying yourselves hugely. Wish I was there, too. Why in thunder some of you did not make a fuss and keep me at home is queer to me, but patriotism was at the bottom of it, I suppose. Eat a little piece for me of your Christmas dinner, and, oh, do write and tell me what it was. Don't think of me in any of your good times, for be sure it will do me no good and only make you feel bad. Let me see, it is about half past two and you are just about eating your dinner. What would you say if I was to drop in upon you all of a sudden, all dirt and rags as I am today? You would think patriotism pretty strong that would make a man love this service, I guess. One thing is sure, I don't like it, no never did. I would not object to fighting, but this laying around loose away from home and never knowing any thing about what is being done or when you are to be at liberty is vexatious in the last degree. "End war! End and let me go home to my wife and babies!" is all I think or care a d—n for. What care I for your nice points of national honor so that the country is prosperous? I care not, and life is none too long to enjoy the good things of Earth with but taking the best of mine days to fight for points of honor that exist only in the brains of politicians. "Let us have peace as soon as we can get it," is the wish of this whole army, the privates, I mean, and so it is with the Rebel army. All that keeps the war jogging slowly along, while thousand upon thousand are buried in the clay of Old Virginia, is because the political ax grinders are not through sharpening up their tools for the next fall's election. There will be a shaking away the dry bones, you can bet. Every soldier here is for the Emancipation Proclamation, at the same time they call it a d——d nigger war, just as it is. But, how Sambo is to blame does not appear, and Lincoln is not to blame. So, who is to blame? Unless it is the South, I can't tell. Yet 'tis a d——d nigger war, so say most of the men here and so say I, but how can it be done away with does not appear so evident.

Kiss the Children and hug my little girl for me. Oh, Es, how I could cry, but it will do no good. I am so lonesome; I do want to see you all so bad. Mother and Laura will snuff up their noses and say, "oh, psha" because they imagine it silly to show my feelings. Father won't say a thing, and sister Sarah will likely enough drop one little tear, and that will end all they will think say or do about this letter. But, you, dear Esther, know well enough how I feel today. Goodbye.

May you ever be happy is the wish of your Charlie

P.S. I don't hear a word from Father, not a word. Your letters are all I get that I care anything about. Hope you will all have a good time at that wedding. I don't know that I care to be there. I should only be in the way for I never was quite nice enough to suit my sisters and I should not like to make them as shamed of me as I should if I was there.

Let her slide . . . time goes on and death gets nearer day by day. I have got too old and worn out to have to do much in this world and I don't know but I had better be dead than in the way as I always have been. D—n Daylor and the farm too. What good was it ever to me?

———

CULPEPER, VIRGINIA
DECEMBER 27, 1863

Dear Esther,

After another hard march of fifteen or sixteen miles, which has completely used me up, I sit down to write a little supplement to a letter I had ready to send you yesterday morning. I got a letter from you dated the nineteenth last night and was glad to hear that you were getting along so well. What made you wean Emma before spring? Why don't you have a stove in your room? Can't our folks afford you the wood? Has Bayard got well of his cold? Get some better ink, for that old ink is so pale that I can't read your letters by firelight. I always get them after dark and have to wait 'til the next morning before I can read them.

I have got rheumatism today so that I can hardly move. I shall have to go to Hospital if I don't get better in a day or two. Esther, I hardly expect to see you again. I have given up all hope, for I can't live long as I am now and doubt that the doctors will do anything for me towards getting any better. If I can get in the hospital, I shall either get better, die, or, though but a mere chance, get discharged. Cursed be the day that saw my name drawn as a conscript and d——d be the hour that I made up my mind to come as a draft. Sick in body and hopeless in spirit, I wish the whole concern were in that pit which has no bottom. I think sometimes that if it was not for you and my children I would blow out my brains. D——n the South. D——n the war and all that had anything to do in getting it up either directly or indirectly. Now I will say what I never said before. No, I won't. I will only think it.

Were I out of this again I think it would take something of a thicker matter than patriotism to get me here again. Rain. Rain for Heaven's sake. Do rain now that we have nothing better to cover ourselves than an old woman's apron. Just the luck of this regiment to be in such a fix as we are at present—out of our quarters every rainstorm, and in them when the weather is dry.

I don't care a d——n how mad Laura is, or Sarah either, and as for the rest of our folks, I think just as much of them as they do of me. Sarah does not care enough about me to answer my letters and she will be some few years older ere she gets another from me. Laura owes me two or three letters and I don't care a d——n if she remains in my debt for all time. I shan't write to her again 'til she writes me a letter worth answering. I suppose ere this reaches you that I shall have another brother-in-law. I hope I shall think something of him, but I don't expect to. I think now the farm is sold and Sarah married. Charlie may go to the Devil. Well, I guess he can stand it.

—·—

IN CAMP NEAR CULPEPER, VIRGINIA
JANUARY 2, 1864

Dear Wife,

Your letter of the 25th came to hand last night and I answer it at once. If you are as anxious to hear from me as I am to hear from some of you at home I know it will seem a long time ere this reaches you, though, I think I write home very often. I am sure when I get letters from home, but whether you get those I send, or not, I sometimes question.

My health is not good, nor am I very sick. I am troubled a great deal with cramping in my legs and my right side. What causes it I am unable to tell. I have asked the surgeon for medicine and he told me he had no medicine that would do me any good. He excused me from duty and I have done no duty since. That was three weeks ago. I shall go to him again in the morning and see if he has got anything for me yet. If he has not, he had better send me to the Division Hospital where I can be helped. I have been troubled a good deal with cough, but have got over it at last and hope I shall steer clear of colds for the balance of the winter. I have been troubled with diarrhea for some time and must try and get something to stop it. It does not do to let it run long in this country, for it fits the system for Typhoid fever and then it is almost certain to prove fatal. I guess I shall get along and live it out, but three years is a long time to be away from home and know at the same time that there is a hundred chances to be killed to one to get home safe and sound. But, I am the only one to blame about it and, of course, must not grumble.

How quick I would give $300 to get out. If the war was over and I home again, I can't say whether I would give $300 to get out or not, and not have the war ended. At any rate, there is not any likelihood of my having the chance. There has been quite a number discharged that came down when I came and perhaps I may be yet, but when or how I do not know.

Provost Marshal Kiner of Canandaigua has not fixed our description lists so that we can get all of our pay. He promised to do it so we could get it this next payday. I think some of writing to Provost Marshal General Frey[38] about it and see if he won't urge Mr. Reimers to give some attention to the correction of his muster rolls. This being cheated is what we do not like, especially as the Government is so very careful to extract all the duty from us that we are able to perform. Guess we will try and see if something can't be done towards getting our hard earned money. Should not wonder a bit if Mr. Reamers found out that there is some of us here that don't mean to be cheated through his carelessness.

So, Sarah is to be married at last. When did you know? Were you all afraid I should know anything about it 'til it is all over? Well, I don't know as I care much about it anyhow. Guess I can get along very well if I never know anything about it. Did Father let B. Herendeen pick those sheep for $10 per head? If he did, I think it too small a price, but as they are not my sheep, I, of course, shan't find fault. Blessed be nothing. If I have got to soldier for three years, I don't want you to suffer for anything. I must try and send you some money after payday, but I have none to send now, not even to buy stamps with. Postage stamps are all gone but two or three and so is my money. Fact is the rations have been so short that we have spent all the money buying off sutlers and commissaries. Hardtack has sold high as twenty cents a piece and raw corn at half dollar the ear, and then we went hungry at that. We lived on nothing, half, and 3/4 rations for nearly a month and our money played out pretty fast. The last I had I gave for ginger snaps. I paid two cents a piece for them. We are having better now and I shall be able to send home some of the next pay I get, though it will not be much for I did not expect to make money by coming here.

Kiss the young ones for me and tell me how Emma looks when you write again. Is she going to be handsome? I hope so. Does Stafford improve any in health? Take care that he does not get any of those disorders like Whooping Cough or Measles this winter and do try and keep him from taking cold. I do so want him to live for I think him naturally the smartest child we have got. Make Bayard stay in out of the wet so as not to get sick, for if he gets sick Stafford will be sick, too, and then you will have your hands full.

Why don't Father take a pair of my old boots to Ripley and have my new one made over the lasts that will fit them. By so doing he will be sure to get a fit, and I want a good fit, for if they are not they will make my feet sore. Send a pound or so of good fine cut tobacco. If he can find a little ax that will weigh about two pounds send it along at the same time the boots are sent. Don't forget the ax for I need it very much. About sending a comforter and pillow, I hardly think it worthwhile for I have got used to sleeping on a cord woodpile and I guess I rest full as well as I should under an extra quilt. And as for a pillow, a tin canteen or a cartridge box is good enough for one. Something to eat in the fruit line I should like very much, but the weather is so cold I suppose it would be in danger of freezing and spoiling. Send me some black thread and a few buttons for my pants. I guess that is about all that I want. Oh, say, send a paper of long carpet nails. I want them to fasten my tent to the shanty with. I don't think of any thing else.

Guess Father had better not come down here for he can't better my condition any. He would go home feeling very badly and I should be homesick as a dog. And then there is a risk in coming out here, for we are clear out to the front and we may move in a day or two, for we are in marching time and under marching orders. Still, we may stay all winter if the Rebs behave themselves.

Our pickets are out next to the Reb line on Cedar Mountain. I guess Old Kilpatrick will be after them in a few days trying to cut the RR between Gordonsville and Richmond. Our Cavalry is a great terror to the Johnnies. They hate our Cavalry and wish the D——l had 'em. All Honor to Hooker. He has made the cavalry of this army a very efficient corps and for the first time since this war commenced our cavalry are of some use to the Infantry Corps in helping keep the Rebs occupied in watching their own rear instead of making raids on our trains.[39] Should not wonder if Johnny Reb went hungry some this winter. I see that Averell has destroyed a large amount of provision for them in Western Virginia.[40]

Write soon.

With much love I remain your Husband,
Chas F Biddlecom

CULPEPER, VIRGINIA
JANUARY 8, 1864

Dear Esther,

Yours of the third came tonight and like a good boy I answer it right off. Esther, the hills (and valleys, too) are white with snow. The face of nature looks quite like Old Ontario County in the winter with the exception that this county is stripped of fence and the wagon roads run in every direction. In fact, our generals make roads from one point to another to suit their convenience without paying any regard to section quarter or lot lines, across grain fields, through door guards, across creeks and rivers, as seemeth to them good. We poor devils travel them sometimes, but generally we march each side with the artillery and the baggage trains in the roads. Frequently the army will move in parallel lines on different roads in sight of each other for miles together. Thanks to General Hooker for regulating the army and establishing this manner of moving, for we are never mixed up one regiment or corps with another. Everybody knows his place and tries to keep it. We never have any jams of artillery, ambulance, or wagons to hinder our marches, but everything goes off smoothly like a well regulated machine.

Every regiment is numbered and each corps has its badge on.[41] The different divisions (of a corps) wear different collars. For instance, the First Army Corps has for its badge a round patch. The First Division wear a red patch. The Second Division a white patch. The Third Division a Black Patch. So, you see, in this regiment each man has on his hat first, his company letter, then the number of the regiment, and under these the corps badge in red (thus, $\overset{A}{\underset{O}{147}}$). The ball under the 147 is red. The Second Corps badge is a clover leaf. We call it the ace of clubs. The Third Corps have a diamond; the Fifth a cross; the Sixth a Greek cross; the Eleventh Corps a crescent or a new moon; the Twelfth Corps a star of five points (as it is hard for me to imitate I won't try, but when you go to Quaker meeting look at Hinckley Tug's house and you will see one right up in the peak).

When I was down here before I belonged to the Star Corps, and properly named it was, too. Yes, I think this First Corps has done more hard fighting than any other in this army. The colors of the different brigades and regiments are so riddled with shot and shell that they hang in tatters and are always carried rolled up to keep them from blowing away in the wind. This (Second Brigade, First Division) is composed of the 76th, the 95th, the 147th NYV's, ~~the Second Wisconsin~~ the 7th Indiana, the 56th Penn, and the 14th Brooklyn Militia (known as the 82 NYV's in the army records).

Anyone that has kept a good watch of these regiments since they came here will know at once what kind of stuff this brigade is made of. For instance, the 14th Brigade has been out since April '61 and was in the first Battle of Bull Run, and the Second, for that matter, and have had something over 3,400 different names on their muster rolls.[42] Though now they show less than two company front when on dress parade. They are mustered in for war and are bound to see it out. The city of Brooklyn is paying upwards of $1,100 bounty to recruits for the 14th. They get men, but slowly, for the regiment has a kind of fatality connected with it that the men at home dislike. They have sent large numbers of recruits home in their coffins in less than a month from the day they left home to join the regiment. Especially at South Mountain[43] and Antietam was this the fate of some of the recruits sent to them. They were as noble a lot of men as ever shouldered a musket in this crusade for freedom. I see I have carried this talk about this brigade too far, so I will stop with saying that the 147th is soon to be brigaded with such a regiment as I have named who have witnessed the heights of Gettysburg and the pine thickets of Mine Run, where to stand was as hard as to advance to the attack.

I said the generals made roads to suit their convenience, and sometimes to the inconvenience of the privates. Especially is this the case with the brigades that last time out (out of the same seven or eight times this fall) we crossed Mountain Run. The bridge was two poles about ten inches in diameter and thirty or thirty-five feet in length, laid side by side from one bank to the other. The regiment crossed in Indian file, one man at a time, and it was after dark at that. Company A crossed first and after marching a regimental distance halted for the rest to cross and close column.

Oh, God, how tired and cold we were. It did seem as though we must all die, but there is no telling what a man can endure and live until they are put to the test. Weary, hungry, and cold as we were, still our dear Uncle Sam had not forgotten us. When we stopped wagons had some express boxes for different high privates sent them from loved ones at home and among the rest one from you to me. A soldier's life is a queer life to be sure. In no other place will a man find such intense bitterness mixed with such exquisite sweetness as here. See for instance the poor, tired, footsore soldier, forgetting all his pains of the great day, and even a smile of gladness on his countenance, as he studies out the lines by the flickering fire light, penned by his wife. That, for a time, fills his heart.

The New Year has come and with it has come another year of war. I fear for this toil worn army, but the end will come some time. If not in '64 or '65, why then, in some of the years that are hidden away in the mystic future. Wishing, hoping, praying on my part cannot affect it much. If I am

well to march, to fight, to die, if God wills it, that I can do, and all that
will be asked of me, in common with others, to do. It does beat all what
an anxiety there is manifested by all the rank, and file, and most of the line
officers, to have this war ended, if possible, without another campaign. I
have heard that our colonel wants to bet his fortune that his war will be
ended in sixty days. Well, God knows I hope it is so, but nevertheless, I
should like to know the grounds for the faith that is in him. Hope, it is
said, is the anchor of the soul, and without hope the heart would break.
But, a groundless hope, a hoping against reason in a past experience, is
worse than nothing. Consequently, I have ceased to hope for the end of
the war this year to come. The backbone of this rebellion has been broken
so many times, and each time managed to get together again, that I began
to think it like one of those little reptiles called the joint snake, capable of
disjointing itself at will and untying again as suits convenience. I suppose
Laura will find some fault with me for writing as I do about this war, but
I must write as I see things, whether it suits or not. I would be foolish to
do otherwise.

Well, the wedding is over, at last. Though, Mother may not call it
making a wedding, still, I guess there was something of a fuss made, more,
I know, than there was when we were married. But then, Gates folks are
grand and you and I were humble. Well, I don't know as I care how much
they fuss. One thing I do know, there is one less old maid in the world.
So, you could not manage a small affair as the wedding without having
Aunt Hannah sent for. Not a very smart lot of women, you, especially as
you were not to make a wedding. Oh fudge, what is the reason Mother
could not have kept that to herself? I wonder what she meant by saying it?
I am sure you don't care how much fuss they make, and as for me, why, it
is but a small matter whether I care or not. Tell me all about the wedding
when you write again, and be sure to tell me about the dinner.

So, I. B. Lapham has enlisted. Well, he will find that he has got something on hand now that he will wish himself rid of many times before
he gets out, if he has the good luck to get out at all. Alas, poor fool, he

little mistrusts what is in store for him. His Michigan experience will be boy's play by comparison with what is to come if this war lasts. I am glad I haven't any brother to enlist. One owl out of the next ought to be sufficient. I don't hear of but two enlisting that I am really glad are fastened. They are Leote Chilson and George Crocker. Both of them are too lazy to be of any account at home, so let them go to war and I will say, "Amen." I think about the only life manifested by the government in this war is in the enlisting of troops and then the killing of them with fruitless marches and drawn battles in which we just save ourselves from being eaten up alive.

Hurry up the boots, for I begin to need them. Probably by the time I get them I shall be pretty much the same as barefoot. Hard place, this, on shoe leather. Peckham is in Washington yet, don't think he will ever come back to regiment again. I don't blame him one bit, for the company he was in, Company F, is one of the meanest I ever saw. I am glad I got in this company, for it is the only decent one in the regiment. I guess Roberts has forgotten that I wrote him, or else, he has taken offense at something I wrote. I can't think what it can be, as I am sure I was as guarded in what I wrote as need be. Well, all I have to say is I can get along very well if he don't write at all, but I should like to hear from someone in that neighborhood. Guess I will write to Mike Bowerman and see if he thinks enough of me to answer.

Esther, how I long to see you and the children again. It seems so long since I saw you that I really can't believe the time that has passed so short. Don't let Bayard and Stafford forget that they have a father. Kiss Emma very often for me, dear little. How I do want to see her, the little chub. Is she fat as ever? And, is she good natured? So, Stafford could not say "thank you," because he was so deaf? Oh, the little coon. Does he get any better, or is he the same as he was when I left home? I hope he will grow up to be a big boy by the time I get home if I have to stay here three years.

My health is better than it has been for some time back and I expect to get along for a few weeks more before having another pull down. It is

p.m. and I must go to bed, for I am tired and sleepy.
y for two nights to speak of. I presume I shall have to
he next 24 hours and maybe on picket for two days and
en I shall need to get some rest. I am as I ever hope to
be your loving husband,

Chas. F. Biddlecom

——·——

[The letter below is from David M. Lapham, Esther's brother.]

SPRINGFIELD, ILLINOIS

JANUARY 11, 1864

Dear Sister Es,

I received your kind letter of December 27 on New Year's Day, which contained a draft for $39.78. It came in good time although I would rather have had it six weeks before.

You ask if I have heard from brother Stephen. I have not and don't know where he is. I have not had a letter from brother Dan for six months either. I must write him. I had a letter from Cornelia a few weeks ago. She was in good health for her, had got on some ear trumpets, which helped her a good deal. I owe her a letter and shall soon write to her.

We have had some of the coldest weather here that I ever experienced, twenty-five degrees below zero. The snow now lies eight inches deep on the ground allowing the most sleighing I ever saw in this state. The cold weather and snow together has thinned out my school, which is a small one at best. I barely average over eighteen scholars. I have taught over nine weeks and have got eleven weeks longer to teach, if the draft don't take me. I am not much afraid of it this time. I shan't go if I can get out of it. I guess Charles has probably had enough of it.

I have not seen any of Round Prairie people very lately. I saw Nettie Woodruff several weeks ago. She has become a large girl, haughty and proud, a perfect fly away. They are all abolitionists (nearly) on Round

Prairie and I'm not so much thought of there, as I am of the other party and a Spiritualist. Please excuse the way I have scratched this off. Write soon. It is half past ten and I must retire. Don't let any one see this letter.

>   *From your Affectionate Brother,*
>   *David M. Lapham*

————

CAMP OF THE 147TH NY VOLUNTEERS
NEAR CULPEPER, VIRGINIA
JANUARY 15, 1864

Dear Wife,

Yours of the 7th ins't came last night and found me in better health than I have had for a long time. I am cured at last of the diarrhea so common to the army and with the exception of the old rheumatic pains in my legs, which I am never clear of, I may say I am well again. I was as tired last night as a poor worn out hound dog, for I had been working for the Quartermaster[44] cutting timber for a mule stable and as he was in a hurry to finish up we put in our biggest licks and got a good word for our pains. Well, that is better than a reprimand. Esther, I am very sorry our folks should take what I wrote to Laura (in such good nature) so much to heart. Well, if they can't take a joke better than that, why I hope they will never crack their dry ones over my head. That's all. Seems to me I can remember some of their talk (that was said in good earnest) some nine years ago last August, but perhaps not. Now my parents and my dear sister Laura will please be so thoughtful as to remember why I am here; it was to please them and their pride in having it to say that their son and brother did not dodge the draft, but walked up to his duty (yes, and a little more than his duty) like a man. For it was known to Father that I had the $300 necessary to exempt me from serving, to be sure.[45] I am well aware that I had my own pride and sense of duty in the matter, yet I think I should not have done just as I did had there been none to please but myself.

Now, I do not wish to be harsh in my feelings towards them, but I do sometimes think that while I am suffering almost to the pains of death in this most trying of all places a man can be placed in, that they do not appreciate fully the reasons why I am here, and have not that feeling for me that it is my right to expect. I may be wrong in my thoughts at times, but I trust that you all know me enough to know that though I suffer ten times what I have already endured, I shall still try to acquit myself with the best degree of honor possible, both to please them and do justice to myself as a soldier.

I should like above all things to get a few lines of encouragement from Father, yet I get not a word. I think I will write a few lines to him and see if he will answer them. I do think it is queer that Laura's sensibilities should be so shocked at what I said about making an Aunt Hannah joke, for she can but remember how Mother has talked about the way Aunt H used to act with Sarah and I and it was to try and hinder the same kind of feeling existing between you and Laura that I wrote as I did. So, if I have lamed her over-nice sensibilities, I am very sorry (not for what I wrote, but that her sensibilities are so painfully acute). I hope she will be as careful of wounding others, as she is fearful of being hurt herself. If she is, there is not much doubt that every thing will go smoothly enough while you live there.

Now, I have used nearly a sheet in explaining away the roughness of former letters and if I ever do the same thing again, i.e. hurt anyone's feelings, why they will have to remain sore for I don't mean to write any more explanations, nor apologies either, unless I purposely insult somebody and then afterwards feel sorry and take back what I have said, which is not likely to be the case.

Mr. Gates and Sarah were married at 2 p.m. the 7th of January 1864 and so "Let it be recorded." I will do more for Sister than she done for me, i.e. I wish her much joy with all my heart and hope she will, even in her great happiness, still kindly remember her only brother in his lonely misery as she "goes carelessly wandering."

Turkey and oysters for dinner. What are turkeys? Are they any relation to salt pork and blue beef? And, are oysters anything like hard tack? Good living, turkey and oysters. I guess I am sorry your fruit froze. You had considerable trouble in fixing it, I remember.

Ira B. put his first smack in it, didn't he? Bit his nose off? Orin would give $1000 to get him out, would he? Well, I guess the government could get lots of such chances right here in the army and not have to hunt much either, especially if they don't furnish more rations soon.

I thought I sent particular directions how I wanted my boots made and if Father has done as I wrote I would risk that they are right enough. Did you pay the charge on the box? If not, I shall never get them, and if I don't get them it won't matter how they are made. I can't pay the charges on anything costing more than a letter, so if the box should chance to get here at all unpaid, I can't pay the charges on it 'til after payday.

Of course Gates would call the baby good looking now, for everything he sees is rather softened and the rough spots smoothed off. He is like all other men when first married: bound to be pleased with every thing having any claims on the wife's side. He will be likely to vote all babies, except his own, a nuisance in the end. So, don't tell me what he thinks, but tell me how Emma looks to you. Is she fat as ever? Does Stafford grown any? Is his head any better? Tell me something about him when you write again, will you? I want to hear about him very much. Bayard has got old enough now so that he will be likely to get along and grow up, but I fear Stafford will not. If anything ails him, be sure and write to me all about it.

There is no news from the paymaster[46] yet and the probabilities of our being paid off before the March payday are growing less every day. If we are not paid off 'til then, I shall have six months pay due me excluding what is due on the old enlistment, making six month pay at $14 per month $84.00, and one month and eight days pay at $11.00 per month is $13.81 more, in all $97.81. If I get all that is due me on the March pay day, I shall send you a nice little sum. What the reason is that we are not paid this month we, of course, can't imagine. For the government must have money enough, else why do they offer such large bounties for reenlistments? I don't think the war is very near its end, for if it is, the powers at Washington would not be so anxious to get so many men in the field for the full term of three years and engaging to pay them such large bounties.

Yes, Esther, it is hard to go hungry and cold, but harder still to do it for the honor of those that don't more than half appreciate what we poor d——ls are suffering for them. But it is always the case that those that live smugly at home with lots to eat and warm places to sleep in think little of the "lone picket" on whose vigilance the safety of the nation may depend. Oh, it is nothing. Has he not sold himself to the country for three years to march, to starve, to freeze, to watch in darkness and storm? Though he die on his post of exhaustion and cold, he must (according to the terms of his contract) fight and die in defense of those that care not for him. That is, unless it be to make a high sounding fuss for few days, or weeks at most, over the downfall of some general that, so far as this suffering is concerned, is a stranger.

I was on picket two days this week, Sunday and Monday. We went out Sunday and came in Tuesday. The weather was fine and not very cold in the day time, but at night it was very cold and as our generals are very fraid that some guerilla, or gorilla, or what is it, will carry them off, we were not allowed to keep fires at night.[47] Fancy, if you can, this standing still and looking out into the darkness after imaginary dangers for two mortal long hours, the thermometer marking minus ten, and then you can come somewhere near what we suffered. Well, when the two hours watch is over, you come in to the post froze almost solid, to turn and twist before the fire like a piece of meat on a turn spit, roasting one side while the other freezes. Tired and sleepy and no chance to rest or sleep, for woe to him that undertakes a nap on the ground at this time of the year, for typhoid fever is almost sure to mark him for a trip to the hospital and likely the grave. Forty-eight hours of misery as severe as the mind can well imagine. I remember of only one other time when it was as bad as it was this time and that was when our pickets laid for sixteen hours in little rifle pits just large enough for two men to lay side by side in, looking for all the world like two muddy logs of wood laying side by side in the ruins of a potato hole. You know how they look after being opened in spring. The time we were over the Rapidan I was detailed to go out and was putting on my belts when the orderly sergeant came to me and said, "As you are not well, you need not go." So, I was saved that frozen trip. The weather was very cold and windy. So cold, that some of the men in the Fifth Corps froze to death. Well, what made it worse for the boys was that the Rebs would not let them stir without sending a bullet after them. So you see, it was lay still and freeze or get up and run the risk of being mustered out of the service by getting a bull in the gizzard. Such are some of a soldier's hardships.

Now for some of a soldier's joys, or at least some of his easy times. Well, I am taking a good large taste of one of them today by writing home. Writing letters when off duty is one of a soldier's diversions, another is making a fool of some convenient greenie, if it is an officer so much the better. Our fool today was the regimental M.D. What fun we had as he rode by on his old mare (said old mare resembling for all the world Hunter's Old Nancy).

We recommended him to give her pills and powders to be taken once in four hours (that is the way he fixes us when we are sick) I have given this Bachelor of Physics a name that will last him as long as he stays in the regiment. I called him The Louse. It is my luck to be calling names that last (it was me that named Old John's residence The Light House, and the name bids fair to out last the house). The reason of my calling this fellow The Louse is this: some time ago, before our old doctor got to be brigade surgeon, and this one was only a kind of roust about chap with a second assistant surgeon's commission,[48] he got so lousy that the old doctor drove him out of his tent. Since then I have called him the louse and he will carry the name for a while. He is the dirtiest looking doctor you ever saw. Mose Bennet not excepted. Well, we have the devils own fun

laughing at him. Though, I guess he is not a bad fellow at heart. His name is Stillman. [49] He hails from the town of Brookfield, Madison County, NY. Maybe Mother will know something of him. I have heard her talk of Stillmans living somewhere.

Another way we have of diverting our minds is telling large yarns. We have got some men here that have travelled further and seen more than Ike Lapham has, and they possess in an equal degree with him those powers of marvelousness so necessary to make a story sound well, especially where the one telling it is one of the principle actors in the story. We have one fellow by the name of Brown that has knocked about the world right smart. He is an old man of wars, has served on the Mississippi Flotilla, been out to China, and Lord only knows where else. Well, he can draw the long bow from morning 'til night and from night 'til morning again. He is going it with all quill set when we wake up in the morning and away he goes before the wind all day and when I go to bed he is still going, going, going. When I get lonesome I just get him started and I am all right 'til I get over the lonesome bit.

Another comfort I have is in talking over old times with a couple of fellows that were out in the old 28th. It seems all most like a going "home to have a chat" over times we had in Albany and Washington two years ago. I wish there were more of the old boys in the company; I should feel more at home if there was. My tent mates are not the most entertaining chaps in the world, still I manage to get along with them first rate. There is four of us in this shanty, the other three are from Oneida County, one conscript and two subs. The conscript is a little waspish Dutch man, but I get along with him first rate, for when he gets peevish I just talk him blind in about two minutes. The next in line is a fellow that is a first rate, good cook. Everything is all right with him, except when he gets a little sick. Then he is so weak and faint that his voice is almost inaudible. You would think him nearly dead, he mopes so. The other one is the meanest old D——l in the world and if he was not a church member I don't know what we should do with him. As it is we let him go 'til he gets so intolerable mean that we can't stand it any longer. Then we just go at him and such another drumming as he gets from the three of us is hard to find every day.

Have been out drilling this afternoon under our new lieutenant (our Captain, the *Old Man* we call him, is sick in Washington) for the first time. I like him first rate. He used to be a private in the 14th Brooklyn, has been wounded in the right arm so that he can't use it even to write his name with. He wears a sabre, but of what use it is to him I can't see, for he can't even draw it, much more fight with it. He is not larger than John Abot, but he is as smart as a ten acre lot full of Abot. His name is Berry.[50] The boys think it unfair his being put in command over this company. For there are boys that belong to the company that have done their duty and fought as well as men ever did and merited promotion, though they have been lucky enough to come out without being hurt. So, his being here causes some hard feelings. Not toward the lieutenant, but towards those that sent him here.

We have just drawn our rations soft bread, hard tack, coffee, and sugar. A loaf of bread and nine hardtack and about three spoons full of sugar for each of us. It has got to last three days. Not much sugar, that, but it has to do. We are to draw fresh beef tonight, so I guess we shall make a life of it for the three days to come. I don't want to loose my appetite again, for I am not sure to find a meal when it comes to me again.

Well, Father need not read this letter for fear there will be some nonsense in it. Posh. The fact is it (that letter) cut close somewhere. If it had not, he would have read it quick enough. Mother had more feeling for Laura than she did for me when I bid them goodbye thinking it would be the last time I should see them 'til this "Cruel War" is over. I was so maddened then at what she said, and the way she said it, that I did not dare speak for fear of choking with rage. I think I would have gone to (——) then rather than to have asked a favor at their hands. People that live in glass houses should not throw stones and I will not hurt their tender sensibilities again if I can avoid it. You will find the bill you sent me enclosed. Nothing but greenbacks[51] are good here. If this gets through before you send the things direct in this way: 147 Regt NYV First Corps Washington D.C.

And pay the charge, which will be about $2.00

With Love to all I remain,

  C.F. Biddlecom

P.S. Two of my tent mates rec'd a box of stuff last night. They are in for a big eat—wonder if I could not have a box of meat cakes sent.

CULPEPER, VIRGINIA
JANUARY 24, 1864

Dear Wife,

Yours mailed the 18th came last night. I was glad to hear from you, as I had been expecting it for a day or two I had become somehow anxious to get it. I have taken another heavy cold and feel a good deal clogged up in my throat and have a touch of the old tickling in my windpipe. Other ways, I am quite well.

Esther, I really think the talk about the Rebels starving prisoners a kind of cooked up dish to keep the conscripts and subs from allowing themselves to be taken prisoner by the Johnnies. There has been quite a number of our men taken by the Rebs that could have prevented it quite as well as not. Some of the men that came under the draft never calculated to do any fighting if they could help it and as a matter of course have taken all kinds of ways to get out of it. One of the ways is to straggle off from the main body while on the march and so get taken prisoner and get paroled by some roaming band of Rebel Calvary. Some of the men that have come back to regiment say that in the main, they were well treated. From all that I can learn, I have come to the conclusion that the accounts we have of starving prisoners in Richmond and Bell Island[52] a fictitious lot of stuff fixed up to operate on the minds of men that have a desire to keep out of a fight at all hazard, even to be taken by the Rebs.

I wish it was possible for this army to capture Richmond, or any other place, but it doesn't seem to be the case. For all this army is likely to do, the poor prisoners in Richmond are likely to pass the remainder of their days in the hands of the South. I do not wish to make light of the Army of the Potomac, i.e. the men in the ranks that do the fighting, but as for the officers (the majority of them), why, God help them to be better and braver men is all I have to say. Our Brigadier is exercising us in the use of the ax, the shovel, and the pick in building a theater for the amusement of himself and his wife. A big production that we all think we would be glad to hear was burned up, were it not that we know we should have to build another one. So, we wish it may stand the winter out. I think sometimes that our Generals are of the opinion that the clay of which they were made is of a finer quality than that of which we privates are composed of. In other words, they are the meerschaums while we are the common penny clay fixture only fit for the common hearth.

Our Colonel has come back to the regiment again after being gone ever since the Battle of Gettysburg (he got hit on the side of the head, just enough to draw blood and show off his limbering to the rear without losing his commission). He managed to get on detached service (to look after conscripts) at Elmira and while there, got his Eagles. Whereas, the man entitled to wear the Eagles, Harney, the officer that led the regiment in the fight at Gettysburg, was severely wounded in the hand and stayed with his command all summer and fall until we were in winter quarters, gets but the Silver Oak Leaves for his reward. Well, that is about the way it is in the army, as well as in private life. Those that do the least and make the most parade about it get the praise, while the real workers go quietly on though life down to the grave and mankind think them but common men at best.

Our Colonel is a gay kind of man, carries his head very high and is very much military in carriage, if not in deeds. In short, he is a first rate, Fourth of July colonel, but is not particular to volleys of musketry or leading bayonet charges. Now this proud, red haired, red whiskered, would be son of Mars, must have everything done up in regular West Point,[52] apple pie kind of order. No matter if the mud is knee deep, boots must be polished, and buttons and brasses brightened in regular grand review or else the D——l is to pay. Probably he will be sick by the time spring campaign commences and will not play off all summer 'til another winter, when he will again be on hand to torment us with his grand military knowledge and ability.

How come on the enlistment business in Macedon is the town likely to revise its quota? Who besides Ira B. has enlisted that I know? How does your Uncle John's folks treat you when you go there? Do they put on those patronizing airs as much as ever, or do they condescend to descend from their lofty perch of pride enough to treat you as one of the same blood as themselves? Es, you know I never did put on airs, nor is it at all probable that I ever shall.

Please write all the news you get from Farmington. The box has not come yet. When did you send it and what besides the boots was in it? Has Father sold any more of the stock? Ask him all about it. Don't be afraid, for I want to know all about it. Ben McVeigh has not answered my letter, neither has Dan answered the one I wrote to him. Probably they will hear from me again soon over the loss. Maybe it's that I can't write a letter that is worth answering, but it has been too long since I wrote to them that I have given up looking for a letter from them. All the letters I get now are from you. They are my only enjoyment and I guess about all I wish for.

We are not paid off yet and probably shall not be 'til March. The order has come from Washington to our company commander to have the men from the Ontario district paid from the day they were drafted. It will put $26.00 in my pocket. Es, there are a great many camp rumors afloat in relation to the time we have to serve. One is that we are only to serve nine months from the day of draft. Another just started is that every man that is father of more than two children is to be discharged of the service. Another is that all that wish to go home shall have the privilege by paying $300. Probably there is not a word of truth in any of them. What action Congress may take in relation to the drafted men is only a matter of conjecture, if they take action at all. We conscripts that came here last fall feel rather cross grained towards the folks at home from the fact that we are compelled to serve or pay $300 and no town, county, or state bounty to sweeten up the bitter dish with. Now, those that come get from $6.00 to $100 for it. If we have got to stay 'til this war is over, I think we should a share in those large bounties. With us it was, "come or pay." With those that are coming now it is, "if you will go, we will pay." Not much honor in a people that will do as the taxpayers in the north are doing. But men will do things to save themselves from conscription that no sense of justice will prompt them to do. I wish I could be a little charitable towards the cowardly, stay at home, do nothing, moneyed men of Old Farmington, but it is not in my composition. In fact, this soldiering is not calculated to soften the heart, however much it may soften the head. I think some times that I (in common with others) am becoming idiotic.

CULPEPER, VIRGINIA
JANUARY 29, 1864

Dear Esther,

Your letter came last night. I suppose it is needless for one to say that I was glad to get it, for I have written the same thing so often that it would be but a repetition and would be no more convincing than it already is. Since I wrote before I have been quite sick with some kind of a bilious difficulty, but I have got over it and with the exception having a snotty nose and a tickling in the throat feel quite well again. No pay yet. We shall not get it now until after another muster, which will be February 29th, just one month from today.

The rumors in camp about our going home at the end of nine months (which will be in April) thicken every day. Were it not for my knowing so well what it is to be disappointed, I should be inclined to believe some of them. As it is, I believe nothing, but hope on that something will turn up so that we can get away before long. Maybe the Rebs will give up and accept the President's amnesty and Congress may take some action that will soften the obstacles in the way of a speedy peace. It may be that when the Rebs see that the Union armies are stronger than ever this spring that they will not make much of a stand, but give it up as a bad job, as it certainly is. For they can never gain their independence, and the longer they hold out the harder will be their fate when driven to submit.

The weather is very fine, more like our April in New York than like January. There is hardly any frost nights and days are so warm that we go in our shirtsleeves. The ground is dry and the roads are getting dusty. How long it is to last is another question.

I was out on picket last Sunday and Monday and could not ask for a nicer time for picketing than we had. There was fourteen of us on one post. The sentinels stood post two hours and were off ten hours. I acted as noncommissioned officer half of the time, and by that means did not have to stand post at all. I had all day and half of the night to myself and used the day time up looking at the Blue Ridge away to the west of us some twenty miles. How I wish I could sketch. I could make pictures of them, though still pictures are a very poor representation (at best) of the beauty of nature. We are so far off from the mountains that they are mellowed down, their tops rounded and smoothed off so that the skyline is but a gentle undulating curve. The sun, as it shines through the gaps and lights one side of them while the opposite is shaded, gives us a truly beautiful view of their different forms. I sat on a large rock and strained my vision trying to see more of them, while at the same time I thought of home and the dear ones that I left behind. When, oh, when shall these eyes behold them? When shall this knee support my little ones again? Who knows? Who will tell me that my heart will be satisfied? Will I ever see them? Oh, will I get home again? Or, is it my fate to end my life on some hard fought field? I know I ought not to think of such painful things, yet I cannot help thinking of them.

Yes, Esther, let Father take all and be satisfied and when I come home we will buy ourselves a home. Be it ever so humble and poor, what we have will be ours. How I wish we had started that way, for we could not have been much worse off than we are at present. The most I fear is that in case I ever get home, my constitution will be so shattered that I shall not be able to work much. But, I can do something, if I am not used up entirely mind, as well as body.

Father does not send a word to me yet, nor Mother either. Poor, poor Charlie has but one in the world that takes more than a momentary interest in him. *Let it go, let it go.* Perhaps it is as much as I deserve, and may be not half I do deserve. Oh, God. Am I always to be thus striving and still met with the same cold feeling from everyone?

I did not send the bill when I intended to and before I wrote again I had used it to buy some onions with. So, you see, it is gone, eaten up and passed away, and is so far as I am concerned, among the things "that were, but are not." I have no money, so you will have to send me some more postage stamps, as those you sent are nearly all gone. I have lots of paper as I bought a lot off a sutler that had more than he could make off with, so got it very cheap, about half price. I have sold some, but got no money yet. Am to get it payday, if it ever comes again.

I shan't write to anybody at home except you until some of them write to me. As yet, I know only through you that my sister is married, as she nor Laura have ever thought enough of me to write a word about it from first to last. If it were not for you, I should not hear from home at all.

The box has not come yet. This, I think, is a little strange, but as I don't know whether the charges were paid for, or not, I only can look and pray that the boots may come soon, as my shoes are almost gone and then my feet will be on the ground. It takes so long to get anything from government that it is almost useless to try for a pair of shoes. I am not going to write another sheet full this time, so kiss my children for me and be sure in the love that I feel for them that I shall try and not disgrace them.

      Chas. F. Biddlecom

————

CULPEPER, VIRGINIA
FEBRUARY I, 1864

Dear Esther,

Yours of the 28th came to hand last night and as I am off duty for the day I will write to you. I came off guard yesterday morning just in time to save myself from being thoroughly saturated. All day yesterday there was one of those old Virginia mists flying that go through and through a poor, rheumatic fellow like myself, causing the joints and bones to ache like a jumping tooth ache. The same weather prevails today and my joints are very sore.

The box and book came all safe and sound last Friday night. The boots are an exact fit and suit me first rate. Only one fault to find, that is they are so small in the leg that I can't draw them on over my pants. I should have liked them better if the heels had been plated as I wrote to have them, but I guess I can make them last until I get home, or what is the same thing, go to the hospital. I should have been there long ago if it had not been for the best care I could take of myself. The rheumatism has taken hold of me in a different way this winter from what it has ever done before. It commences in my hip joint and then extends up along the back of my shoulders and around my ribs. When it gets to my ribs it affects my stomach so much that my food does not digest, but passes almost as I ate it, causing me much pain for two days, and then gradually subsiding so that I am sick today and tomorrow, and then well again for a day or two.

Rumor in camp this morning is that we are going to move in a few days. Some say further to the front, and some say that we are going to the Army of Tennessee.[54] I give them as rumors, not believing or disbelieving them, for I have learned not to have any belief in camp stories. Still, I should not be surprised if we move to either place, nor do I fear much. Only, I won't like having to build up quarters again this winter and hope we shall not have to do so. Day after tomorrow will be my day for going on picket again and I am glad, for this storm is coming down now and it will likely be over by the time I go out again. The peaches you sent me helped fix up a lot of dried apples we had on hand so that they tasted first rate. I wish there had been more of them, but perhaps it is well enough as it is, for the longer they lasted, the harder it would have been to go without again. The little ax is very nice, but is not quite what I wanted. What I wanted was a regular little chopping ax. This will do very well, and if it stays with me I will fetch it home for Bayard.

We have all kinds of rumors about going home, or reenlisting at the end of nine months. Sometimes I almost think there may be something in it; still I can't see any law for it. I wish I could. My idea is that we shall have to stay 'til this war is over, i.e. if it does not last the three years out. How I very much wish to get home, but when I do get there I don't want to have to turn out and come down here again. I had rather stay a little longer and have an end of it. I think from appearances that this war will fall of its own weight in a little time, for there is no mistake but the Rebs are very sick of it and rations are very scarce with them. I should not be much surprised if they side for peace in a little while. But again, we may have to war with them another summer and starve them another winter before they will give up. I sometimes think the Washington political policy is to keep the war running 'til after another election. If such is the case, we shall not do much that will hurt the Rebs for some time, not before another fall. Oie Gads! How it does want some Oliver Cromwell to kick up a dust with the government officials in Washington. I do think Washington beats Dickens' Circumlocution Office in devising ways and means how not to do it. One thing is sure; the administration has had bad success in finding out how to end this war satisfactorily. It is enough to put an extinguisher on any man that really fights or even talks in earnest about ending this war in any way except in the old regular patauger[55] way of doing business. I do think an honorable peace attainable by the means of a conference of the two governments. I say two, for no one is foolish enough, I hope, at this late day to deny that Jeff's government, if not legitimate power, is at least a very troublesome thing to wholly ignore, and still a worse one to put down.[56] I don't want to find fault with the government, and I am as ready as ever to fight, but I want it to be in earnest and for a definite end—that end being the putting down of the Rebellion and not for the purpose of adding stars to any man's shoulder straps. There is altogether too much fishing for promotion and too much of a desire among officers for distinction to have an end of the war as long as the Rebs can make a fight. Though, I am in hopes the Federal generals have so pressed upon them (by mistake) that they are nearer their death than our officers are willing to admit.

If you can get a list of the boys that have enlisted in Farmington and for what regiment, I should like it very much. Some of them may come to this corps and if they do, I should like to know it so I could hunt them up. So, you think Sarah will write to me? Well, perhaps so, but I don't think it. She has got somebody else now to think about besides her rip of a brother. Laura, I don't know what to think of sometimes. I am not as well acquainted with my own folks as I am with a great many others. One thing is sure; I am getting like mother, suspicious of everybody except my wife.

Thinking that I shall get another letter in a few days I will close this by saying that if anyone wants to send me a box of provisions they are at liberty to do so, but don't send any onions, or anything that won't keep good for a week or ten days. Ham would be nice, some good butter not bad, nut cakes, or any kind of cake, biscuits, short ones, any kind of dried fruit except apples (those we get enough of, but they are flat things just stewed) would be very acceptable, pickled cabbage, or anything of that kind. Whatever is sent (if you send a box) be sure and pack the box full so it can't shake to bits and secure the box with hoop at the ends.

I remain your,
Charlie

CULPEPER, VIRGINIA
FEBRUARY 6, 1864

Dear Esther,

Your last came to hand last night and as I am on the sick list, I hasten to answer it. Yesterday was my regular day for picket duty. I went to the doctor to get some medicine for the diarrhea and he put me on the sick list against my will. For as the weather was fine, I wanted to go and I was fearful it might storm the next trip out. Perhaps it is well as it is, for the regiment left camp this morning on a three-day trip to try out what the Rebels are at.

. . . Well, the doctor's call was not sounded this morning and as my stomach and bowels were badly out of order I did not fall in with the company, but just remained in camp thinking in this way — that if I was not fit for picket yesterday, in as much as I was no better this morning, I was not fit to march. So, I stayed in camp and so far have had busy times running to the sinks and back. Yesterday evening I had a terrible time vomiting and have eaten comparatively nothing since. How long this fit of indigestion will last me I can't tell, but it has hung to me pretty close for the last two weeks. Something is radically wrong with my stomach as most everything I eat passes my bowels without digesting. I puke and purge a great deal. I am troubled at the same time with severe pains in my back and shoulders and chest and what is very strange, nearly every one of us is troubled with cramps in the legs and arms. What causes it I can't imagine; only that it is something in our rations.

One thing I am sure of is that is there is something in our soft bread that is not wholesome and tastes like soap and is apt to make me sick. The hardtack are the same as before, but we don't get enough of them and nothing else in the bread line. Of meat we get 3/4 lb. of pork as a day's ration and it is as a general thing pretty good. The fresh beef is very poor and tough and it is almost an impossibility to cook it so as to have it fit to eat. Of the rest of the rations I have no fault to find except that they are too small. The beans are good, but the way they cook them here is sure to make men sick with colic and diarrhea. We soak ours in weak lye rinse, par boil in two waters, then boil to a mush. Still, they will make me sick in spite of all that. I rather think the coffee we get is an adulter- ated fixed up mess that is hurtful to me, for after drinking it I almost always have a bad feeling in my stomach. I drink as little of it as possible. We get potatoes and onions once in a while, but in such small quantities that they don't seem to satisfy our appetites for vegetables. The potatoes are small and a good many of them are touched with rot. The onions are these little, strong things called multipliers. Between the rotten potatoes and strong onions, our vegetable diet is quite poor. About once in two weeks we draw rations of rice and molasses, and if we got it every day we would be the better of it. But, we have to eat such as we can get and make the best of it, for there is no way of improving the rations. So, if I am sick and unfit for duty, the government may charge it to the account of bad rations. As long as I had money I managed to keep along, but as I have none now and would not use it to buy things to eat with, why, I am sick just about one half of the time. If they don't feed us better, they must get along with what service men that are sick half of the time can render. I don't know any other way.

I understand the regiment has gone to Raccoon Ford on the Rapidan. From the sound of things I guess they are having a bit of a fight, as we can hear the report of cannon. Whether it is any more than our artillery shelling the woods I cannot tell.[57] If it is a regular get go they are having,

I hope they will finish the war. I think a very little sharp fighting would make a finish of it, for the army under Lee are very discontented and are trying to desert to our lines. 'Tis said they have had some severe brushes among themselves to keep their troops from deserting by regiment. I will write again as soon as I hear the result of this reconnaissance in force, for 'tis said we have 103 pieces of cannon and a correspondingly large force of Infantry and Calvary. With much love to you all I remain as ever your affectionate husband,

> *Chas. F. Biddlecom*

—·—

CULPEPER, VIRGINIA
FEBRUARY 7, 1864

Dear Wife,

Everything in camp remains as it was yesterday when I finished writing to you. All we know of the battle yesterday is that the First Corps were held in reserve[58] and, of course, were not in the engagement. As yet, the 147th is as good as ever, i.e. it has not lost any men so far.

The fighting late yesterday afternoon was very severe judging from the noise. We could hear the sound of musketry very plainly as one continual roar for over two hours. We could hear above the roar of the infantry fire, the louder report of cannon in quick succession, as often as one every five or six seconds. From the reports of guns, we thought they were using canister[59] or grape.[60] It is very easy to tell the difference between shell and canister, for there is a second report from the shell almost as loud as the first report from the gun. With canister there is a louder report from the gun and no second one from the canister. Another way of telling is by the rapidity of the firing. It is a great deal rapider in firing canister than in firing shell.[61]

I hear that our troops were successful yesterday and are following the Rebels up today. As yet, we hear no cannon. Maybe the Rebels have fell back so far that our men can't come up with them today so as to have a continuance of yesterday's battle. I hope our men will make a finish of 'em this time and I shall not be sorry that I was not with the regiment. I can't say that I have any great desire to be a mark for the Rebels to shoot at. As for the glory to God in war, I care not for it. I shall never force a fight if I can help it, but once in I will do my best. I shall not skulk to keep out of battle, nor shall I volunteer to be one of any *forlorn hope*.[62] I am, as I always have been, willing to do my share to put down this rebellion, and so far this fall and winter have done my best to be up to time. Now and hereafter, as long as I am here, I calculate to do the same. But, if I am sick, I shall get excused by the doctor, if possible. Life, limb, and good health are of considerable importance to me yet and I calculate to take as good care of them as I can. Let them blame me that have sacrificed as much in this war as I have and for as little pay, and not those very patriotic, stay-at-home folk that think to place a money value upon a man's life. Don't you think that a fair position?

If anything transpires or not I will write at once, if so situated to be able to write.

> *With much love I am your husband,*
> *Chas. F. Biddlecom*

————

CULPEPER, VIRGINIA
FEBRUARY 9, 1864[63]

Dear Esther,

I write to let you know that I have survived the great scare that we had the other day and that my nerves have not suffered a shock so severe that I am likely to become insane. Though, I fear some of the officers that remained in camp have suffered so as to sadly derange their minds if not totally craze them. A big scare and a canteen of commissary whisky are enough to fix out the strongest intellect, but as some of our junior line officers are not very strong in body or mind, I fear they are done for.

Word about the scare I wrote to you about (the movement of last

Saturday at Raccoon Ford on last Sunday afternoon). Orders came from Culpeper to have everything ready to move at a moment's notice. The headquarter wagons and regimental wagon train all moved off to town and a wagon was detailed to move the sutler's goods to the depot. Well, it came and we loaded it full in about ten minutes and got as our reward five apples and a haversack[64] full of soda crackers a piece to tramp with in case we had to leave. Well, well, I have found out what will open a Jew's heart and it is nothing more, nor less, than fear of loss. I was very much amused to see him bluster about, out of breath and supporting his head on his hand in great distress, thinking of the loss he was in danger of. I could not help thinking it was a punishment sent to pay him for charging three prices for his goods (three prices if he would be contented with three, but he oftener takes six). Guess his conscience is one of those case hardened ones that can't be touched with anything short of the rough hand of adversity. At any rate, he got a good scare and it served to open his Jewish heart. I often think of what O'Connell said of the Jew in the British House of Commons,[65] i.e., that he (our sutler) is a direct descendent of the impenitent thief that was crucified with our Savior. Perhaps I am prejudiced, but I dislike the whole Jewish race and will go without before I will buy anything of them.

We had everything ready for leaving camp before dark (Sunday) and we were to burn up everything we could not carry with us in case we had to leave. After packing up my things, bundling up some of my chum's things, and being ready for a start, I laid down thinking all the rest I could get would be wanted in case we had to take a run for our life. I had hardly lain down before I heard a noise, faint and indistinct, away off toward where our advance was supposed to be. At first, I could hardly make out what it was, but as I listened it came a little louder and nearer, and I could plainly distinguish the shouts of our men. At first, we all felt like returning it, thinking it the sure sign of some very favorable news, but as cheering is not played out in the army unless the men are certain that the news is reliable, we held our breath and awaited further developments. I don't believe anything less than positive news of peace would start a shout among the old members of this regiment.

Well, we did not have to wait long, for news came that the regiment was on the march back to camp and pretty soon some of the men came into camp with orders to have supper cooked for the officers. Our wonderful, smart lieutenant sent a messenger to Leafler, our company clerk, to have some ham and apple dumplings cooked for his supper. Well, the clerk did the best he could. He cooked the ham, but as he was out of soda he failed to have ready the dumplings. Lieutenant Farling[66] was so enraged that nothing but dire vengeance on Mr. Clerk could appease his wrath. So, next morning he put the clerk in the ranks again. Poor, babyish, little dunce of a lieutenant. Instead of apple dumplings, he will have a large slice of humble pie to eat when the captain gets back again, for he will tumble this new clerk out and have the old one in again.

The regiment reached camp about ten o'clock p.m., a muddy looking set as ever I saw in my life. Such shouting I never heard in my life they kept up until they got into camp. Then they took a turn and swore nearly as loud as they had cheered. I did not wonder much, for the whole move, so far as we know, resulted only in tiring out the men and did not have any weight in subduing the Rebellion. I do not know of anything that will enrage volunteers so much as tramping through the mud without having some definite good come of it.

Well, after sleeping over it and resting yesterday, the men are feeling first rate again and are having a game of football in which the officers are taking an active part. So, you see we had something of a scare and all for nothing. The sutler of the 95th NY Volunteers had a worse fright than our Jew did. He was so badly scared that he burned up what stuff he could not move in one wagon. He burned his tent among the rest of the things. I hear that is the policy of these sutlery to burn up their goods, rather than let the men have them. I suppose the reason for this is if the men get a supply of things such as they want it would prevent the sutlers from selling their stuff for such extravagant prices. If they should sometime find themselves cleaned out by the guerrillas we should not care much for the sutlers, but should object only because the Rebels would have so much more stuff to keep their lives in their wasted bodies.

FEBRUARY 12, 1864

Can't write much, my head is sympathizing with my stomach. My food does not digest at all. I either have a looseness of the bowels and everything I eat goes right through, or else it comes up. Yesterday, I went to the doctor for some medicine for diarrhea and he gave me some that stopped it, but ever since I have been vomiting up everything I take into the stomach.

. . .

Your letter came last night. I had one from Mr. and Mrs. Gates the other day and I thought when I read it that he, Gates, was taking the privilege of making game of me. I shan't take any notice of his letter. Sarah thinks me a very ungrateful dog because of something I wrote in some letter to you about Father selling off the stock. Well, I did not intend to be understood as claiming any property, nor having anything to say about what should be done with it. Sarah thinks I ought to be truly grateful for what Laura is doing for Bayard. Well, perhaps I am, who knows? Then Sarah gives me a great lecture about being insensible of all Father is doing for my wife and babies. Now, I think I have a due appreciation of that fact and I am not aware that I have intimated anything to the contrary. Why they should be so prompt to pick flaws in my letters and try to make me out an ingrate I am sure I can't tell. Of this much they may be assured, I will try and get along in the future without hurting their feelings. I shall not write to any but you and then they will not be wounded. My head is so dizzy I can hardly see the lines and I must quit. I will write again Sunday if I am well enough, which I hope I shall be. Accept this from your own,

> *Charlie*

P.S. Betsy Cole's son, Myron Strong, is in the 8th Cavalry. I expect to see him tomorrow.

Dear Esther,

I have nothing new to write and I have got tired of writing about nothing. I am off duty yet on account of my health. I don't think I shall be much better as long as I stay here. I was advised by a friend of mine to call for an examination before a board of doctors and see if they would not discharge me from the service. I think I shall do so, but not yet, for I want to get my pay first. We shall get paid about the 15th of March and if I am not sound by that time, I shall make an effort to get out of this. I have no expectations of being well.

There is a division review today. The company are all gone except three or four that are sick. These reviews are the forerunners of some extra move. General Meade is at home sick. Sedgwick,[67] the second in rank, wants to do something to get his name up and will have another move to the front if the weather is suitable. Thank fortune it is snowing now, for if it continues on snowing it will put a stop to General Sedgwick's fine plans for gaining notoriety. I hope the weather, or something else, will keep us still until the new troops arrive to reinforce us, for this army is very small now in comparison to what it was when the fall campaign closed. The regiment that has been out two years are nearly all reenlisting and going home on furloughs so that the real number in the field (for stats) is smaller than many of us suppose. Then, take out the sick in camp and hospital, together with those on detached service, and the regiments left for duty are quite small. For example, this 147th shows a full regiment of 1000 men by the book, but in reality we have but about 500 men for service. The rest of them are, so far as fighting is concerned, are out of the play. Now, the 147th is the largest regiment in the brigade and I guess as large as any in the army corps.

The picket duty comes very severe this winter. This regiment furnishes from 90 to 110 men for picket every two days and 25 men for guard duty all the time. This is considered very heavy duty and most of the time it is done on a very short allowance of rations, which makes it worse than it otherwise would be. We have been making up for rations that were issued to the men and thrown away (by the quartermaster) the time the army retreated to Centerville last October. How much longer will it take us to make up the loss we can't find out. When the quartermaster commenced issuing short rations we were said to be but eight days behind. Now, they still say eight days. Behind or ahead, I should have said of the quartermaster. We have been over two months living in this starvation kind of way and don't seem to get ahead a bit. Something is devilishly out of gear in the feed works. We are all calling for Hooker and lots of grub. Hooker is the man most thought of by this army. We think Hooker the man that made Gettysburg possible and we think him a much abused man. Abused by those that should have a better appreciation of his services.

I am thinking our Father Abraham will fare slim in the next fall election, if he is to be elected by the soldier's vote. The army are going in for Grant or some other general. The quicker the folks at home find it out the better. Old Abe has got to be dropped or beaten and I don't care which. He has fooled away too much time in this war already. Next March '65 his turn is out and some man with more energy will take the chair. Abe never will end this war unless he does it by mistake. I have come to the conclusion that it is not his policy to end it.

. . . Your letter of the 10th came in last night and I was very glad I had not finished writing you yesterday, for I shall save a postage stamp. I am glad the box is on the road, for I think a change in diet will do me good. Do try and get that spot off Bayard's eye. I wish I was at home to go into the grocery business, and maybe I shall be. I think I should like the business first rate, much better than farming a stone farm. I meant to tell you not to put any vinegar on the cabbage, for we have plenty of it here. I am afraid it will spoil the cakes, unless you have secured the kegs very securely, but it can't be helped.

I wish the government would pay us off then I could send you some money and buy some flour and have apple dumplings. The boys make first rate ones here. The sutlers keep a kind of baking powder that make them light and good. For shortening we use pork fat. The flour cost five cent per pound and the powder the same. I will write again Sunday. Until then, I bid you goodbye,

Chas. F. Biddlecom

———

CULPEPER, VIRGINIA
FEBRUARY 22, 1864

Dear Wife,

I write to you again today knowing you will be looking for a letter from me by the time this reaches you. My health is some better than it has been. I am doing duty again. I was on picket last Friday, Saturday, and Sunday. We came in Sunday about 2 p.m. The weather was clear, but quite cold Friday night. I took a cold and am considerable hoarse, my throat filled with phlegm. I am not doing anything for it, nor do I calculate to for this reason: the doctors are just as likely to give the wrong medicine as the right one. I rather think they have had me about as long as profitable to the service. I know I have stayed as long as is profitable to me.

This is Washington's birthday and as a matter of course we have had a Division Review. We should think we had got off very nicely if the review ended our days work, but our Spread Eagle Colonel must have a short battalion drill this afternoon just to air his military and please his soft headed wife (who is here, and is our real commander). I wish the Devil had all the soft pated men and women connected with this army, and especially this brigade. If he had, we should have a day's rest once in a while. This, Washington's birthday, is supposed to be a national holiday and will be kept as such in the north, but here we have no such thing as holiday. Last Fourth of July, the armies of the north kept with a vengeance. Thanksgiving Day was recommended by Governor Seymour to be kept by all the New York regiments and the governor ordered his proclamation read to every regiment, but instead of that we got orders to pack up and march to Mine Run. Christmas Day, we left camp at Kelly's Ford and came here.

I have told you part of what has been done today and when the day is spent I will record the rest. When, oh, when will the cursed fools have done with parade and go to work in earnest? Who can tell? Say, Old Abe and his crew are played out in this army corps and his nomination to be the next president will be his political death. "Next summer's campaign is to end the war," Lincoln men tell us. And so they have been telling the people at home and the army ever since the first summer and they know they have lied all the while. For whatever Lincoln may have desired, some miserable curse of a general has managed to be out of his place just enough to let the Rebs recover from their losses and get ready for another campaign by the time our troops were fighting again. And so it will go on for years, unless some man of more penetration and better judgment is given the charge of affairs at Washington. Let us have Frémont or Grant and we shall have done with this war before the end of time. But, with Abe, and the like of him, eternity is not long enough to conquer a peace.

I received a letter from Andy Roberts last night and one from Ben McVeigh one day last week. He wants us to go to Illinois and buy the Thompson place. Can't see it, can you? Don't mean to go west to farm anybody's land but my own, and as I have no money to buy with, I shan't go. I don't mean to farm it again if I can find anything else to do. Next to soldiering, farming is the hardest work in the world for me to do, especially as stony land as the last farm was.

I have mailed to your address a company register of this Company A 147 Regiment. I thought it would please you all at home to have one. The cost was $1.50. All the men are sending one of them home. Please take good care of it for if I get home I shall think a great deal of it. Roberts writes that wages are very high and help very scarce. I don't know what there is of interest more to write. That Box of provisions has not arrived yet. I am expecting it every night. My boots are just the thing.

Esther, I think I never was as thin in flesh as I am now since the

winter I had the typhoid fever. I am looking a great deal thinner than I
did when I came home from Harper's Ferry. Still I am not dangerously
ill at any time, but I am worn out and tired all the time. How long it will
last, I can't tell, but the first spring march will use me up and then I am
coming home, if such a thing is among the possibles. Who was that Mr.
Wells that had charge of the Box as far as Baltimore? I saw Betsy Cole's
son, Myron. He is in the 8th Cavalry. He is looking first rate. Did I ever
tell you that there was an Irish boy from Macedon in this regiment? His
name is Foley. Father knows him.

Believe me your loving Husband,

Chas. F. Biddlecom

———

CULPEPER, VIRGINIA
FEBRUARY 28, 1864

Dear Esther,

I will write you a short letter today hoping that I may have another opportunity in a day or two when I feel more like writing than I do today. I
have just come off guard and do not feel very wide awake. Yesterday the
3rd and 6th Army Corps moved past us to the front and last night we
were ordered to draw three days rations and be ready to march at an early
hour this morning. It is past noon and we are here yet and, I guess, are to
stay another night at least.

There are the usual amount of rumors in camp, some of which I wish
were true, but I can't trace any of them to a responsible source. One rumor
that is very much talked over is that this corps is to be withdrawn from
the front and troops that have always been in Washington sent to take
our place. I hope it is so, but it is too good to believe. What the army is
gone out to the front for is only a surmise in our camp. Some think the
Rebs are falling back on Richmond. I guess not, but think they are at some
of their old flanking tricks. Time, however, will only tell. We know less
of what we do our selves, than you do that take the daily papers. I hope
there is not to be a general move of the army at this time, for a move of

infantry at this time of year is sure to cause a great deal of sickness and rarely, if ever, are they of much use. Our Captain has come back to us. He has been gone home sick for about two months.

The box came through all safe and nothing in it damaged in the least. I think the victuals saved me from being down sick. At any rate, I am much better than I was before the box came. How we did go in on the biscuits and butter! I fixed a stewer out of the largest oyster keg and I tell you, if I did not have some steamed biscuits that were about right, then there never was a good biscuit. Biscuits and butter, stewed peaches and tea, and three kinds of cake made a grand display and were duly appreciated by us four poor devils that had almost lost our natural tastes and found an appetite for hard tack and salt pork.

I have received a letter from Roberts, but have not answered it yet. Had a letter from George Peckham, he is in the hospital yet. Smith Crocker is in the 146th NY Volunteers, commonly known as the Garrard's. They are from Oneida County and are in the 6th Corps there. There are quite a number of the boys that belonged to the 28th scattered through this corps. I saw one of them the other day. It was almost like going home to talk with him of old times.

Church call has sounded. I don't know whether I shall go or not. I guess not, for I have come to believe that soldiering and Christianity do not go very well together. I can't reconcile the two as well as I used to do. No, I don't believe God hears prayers that are as one sided as those we give. One thing is sure, there is not much of the "Father forgive us, as we forgive those" in them, and very little charity for the poor Rebels. I can't go for such kind of preach and pray, even mean as I am. I have almost come to the conclusion that the evils of this war are as great as the good that we expect to come of it.

Esther, I do not say this because I am afraid to fight, for I am not, but, I see so much that is evil connected with the war, and so little of true patriotism in the army, that I am not at all satisfied that going to war with the South was the best policy. I sometimes think it would have been better in the end to have let the South go out peaceably and tried her hand at making a nation.

I must stop and get some dinner. So goodbye, my Esther, for a few days.

> *Your own,*
>
> *Chas. F. Biddlecom*

———·———

CULPEPER, VIRGINIA

MARCH 4, 1864

Dear Wife,

By the time this reaches you, you will begin to be anxious to hear from me and will be wondering why I have not written. Well, Esther, I delayed writing after receiving your last one day too long. The day that I intended to write I was sent out as one of the picket to keep watch of the Johnnies and I only came in yesterday evening and was so tired I could not write. We had a very rough time. It rained and snowed and sleeted forty hours out of the forty-eight that we were out. The trees were covered with ice and though we did not suffer much from the cold, still we could not keep from getting wet to the skin.

How it is that men can stand so much misery as we do here in the army, and still live, is a great mystery to me. If any of the folks at home were to take a week's time of such life as we live here all the time, I am sure it would be the death of them. How do you think they would stand the victuals and lodging, to say nothing of the drill, picket, and guard duty. I am sure of one thing, there would be some howling done at first, but it would get to be an old story after a little and they would do the same as we have been doing for the last two months, i.e. curse the war and everything connected with it.

Of one thing let me assure you, that is Abe and his satellites would come in for their full share. We, all of us, feel that this war is not to end in Abe's time and groan when we think that it is one year from this day before we can have a change. No one need talk to me thinking to convince me that Abe has done his duty and that he has not failed to do for the best interests of the people north. No use telling me what has been done when the great thing remains undone and so far as we can see, is likely to remain undone for at least another year. If Abraham wants to rule for another four years let him put his best foot forward and end this war before another nominating convention meets, or else he will have to take himself out west and that pretty fast, too.

You ask how we manage to keep clean. Why, my dear, we wash ourselves with soap and water, of which there is no lack. As for lice, we hunt them off and when we wash we give our clothes a good boiling. Can we keep clean? Well now, you should see us at morning inspection with boots and belts polished, box, belt plates, and buttons as bright as a new cent, our coats, pants, and hats brushed up in regular go to meeting style. I think you would come to the conclusion that a soldier can keep clean as well as anybody else and so he can . . . when in camp. Though, once the campaign commences a soldier is as dirty a man as can be found. As for lice, he will have lots of them, and unless he manages to have a skirmish with them every day or two he will be devoured by the graybacks.[68] How it is that lice live and flourish so universally in the army is beyond comprehension. I don't believe there can be the same amount of vermin found on the face of the Earth that there is in the army while they are on the move every day or two. I have so far kept myself clear of them, or nearly so.

We are having fine weather again after the storm. The robins and bluebirds make the morning air vocal with their music and the night of the first of March I heard a frog trying hard to raise a peep, though it seemed to stick in his throat. Guess the frost was not quite all out of him, but a few warm days will limber him up so he can make a go of it. The day is so warm I have half a mind to go fishing this afternoon, though I guess I will wait a day or two for fear that the water is too cold for the fish to bite.

I am feeling pretty well these days and hope to keep well, though I do not expect to. When you write again tell me all about our folk and tell them for me that after this I shall write only to you, for it seems that I have given some offense to some of them every time I have written. To prevent the like happening again I shall not write to them again. Sarah gave me a tongue lashing and seemed to carry the idea that I was in some way ungrateful for what was being done for you. I suppose it grew out of something I wrote about living by myself when I got home. She gave me very decidedly to understand that I was to consider myself eternally obliged to Laura for what she was doing for Bayard. In fact, she intimated to me that I was obligated to all our folks and that I had done some outrageous wrong by not going down on my weary bones and acknowledging it. Well, perhaps. In fact, quite likely I am a mean fellow, but I am not nearsighted, nor have I a breach in the groin. Consequently, I am what I am: a poor, d——d soldier, and as such, met with the same degree of appreciation that all the rest of the soldier boys get. If I come home minus a leg or an arm it will be but little. And, won't the government pension me? Perhaps so, but I had full as soon they would pay as we go. Oie Gods! I wish every man in the north had to take a hand's share in this miserable war. Then we would all be on par and would be able to see what one had sacrificed for the other. Thirteen dollars is rather cheap for murder, but by the most of folks at home, considered very fair wages.

I believe Congress has forgotten us for the great matter of selecting the next President.[69] I wonder if they intend to raise our wages as the money gets poorer. If they do, they may as well leave it as is, for the $13 per month we get now is not as good as the old pay of $11 in gold by a matter of about $5.50. For $5.50 in gold at the same time the war commenced would buy as much as the $13 in Greenbacks will now. Write a long letter full of news next time and I will answer promptly. The 3rd and 6th Corps has been out on a reconnaissance. They came in yesterday.

I remain your loving husband,

Chas. F. Biddlecom

Kiss the babies for me.

CULPEPER, VIRGINIA
MARCH 5, 1864

Dear Esther,

I received your last letter last night and as I may have to stand guard tomorrow I will write to you today. I am not quite as well this morning as I have been for some time back. I have a run of diarrhea often and it is giving me a pull down again today. I had considerable flesh for the last week or two but shall probably lose it again. Esther, my right knee is quite lame and swollen this morning. I am afraid it is going to trouble me as long as I live. The veins are swollen very much and are more knotted than ever before. The most I fear is that it will get just bad enough to send me to the Invalid Corps, but not quite bad enough to get me sent home and discharged for good.

However it may go one thing is sure, I shall be sent from the front before the spring campaign opens, for I understand it is the policy of the government to have all the inefficient men sent from the front before there is any movement made. The doctors are examining men now to see if they are fit for active service. When my turn will come I can't tell, but I think before long. I am not sanguine of being discharged, but I shall try hard to bring it about and do not think I shall be wrong in so doing. For it is very plain to me that I am not strong enough to stand a summer's campaign. My captain is convinced of it and on him as much as anybody depends the results of the examination.

It is raining this morning and as we have had a very fine dry winter it is believed we are to have a wet spring to make up for it. If such is the case, the spring campaign will not open before the first of May. Most of the old men are hoping it will rain all summer and keep the roads so muddy that the army will have to lay still. I don't know that a rainy spring and summer would not hurt the Reb as much as we should by fighting them. For if it is really a wet season, the Rebs will be unable to raise much of a crop and unless they do, the next winter will starve them into submission.

Kilpatrick[70] is somewhere down toward Richmond with a large force of cavalry and it is thought that he and Butler[71] may succeed in releasing our prisoners, even if they do not take and hold the city. I am afraid it is too much to get at once. It is said by some that it "never rains, but pours." If it should so happen that our poor fellows are released from the Rebs, we shall think there is nothing too hard for us to undertake. There is no mistake, but this army is scared of the Rebs under Lee and something has got to be done to raise the spirits of the men. A raid to Richmond would be just the thing. We shall know in a day or two what the results of Kilpatrick's raid are and we can only hope for the best at present.

. . .

Sunday morning March 6th and as fine as a May morning at home. What fine weather we have had for almost two months. The rain will come by and by, and then, oh dear, what mud we shall have, but we must have some bad with the good and some bitter with the sweet. I guess we shall find better enough before another winter. I do not happen to be on guard this morning and it is really a wonder, for it is guard or picket nearly every Sunday.

Keep all the money you have got, or can get, for your own use and don't send me any more. I must get along without and you will need it more than I shall. I am glad to hear that Bayard's eye is getting better. How is my little man, Stafford? Is he gaining slowly? I do so wish he would get stout that I can hardly wait for him to grow up, he is so cute. I think he would make a very smart man. How is my little girl? Mischievous as ever, I will venture to say, and lots of trouble to her Aunt Laura. Well, I hope the fates will so order it that I can see them all before long and live at home with them ever after without having a merciless Conscript's Act to take me from them. I will write again the middle of next week. Until then, goodbye.

> *Kisses for you all.*
> *Charlie*

CULPEPER, VIRGINIA
MARCH 11, 1864

Dear Esther,

Yours of the 6th came to hand last night and, of course, I was glad to get it. I was calculating to write you today, and should have written yesterday if it had not rained so hard as to make it very uncomfortable to do anything. It does not rain today, but it is quite foggy and cold. My joints ache so that I could cry, if only it would do any good. As it is I grin and bear it as well as I can. I am fixing things for a discharge as fast as I can and I think things are working very favorably for once. You can tell Father that I expect to be at home by the first of May, and I don't mean to be disappointed in my calculations either.

I suppose I might find Dave Richardson, but I hardly think it worth the trouble it would cost, for he is an officer and I am but a poor conscript and after I had found him he might refuse to see me. I tell you what; it makes a great difference whether a man is an officer or private. Shoulder straps elevate most men to such a tremendous height that a "poor d——d private" looks very small in an officer's eyes. Perhaps a doctor may be an exception to the rule, but if he is, it is only the exception necessary to prove the general correctness of the rule.

We are getting enough to eat once more and if my stomach was right I should get along first rate. As it is, I do not get along at all well. I don't mean to do duty in this army this summer if it is possible for me to avoid it, and I'm sure it is.

I have not received an answer to the letter I wrote to Steven's folks and I don't know as I feel at all bad about it. I don't believe I shall write to anybody but you unless I have to stay here through the next campaign. I am glad Bayard's eye is getting better, but you don't give me any encouragement about Stafford improving any. Do tell me, is he sick and is that the reason you do not mention him? Emma is smart, of course. So, you think Gates not smarter than some other folks? Well, I think something similar, but Mother thinks him the top knot, and that's enough. Why should you or I care, so long as the rest of the folks at home are suited? He meant to insult when he wrote, or else he is a devilish fool, and I care not which. I am glad I did not answer it, for if I had and given him his just desert, I should have committed the unpardonable sin. As it is, he goes scott free and is welcome to think of me as he sees fit. So much for him. I have written more about him than I ever meant to.

When does your brother Dave leave for Iowa? Or has he gone? Do you hear from Cornelia? Good luck to them, and that is more than they will wish me. How pleased they would be if they could make a willing slave of me. As it is, there isn't any love wasted between us. I just wish them well and will think of them no more, if I can keep from it.

So, the poor Copperheads[72] are dead again. Well, well, the only way to kill them is to pound away as long as the tail wiggles. That used to be the rule for killing snakes when I was a boy. So, let the Unionists pound away, for they may be sure that their blows are not wasted on the air.

I have mended two pair of socks since I came to this camp and shall have to mend again the first chance I get, as they begin to want mending again. I have yarn enough to last some time yet, probably all I shall want. The victuals are all gone except the beef and dried fruit. You may laugh about my oyster steamer, but I have seen poorer ones at home. Folks don't need half as much to get along with as they think they do. Many a woman spends half her time scouring pots and pans that she could get along without using at all, and would be better off if she hadn't them at all. I often think of the old pots and kettles we had and wonder what in the world you done with them all. No news here, only that I shall have to go on picket tomorrow.

> *Your, Charlie*

CULPEPER, VIRGINIA
MARCH 19, 1864

Dear Esther,

Yours of the 12th was received last night and as this half-day is my own

I will use the opportunity to write you another letter. My general health is better than it has been for a year and with the exception of my right leg I am getting along first rate. The rheumatism seems determined on setting in my right ankle and knee joints. My boot leg is filled every night with swollen leg and the swelling is dropsical, so much so that if I pinch it the prints of my fingers will remain for hours. I am afraid I shall be a crippled in my right leg yet. The veins are very much more knotted than they were when I left home.

The latest news here is that we are all to have a thorough examination by a Board of Surgeons from Washington before the army takes the field. Those that are not fit for active service are to be sent to the rear, and those that are not likely to ever be efficient in the field are to be discharged, if they so desire. I hope to be one of the condemned soldiers. Still, I can't tell how it will be as very much depends on who is in command of the company at the time the examination comes. If everything works agreeably, I think I shall be in Macedon one of these fine spring mornings. At all events, I shall try to get out as hard as I can. If Uncle Abe wants to grind politics with this army all summer, as he has done for the last year, why, he may go to —— for the boys won't stand for such fooling as they have had for the last six months.

Already we hear from the Blue Ridge Corps of those that are calculating to desert just as soon as the weather gets warm enough to lie out nights. Then, there is the Coffee Brigade, or those that are always five or six miles back from the front cooking coffee. Then, there is the Corps of Confirmed Dead Beats that are in the hospital or riding in the ambulance. This corps is likely to be well filled this coming campaign and there isn't a doctor in the army that can find out who is really sick, or who is making themselves a little sick and feigning a great deal that does not ail them. As a general thing the man that plays off gets the best treatment from the surgeons. When we first came here last fall, the doctors treated us very mean. The first question asked would be, "are you a conscript or sub?" If the answer was drafted, the doctor would ask, "why didn't you pay $300?

You ought to be sick." If the poor devil was a sub, the doctor used to say, "didn't you get paid for coming? Go and drill. I can't do anything for you." Well, after a time, men would come in from duty and just lie down and die. After two or three had died, the doctor got scared and commenced doing something. Since then, it has not been hard for a man to get excused by the doctor.

Esther, the chimney has taken a notion to smoke and I shall have to stop for a while 'til the wind goes down.

. . .

. . . *Sunday morning* and the wind blows as usual and the chimney smokes as bad as ever, but I must try and finish this. The Devil is to pay with the pay department and it is very doubtful whether we get any pay or not. One thing is quite sure, if we are to have supposed rations and supposed pay, then the government may suppose our service. For I think we shall all belong to the Blue Ridge Corps and take French leave of the service and trust to luck to get off. One thing is certain, most of the men have been humbugged to such an extent that they will suffer death rather than submit to it any longer. It is said that we are to get no bounty, and what we have got ($25.00) is to be stopped out of our pay. Now, I am very much like other men and hate to be cheated out of any money that is just my due. If the government is into any of their stealing operations with me, they may "go to ——" to find somebody to shoot at Johnny Reb, for I just won't do it, even if I rot a prisoner on Belle Island. But, we shall see what we shall see, and in the meantime hope for the best.

Esther, keep good heart, for I shall come home some of these days when you least expect me. Give my love to our folks and tell them Charlie is well enough and means to come through this God accursed war all right. I could not vote for Lincoln again, or any of the crew that infest the high places in Washington. Not that I have changed my politics, but when men fail to do their duty, as Lincoln and his miserable crew have done, then I, for one, am done voting for them. Give me Frémont or someone like him and I will go, but none of you slow and go easy set for me!

My head is full of smoke and my mind is all mussed up so that I can't write a decent letter. All I can say is that I think of you and the children almost constantly and long for the time to come when I can be with you.

> *I am your husband,*
> *Chas F Biddlecom*

P.S. send some postage stamp

———

[The following letter is from Esther's brother, Stephen E. Lapham, on the front lines of the Western theater serving the Union Army 25th Michigan Regiment Company C Infantry during the beginning of the Atlanta Campaign.]

> 25TH INFANTRY MICHIGAN COMPANY C
> MOSSEY CREEK, EAST TENNESSEE
> MONDAY MARCH 21, 1864

Kind sister, your letter of March 4th I received a few days ago, but have not found time to answer it 'til now. I am pretty well with the exception of a little cold which soldiers in the field are accustomed to, more or less, on the account of their fare. I am glad you wrote me such a good long letter, they was lots of news in it to me. Who is Aunt Amy? I am sorry Charley's health is so poor and hope he will get a discharge. I don't get much news here about the war. Only our own department that we know pretty much, and what we don't know Brownlow's paper of Knoxville tells us. One thing we know, we have done some hard marching. We have followed the Rebs up as far as Morris Town twice lately and we have fell back to here both times. The boys felt somewhat discouraged for we expected to make towards Richmond instead of falling back, unless whipped up by the devils. But I still think Old Schofield[73] knows what he is about. The Rebs headquarters are said to be at Bulls Gap about 10 miles from here.

We have no doubt in the least but that we could drive them out of here if we was let, but Old Grant, the head commander, is giving some good plan, I hope, on the Rebs. Our cavalry and the enemy's are skirmishing every day. They is one thing certain, they will be more blood shed this summer than last, or the Rebs will get whipped without fighting much.

I got a letter from Olive the other day. She and the boy was quite smart. She had been quite busy sewing for Mary to help them off to Iowa. They had gone for good. I hope they will do well out there and get a good home, although I think Dan has missed it. I hope Cornelia will regain her health and hearing. If I know where to direct to I would write to her. I wonder why she and Dave don't write to me. I am a going to write Walt Gage a letter to day. I believe I have wrote to him last, but he don't want me to wait every time for a letter from him. I don't know but that some of our folks are mad at me. I have not tried to harm them in the least. I think Walt thinks something of me. I do of him and his women anyway. I believe Walt would accommodate me if it lay in his favor on anything. I know they all think a great deal of you, Esther, and you must go and visit them.

We have had disagreeable weather ever since March came in. Cold, rainy, windy weather. It is windy, damp air today and the fire feels good, although it smokes like everything. We have nothing but our little dog tents to crawl into. We are well smoked up, look very greasy and dirty, besides we have got a few graybacks. The Army can't get clear of them entirely, it is impossible. Even the big feeling shoulder straps are somewhat troubled with them. I could have had lieutenancy when I enlisted if I had fished for it. Even my company officers says I am as capable of an office as any man they have got, but my ever lasting temper keeps me from it. They know I don't care a darn for any of them. Even if I do look kindly dirty and rough, I think myself as good as they. As long as I behave myself well my officers and company seems to think a good deal of me, even if I am a private. They think I ain't to be fooled with.

They have just commenced furloughing from this department, one and two from a company. Our Captain told me a few moments ago he had a furlough for me. The boys wants me to wait two or three days before I go. We expect to be paid off day after tomorrow and probably I will start Thursday. If you answer this inside of three weeks direct to Pipestone. It is upwards 500 or 600 miles from here around to Niles. It cost not less than $25 soldier's fare going and coming. If it would not cost so much I would go to Macedon and make you all a short visit.

I want to settle with Walt so that it will be all right there after. They is between 100 and 200 dollars back yet on the note of Uncle Ebenezer from Father's Estate, besides what grandmother's estate was. I don't suppose I will see anything of the horse harness and buggy Uncle E. promised me if I had stayed with him until of age. If I had known I never would have gotten it I would have left him when I was 18, or sooner. But never mind. I want what is my due in such a shape that it can be got even if I should loose my life while in the army, for Olive and the little shaver would need it. If it was not for some business at home I would not go, for I know Olive will feel worse for me to go home and then have to come back again, than if the war should end by fall and I go home for good. But, life is uncertain, especially in the army, and I want to see Olive and the child very much, and you, Dan, Cornelia, and Dave, with some others in your state, also.

Write me a letter to Pipestone. Your affectionate brother,
Steven Lapham

———•———

CAMP OF THE 147TH NEW YORK STATE
VOLUNTEERS
CULPEPER, VIRGINIA
MARCH 31, 1864

Dear Esther,

Yours of the 24th and 25th was duly received and should have been answered a day or so ago, but my head was so much out of fix that I was not fit to write. I sometimes have a fit of indigestion and at such times my mind is so much in sympathy with my stomach that I do not write such letters as I should were I to take the sober second thought. Now, I would like to be out of this and home about my proper business, but at the same time I know that I am no better to be here than any other man and I trust the good God I shall not desert from the army or from my friends in this regiment (and they are numerous). Though at the same time, I think the government has used us mean. Let me say that I do not blame any conscript for taking a French leave of this army and the country, too, if he can make an escape.

Tell the good folks at home that we know the difference between being conscripted and having to come or pay $300, or volunteering for $600 and $1000 and our actions will in a great measure be governed accordingly. In fact, I think many a man will try to keep his body out of the way of stray bullets and out of the way of fragments of shell this coming campaign that would, and in fact did, fight nobly last fall. The cause of this can be found in the acts of our Father which are in Washington (I wish he was in Illinois splitting rails) and his d——d political tricksters of a Cabinet Congress. "May the D——l (if D——l there be) claim his own and take the whole of them to his dominion to grind politics to all Eternity," is the prayer of every conscript in this regiment, if not the whole army.

How wonderful easy it is getting to be for our national government to make unjust laws. I wonder how much better soldiers the costly volunteers will make than the conscripts would have been had they been treated like men and not like so many convicts from the time we arrived at Elmira up to the present. Every man the government has enlisted this last four or five months at the time of his enlistment by some hook or crook, was able to keep himself out of harm's way while we poor d——s were led to the slaughter. Well, God bless their dead souls. We will see how long it will take to put them through the drill enough to get them into two straight rows (as the Dutch captain said) and then perhaps we of the 147th will have the honor of supporting them while they charge some Rebel battery (supporting means standing by to shoot down men that show a disposition to run or as we call it, limber to the rear without orders). Of one thing they may be very sure, if there is any fighting done hereabouts they will get their full share of it. Wonder if the folks at home ever think that we poor miserable conscripts are as much entitled to bounty as the volunteers that have enlisted this winter. Well, as we are all reckoned in this call for "500,000" more, why not give us as much as anyone else?

Esther, I am particularly glad to hear you are all so well and I am very sorry to hear that things go cross grained between you and the folks at home. Try to get along a little while longer and we will hope to have it better for all of us. I can see how I missed it in coming here, but I did not know everything then as well as I do now. I should really think some folks had lost some part of their unlimited patriotism and generosity toward soldiers that they had so much of last September. Well, we will try and remember all the good deeds they do for us and forget the inconveniences we suffer at their hands hoping that when this Hellish war is over to get our fair reward. Until then it is useless to expect anything certain.

I will send you some money in this letter and maybe some in the next. I do not like to send it all in one for there is a great deal of money lost on the route from here to home. One of my tent mates has lost $22 and the other $20 since we were paid. It was stolen from the mail. I will send $10 this time and see if it will go through safe and if it does, I will send some more.

Esther, the Blue Ridge are covered with snow and the weather here is quite cold and we are down in Dixie. Judging from what we are having here the weather must be very cold north at this time. The nights are colder now than they were through February and March. The grand skedaddle of deserters has not commenced yet. The reason is cold weather and snow in the mountains. Es, it is not very likely that I shall ever take French, still a poor devil don't know what he won't do sometimes to rid himself of the misery these cursed friends in shoulder straps sometimes put him to. I never have had any fuss with any of them and hope to always keep out of them, but before I am abused as I have known men to be by their officers, I will take the Blue Ridge or some other route to a land where drunken captains and lieutenants are unknown, or at least where their commissions are not sufficient for oppressing whoever they please. Keep up good heart. I shall get out of this all right yet, I hope. Kiss the children for me and tell the folks I think of them very often.

> *Your Husband,*
> *Charles*

———

CAMP 147TH REGIMENT NYS
VOLUNTEERS
NEAR CULPEPER, VIRGINIA
APRIL 13, 1864

Dear Esther,

Yours of the 6th came to hand last night and I was very glad to get it. Say, as glad as you will be to get this, for before it reaches you, you will begin to wonder why I have not written. Well, the reason is this. The floods have carried off some of the railroad bridges between here and Alexandria and last night we received the first mail we have had for several days. I have in my portfolio two letters that I had written to you, but could not send in time to have them interesting (a cold letter is like a cold pancake —just fit to throw a starved dog). So, I have concluded to write a fresh letter and get it off in the afternoon mail hoping it will reach home before you begin to get over-anxious about me.

We have had a wet time this month so far and as a natural consequence the Old Dominion is one extensive mud hole almost as deep as the Slough of Despond that we hear preachers talk about sometimes when they wish to frighten some soft brother or weak sister. I think from appearances that the spring campaign will not open before the middle of May and perhaps even later than that. I have but little hope at this time of getting home this spring. My health is very good and I can say with truth that I have not been as healthy for five years as I am this spring. I have some rheumatism, but not enough to unfit me for service in the field. How marching will affect me I do not know, but I am fearful that I shall be unable to stand it as well as I did last fall. The course of this will be that my muscles are not hardened sufficiently and we are, all of us, too fleshy and gross to stand fatigue as well as we did last fall. Living on short rations last fall and the first part of winter gave us such appetites that when we did get the provender we fattened like pigs. Not having the proper drill on account of bad weather we are fat, soft, and lazy. I fear there will be much sickness and death in this regiment when we break camp and take the field. For as soon as we do our fare will be changed from soft bread to hard tack, all rations of vegetables will be stopped, and our food will be hard bread, salt pork and fresh beef, coffee, and sugar, perhaps for the whole summer. I am told by old soldiers that changing diet always causes sickness at first. I know such has been the case with me so far and I am anticipating a fit of sickness as soon as the change takes place.

I am sure that I never will stand such marching as this army done last fall. I think I shall be home before the summer is past. Still, no one can tell what is in store for them and perhaps it is decreed that my bones are to molder to traces of white lime in the red soil of Virginia, but we will hope for better things. When I have good health, I am quite patriotic and desire to have the war prosecuted with that vigor which will soon end it, even should I have to suffer some. But when I am unwell I do sometimes almost wish the whole concern in the lowest corner of [——].

Tell Father to put a veto on Laura going to Vicksburg,[74] for little does she imagine the trials she has got to endure if she goes. Furthermore, one owl out of a nest of only three is quite enough to give in this war. There are those that wish for such situations and would be much benefited in a pecuniary point and, moreover, those that possess the physical strength necessary to withstand the hardships incident to a life at any of the posts where freed men are located, let alone Vicksburg, which I think the very worst of all. Don't go. Just stay with Father and Mother for you are the last one left at home and Father and Mother are not as young as they were "just twenty years ago." In other words, they are growing old faster than we can appreciate. Laura is the youngest of us and has, of course, more of life to live than either Sarah or I. Stay at home Sister, your duty is at home and not at Vicksburg. Don't think you are to become great by teaching picaninnies, for such will not be the case. As for the love you will get for your pains, it will be just about as rational a lion's purring and not any more so.

Esther, the snow is white on Virginia's mountains this morning and here in the low lands the air is chill and nature gray in winters sleep. Hardly a green thing is seen except the evergreen pines and cedars. The season is very late I conclude, or else there is but very little difference between the seasons here and at home. I can't think of any thing of especial interest to write to you, but will write if any thing of interest occurs.

My children, how I long to see them and you, my dear wife, my only real sympathizing friend. How I long to clasp you to my heart and tell you how much I love you and my children. My four darlings. O, may the good Father grant us a happy home, however humble, when this cruel war is over. Then men shall scar the earth with the rural implements of peace instead of the howling shot and whirring shell.

Kiss my children for me, tell Bayard and Stafford that Charlie, their father, thinks a great deal of them and wishes them to be good boys for his sake!

Sad and Lonely is my heart as I write and my thoughts, my hopes, and wishes are all with you, my dear ones. Kisses for you all and a hope in a union soon.

I am as ever, your Charlie

———

CULPEPER, VIRGINIA
APRIL 20, 1864

Dear Esther,

I am off duty for the day, having been on guard for 24 hours just past. I received Mrs. Catkamier's letter enclosing a few lines from you. I was very glad to hear from you and glad that you were having a good time, but I am afraid the children will have the measles and kill my little Stafford. Do be careful to not expose the children to any contagious disease for you know that Stafford is too frail to stand another such time as he had with the scarlet fever.

I am very well, only a little lame. I do not expect to come home for a long time and perhaps I never shall see you again. I will try and keep up courage and hope for the best, though, I fear the best will not be enough. Everything is looking like fighting and if we fight Lee where he is now we shall get a terrible thrashing. His position is naturally very strong and he has not let the winter pass by without making it stronger and fortifying. He holds the same ground he did last November when we were over the Rapidan and he means to stay there until he is driven out.[75] To take his position will cost us 20,000 lives and perhaps my life is one of them, but I do hope not. It is the opinion of the officers that we are to take a thrashing the first thing this spring. Whether it is because they have been accustomed to getting flogged every spring or not I can't tell, but I guess former springs have had the effect to make the officers scared.

The Blue Ridge Corps have commenced moving in squads and hardly a day and night passes without some two or three passing away with them. They go quietly and are not missed by the officers until they have been gone from 12 – 18 hours. I hear these discontented ones talk a great deal and keep it all to myself, for it is a soldier's religion not to inform of a private. But, Mr. Straps has to keep his eyes open or he is reported at headquarters. I can see most any time of day groups of men on the top of the hill in earnest council and what is peculiar, every one has his face towards the Blue Ridge. They are locating a line to limber to the rear on. After taking a good survey of the hill they go to their shanties and consult over the map for eastern passage. Most of them have ere this determined the route they intend to travel and more of them will go through than one would suppose could make an escape. I have not the least doubt that there will be 150 men lost from this regiment before the first day of May. For all of the men think the government done an unconstitutional act in drafting them for three years. They also think that nine months is as long a time as the government has any law for drafting. Consequently, when the nine months is up they intend to leave and let Uncle Sam catch them as best he can and then try and see if the law can't be brought before the proper court to decide on its validity.

However much I may desire to be out of the army, one thing I think I am incapable of and that is deserting. I could refuse to do duty and stand out as long as any man if it was even to death, but this sneaking off I do not fancy. Now, did I believe as these men do, I would not do duty, but would stand a Court Marshal and go to the ripraps before I would be compelled to do a thing I really thought was wrong. To do wrong is bad enough, but to be a coward besides is really too bad. The weather is very cold for the time of year. The mountains are still white with snow and the woods are as dead looking as they were a month ago. I hurt my leg last night while on post and it aches a good deal today, but I guess it will be all right in a day or two. How I wish it would keep lame a week or two so I could beat the doctors out of a few days duty, if nothing more, just as one of my chums is doing with a swelling on his neck which he cultivates with a stiff brush. I should not wonder if he succeeds in having a truly sore neck if he keeps on. Well, well, it is all right so long as he does not get caught.

D——l take the MD's. They are mean enough to merit any thing that we can do to them. Next to the sutlers they are the meanest men in the army. The boys made a rally and charged our sutler's shanty and relieved him of goods to the amount of $400 or $500 so that his winter profits are somewhat lessened. I had nothing to do with the scrape, being in bed when it came off and too lazy to get up. I can't say as I think the boys done him any wrong, but was just taking vengeance in their own hands. 'Tis time for dress parade and I hear the old Dutch drummer cording up his drum to beat the call, so I must quit. If you should not hear from me again 'til I write from some hospital, don't be anxious.

. . .

I have been to dress parade and my hand shakes with cold. The sky looks threatening and I think we are to have another storm. I hope so for I had rather it would rain 'til June than to have to break camp while it is so cold. We are getting worse weather now than we had in March. Peach trees are in blossom where they are sheltered, but I rather think Jack Frost will nip the tender fruit if it holds cold long. We have some fun with all our misery and on parade tonight we came near being caught in our mischief by the Colonel. If we had, the D———l would have had to been paid off for it or the whole company would have gone to the Guard House. Well, time will make all things even and when we have to march nights his Eagles will not protect him from being black guarded by all his good friends in the regiment, and they are numerous. I would not be in his boots this summer. To be general in command of all creation . . . wiggle, wiggle. Two or three men have had a time fussing round the seat and I have made a crooked mess of this letter.

'tis said we are under marching orders, but I think we shall stay here a while longer, for I am sure that it is going to storm like sixty.

Kiss the Children for me, will you? My dear Esther, I am still your loving husband,

Chas. F. Biddlecom

———

APRIL 22 1864

Dear Esther,

Yours of the 18th was received last night. I was expecting it and should have been disappointed if it had not come. I went visiting yesterday for the first time since I left home, over the hills to the Fourth Heavy Artillery. I saw Henry Cline and another fellow that was out of the 28th, the same company that I was in. He tells me that most all of the old boys have enlisted again. Most all of the conscripts are very mad because of the unfairness with which the government has treated them. One in the regiment whose nine months is out has turned in his musket and belts and swears he will do no more duty. Now comes the fury of war, steel against steel. What will be done with him remains to be seen.

Lots of the boys are deserting. Two from my tent are ready for a start and will be off the first rainy night. They are very anxious that I should go with them, but I can't see it. If I ever get desperate enough to desert I shall go on my own with only a bundle on my back. Deserting is reduced to a regular system and but very few are caught. I think the government would have more men the first day of July if they were to discharge the conscripts and subs and let them enlist in such regiments as they wish. These deserters are a nation of thieves. They have stolen lots of Colt's Revolving Pistols from the 8th Cavalry and they propose to shoot any man that attempts to stop them after they once get outside of the pickets. I think they will do as they say for most of them have been misused like dogs. They have come to the conclusion that they would make an effort to be free again and argue in this way that they had as soon be dead and done with it as to stay here the remainder of the year. So, here he goes for the North and freedom again. Well, let 'em go. If it was not for the regard I have for my family I might perhaps try the same route, but never shall it be thrown in my boy's faces that their father was a deserter. I can stay 'til I die, but I can't think of the disgrace of taking a French.

Things are beginning to look war-like and if the weather holds fine we shall have at the Johnnies some of these fine days. It is the opinion of the officers and men that we are to get a thrashing the first battle this spring. I am afraid Grant's western laurels will turn to Potomac willows.

Write soon.

C.F. Biddlecom

CAMP 147TH NY VOLUNTEERS NEAR CULPEPER,
VIRGINIA
APRIL 30, 1864

Dear Esther,

Yours mailed the 25th came to sight last night. I will write today for fear that I may not have another opportunity soon. There is nothing new to write and there will not be until the next battle comes off. When that will be is, of course, unknown. We are in hopes this division will be left here to hold Culpeper, but Wadsworth[76] is so much of a fighting general that it is doubtful whether he consents to remain inactive or not.

My health is not as good as it has been. Though, I am still fit for duty and probably shall be for three years unless I get shot. I wish the war was over and I could come home, but I do not believe it will end in five years, if it ever does end. I hope on (even against reason) that the war will end soon. Though the prospect be dark I will continue to hope, for it is all that we poor soldiers have to comfort us.

Everything indicates an early move and when you will hear from me again I cannot tell. Perhaps never, but I will try and not expose myself to danger that can be avoided. Esther, if I am killed do not mourn, but try and think that everything is ordained for the best. Teach my children to believe that Charlie died a glorious death and above all things, teach them to hate and despise a slaveholder as the meanest of all beings (I was going to write human beings, but that would have been a lie).

I will write again as soon as possible. Until you hear that I am dead, believe that I am safe and do not let fear and anxiety on my account trouble you. Kiss the children for me and give my love to my parents and sisters. Be assured of my never failing love for you, my dear wife. Accept this from me this time for my heart is too full to write any more. I am as here before,

Your Charlie

NOTES

1. The Conscription Act of 1863 allowed a man to be excused from the draft by paying a $300 commutation fee or hiring a substitute, exemptions that favored those with money and instigated a major outcry and riots against the Act.

2. 147th Regiment New York Infantry was organized in Oswego by Colonel Andrew S. Warner and mustered into service on September 22, 1862. Charlie enlisted in Canandaigua and eventually ended up in Elmira, N.Y., with other regiments.

3. Pollock's Mill Creek, more commonly called Fitzhugh's Crossing, took place on April 29, 1863, about two miles downstream from Fredericksburg, Virginia. The Union First Corps crossed the Rappahannock River in boats, against modest Confederate resistance, for the purpose of building bridges in the maneuvering that led up to the Battle of Chancellorsville.

4. The Battle of Chancellorsville was fought from April 30 to May 6, 1863, around the crossroads of Chancellorsville, Virginia, with two other battles taking place on May 3, in the vicinity of Fredericksburg. General Robert E. Lee's audacious decision to divide his army in the face of a much larger enemy force, combined with General Joseph Hooker's sudden reluctance to attack resulted in a stunning Confederate victory. It was here that the famous "Stonewall" Jackson was mortally wounded by one of his own men.

5. Miller, Francis C. (Frank). Enlisted on May 1, 1861, Oswego, N.Y., as captain 24th Regiment NY Infantry Company C; discharged for promotion on November 4, 1862; commissioned into Field & Staff 147th NY Infantry October 4, 1862; POW May 5, 1864, at Wilderness, Virginia; confined at Macon, Virginia, and Columbia, S.C.; wounded May 5, 1864, at Wilderness, Virginia; paroled December 9, 1864, Camp Asylum, Columbia, S.C. Miller was incorrectly reported dead, but later found instead to have been wounded and captured. (*See note 17, Chapter 6*)

6. Harney, George, age 28. Enrolled at Oswego, N.Y., to serve three years; mustered in as captain 147th Regiment NY Company B on August 30, 1862; major March 1, 1863; lieutenant colonel on December 25, 1863; captured in action October 27, 1864, at Hatcher's Run, Virginia; paroled, no date; mustered out with regiment June 7, 1865, Washington, D.C. In the Battle of Gettysburg, it was Major Harney who bravely held the 147th Regiment in position until they finally received the missed order to retreat.

7. The New York Married Women's Property Act (enacted 1848, expanded 1860) limited male-favoring Common Laws related to marriage, property, and child custody, and (at least to some degree) property rights, including a woman's right to her earnings, and joint guardianship of her children, though

in practice these laws only protected women with the means to see them enforced. In 1862, the laws were repealed.

8. Peckham, George A., age 30. Enlisted at Canandaigua, N.Y., August 2, 1863, to serve three years; mustered in as private Company F; transferred to 22nd Regiment Company K Veteran Reserve Corps, no date; discharged, July 28, 1865, at Camp Dennison, Ohio.

9. Crocker, Smith, age 19. Enlisted September 19, 1862, as private, 146th Regiment NY Infantry Company B; promoted to corporal, February 1, 1865; sergeant, June 2, 1865; discharged July 16, 1865, Washington, D.C.

10. *Pea coffee:* Coffee was considered one of the most important staples. If it could not be had, several substitutes would pass as good enough: roasted English peas, chicory nuts, or almost any kind of nut or substance that mimicked the color or bitterness of coffee.

11. As Lee retreated from Gettysburg, the Army of Northern Virginia and the Army of the Potomac faced each other across the Rappahannock River. There were two campaigns that autumn: The Bristoe Campaign was a series of strikes and counterstrikes between Meade's and Lee's armies fought in Northern Virginia between late September and early November, 1863. Although considered a Union victory, Meade's army was pushed back 40 miles and lost use of the railroads destroyed by Lee's retreating army. However, Lee was unsuccessful in his attempt to prevent the Federals from reinforcing their troops in the Western Theatre. The Mine Run Campaign fought in the cold rain on the muddy roads of late November, was an unsuccessful attempt by Meade to attack Lee's flank south of the Rapidan River. These indecisive campaigns in the autumn of 1863 illustrated the exhaustion of the Eastern armies after the Gettysburg Campaign that summer.

12. *Bivouac:* A makeshift camp typically in the woods under a covering of branches, sometimes with no shelter at all.

13. Lee, Robert Edward (1807–1870) West Point graduate 1829, rank 2/45. Audacious commander of the Confederate Army of Northern Virginia said, "I shall never bear arms against the Union, but it may be necessary for me to carry a musket in the defense of my native state, Virginia . . ."

14. Meade, George Gordon (1815–1872) West Point graduate 1835, rank 19/56. Though an engineer by education and preference, Meade was a competent leader and distinguished in battle, rising through the ranks to major general in command of the Army of the Potomac in June 1863.

15. Meade was being pressured by Lincoln to destroy Lee's weakened army, but being a relatively cautious general, he did not wish to waste his army on futile attacks against Confederate fortifications, instead hoping to maneuver Lee

into attacking the Union army while it was in a defensive position. Audacious as he was, Lee was willing to attack and suffer grievous losses to achieve his aims.

16. McKinlock, John, age 29. Enrolled at Oswego, N.Y., to serve three years August 30, 1862; mustered in as captain 147th Regiment NY Company A; mustered out with company June 7, 1865, near Washington, D.C.

17. French *leave*

18. Fry, Sampson, age 29. Enlisted August 12, 1862, Rochester, N.Y.; First Sharp Shooters Regiment Company Six; mustered out May 13, 1865, Washington, D.C.

19. *Sutler:* Private merchants who established stores outside of camps and often followed the armies on their campaigns selling food, clothing, and equipment.

20. *Secesh:* A derogatory term short for secessionist, a person who was in favor of the Southern states leaving the Union.

21. *Hardtack*: A staple in the diet of Civil War soldiers, both North and South. Flour, water, and sometimes salt, were combined and pressed into two- to four-inch square thins, then baked; similar to a cracker. A replacement for soft bread because of the ease with which it could be packed, stored, and carried.

22. *Provost guard:* military police

23. A line of communication is not only used for communication, but as a supply line for the army and as a potential route of retreat.

24. January 20, 1863, following his a terrible defeat at the Battle of Fredericksburg, General Burnside made a ill-considered attempted to cross the Rappahannock River and cut Confederate supply lines. Days of heavy rain made crossing impossible and stuck Union horses, wagons, and soldiers in knee-deep mud, causing heavy loss of supplies. Confederate troops watched and taunted from the opposite banks. As a result of the debacle, Burnside was reassigned to the Department of the Ohio.

25. The Second Battle of Rappahannock Station and the final battle of the Bristoe Campaign was November 7, 1863, resulting in the capture of over 1,900 prisoners.

26. Following the defeat of Union Major General William S. Rosecrans at the Battle of Chickamauga, Ulysses S. Grant was placed in command of all of the Western armies and moved reinforcements to relieve the besieged Union Army at Chattanooga. The Confederate Army of Tennessee under Braxton Bragg was defeated there on November 25, 1863.

27. Quincy Gilmore actually failed to take Fort Sumter. It remained in Confederate hands (reduced to rubble by Union artillery) until February 1865. Fort Wagner on nearby Morris Island was, however, taken on September 7, 1863.

28. Meade had hoped to surprise Lee by striking his right flank at the Battle of Mine Run, but a delayed advance gave Lee enough time to build significant fortifications behind Mine Run Creek. Meade ordered Warren's Second Corps to attack, but Warren thought the line too strong. Meade agreed and the attack was called off.

29. Hooker did not return. He had been sent to Grant in Tennessee and served under William T. Sherman for most of the Atlanta Campaign before resigning from the army.

30. Draime, Henry J., age 38. Enlisted May 9, 1861, Palmyra, N.Y., as second lieutenant 33rd Regiment NY Infantry Company B; promoted to first lieutenant November 11, 1861; captain May 20, 1862; mustered out June 6, 1863, Geneva, N.Y.

31. Regiments of the United States Colored Troops (USCT) had white commissioned officers.

32. *Harper's Weekly:* A popular illustrated American magazine that leaned toward the Union cause, but maintained enough balance not to upset Southern readers.

33. The Invalid Corps was created to use soldiers who were unfit for rigorous field duty because of injury or illness, but still capable of lighter duty. In March 1864, the Invalid Corps was renamed the Veteran Reserve Corps.

34. Stephens, Alexander H. (1812–1883) Vice President of the Confederacy and an old friend of President Lincoln. Under pretense of discussing peace and prisoner exchange, requested passage through Fort Monroe and into Washington, D.C.; Lincoln refused to allow the party to pass through the lines.

35. Berry, John, age 18. Enrolled April 18, 1861, in Brooklyn to serve three years; mustered in as private 84th Regiment NY Infantry Company C, on May 23, 1861; promoted to corporal March 1, 1863; sergeant June 1, 1863; shot in the head on the first day of battle in Gettysburg; mustered in as second lieutenant, 147th Regiment Company A on December 19, 1863, promoted to first lieutenant on January 25, 1864; mustered out on June 7, 1865, near Washington, D.C.

36. Brooklyn Regiment is also the 84th Regiment New York Volunteer Infantry.

37. Frémont, John C. (1813–1890) First Republican candidate for President in 1856. His loss to James Buchanan likely delayed civil disunion another four years. Appointed major general of the Union Army early in the war, but

resigned in 1862 after several strategic failures and political disagreements.

38. Fry, James B. (1827–1894) Graduated from West Point 1847; rank 14/38. Fry rose through the ranks from captain and assistant adjutant general, colonel and provost general, brigadier general, then to major general. As the provost marshal general of the Union Army, Fry maintained frequent correspondence with influential political figures, including Abraham Lincoln, throughout the Civil War.

39. Hooker, Joseph (*a.k.a.* Fighting Joe) (1814–1879) Took over and reorganized the Army of the Potomac from Ambrose Burnside in January 1863. Among other efficient administrative improvements, one of his alterations was to consolidate all of the cavalry of the army into a single Cavalry Corps.

40. Averell, William W. (1832–1900) Led a victorious cavalry raid on Confederate railways at the Battle of Droop Mountain on the border of Western Virginia in November.

41. Unit badges were first introduced in 1862 by Phil Kearny for his division. Daniel Butterfield (also the composer of "Taps") is responsible for establishing badges throughout the Army of the Potomac.

42. The Second Battle of Bull Run or Second Manassas was fought August 28–30, 1862, between Lee's Army of Northern Virginia and Union Major General John Pope's Army of Virginia. Though waged on the same ground as the First Battle of Bull Run, it was much larger in scale and numbers. Both were Union defeats.

43. The Battle of South Mountain, referred to in the South as the Battle of Boonsboro Gap, and the Battle of Antietam or Sharpsburg, that Charlie is speaking of, were two of the four battles fought in mid-September 1862, as part of the Maryland Campaign, the first being Harper's Ferry and the last being the Battle of Shepherdstown. On September 22, 1862, days after Confederate General R. E. Lee withdrew his army back across the Potomac and brought the campaign to a close, Lincoln (his public image now solidly shored up by the Union victory) announced that if the rebellion did not end by January 1, 1863, he would issue an order to emancipate the slaves in Rebel states. On January 1, 1863, the Emancipation Proclamation went into effect freeing slaves (but only in certain states and regions, particularly those not under Federal control at the time) and allowed for *"such persons"* to serve in the Union Army. Though it had limitations, the Emancipation Proclamation was a major step toward declaring that the war was about slavery and securing Europe's support.

44. *Quartermaster:* Either an individual soldier or a unit specializing in the distribution of supplies and provisions to troops. The senior supply officer is referred to as "the Quartermaster."

45. Commutation Fee: $300 fee paid by a draftee in exchange for exemption from duty during the American Civil War; seen as class oppression by many and caused riots in New York and other Northern cities.

46. *Paymaster:* During the Civil War, the federal army had nearly a million men on its payroll and 447 paymasters to hand out wages. Transportation, crime, and lack of funds often led to undue delays in paying wages. Despite the chaos, the Army reported less than one-tenth of one percent of the funds were misappropriated or embezzled during the war.

47. This fear was relatively well founded. Confederate guerrillas (usually called partisan rangers), most notably under the legendary Colonel John Mosby, operated freely in this area.

48. *Contract surgeon:* Local doctors who volunteered to "help" during the war and worked mostly in the rear hospitals attending to less complicated medical needs using their own personal equipment.

49. Stillman, John T., age 34. Enrolled at Oswego, N.Y., to serve three years; mustered in Assistant Surgeon, September, 23, 1862; by promotion to surgeon, December 27, 1864; commissioned an officer in 88th Infantry, January 5, 1865; discharged January 5, 1865. He is the author of *Stillman's Pills.*

50. Berry, John. (*See note 35 above*)

51. Paper currency. As a result of the expense of the Civil War, gold and silver became scarce. On February 25, 1862, Congress passed the first Legal Tender Act and implemented the use of a national paper currency.

52. Belle Isle, in the James River within the City of Richmond, Virginia, served as a prison camp during the war for approximately 30,000 Union soldiers. Upon seeing men returning from Belle Isle Walt Whitman asked, "Can those be men? Those little, livid, brown, ash streaked, monkey-looking dwarves? Are they not really mummified, dwindled corpses?"

53. United States Military Academy at West Point, New York, situated above the Hudson River north of New York City. Originally an army post, it became the nation's training place for cadets. Many of the Civil War's senior military leaders, both North and South, had come through West Point.

54. The Army of *the* Tennessee (named for the Tennessee River) was originally commanded by Ulysses S. Grant, but at this time by William T. Sherman. The Army of Tennessee (named for the state) was Confederate, commanded by Braxton Bragg at Chattanooga, and General Joseph E. Johnston at the time of this letter. It is possible that these rumors were swirling around because the Army of the Potomac was one month away from a large reorganization.

55. *Patauger:* French, "floundering"

56. Lincoln's policy was not to recognize the Confederate States of America (or Jefferson Davis) as legitimate political entities, instead focusing on them as rebellious states and citizens.

57. The day Charlie wrote this letter the Union attempted to divert the Confederate Army's attention away from a planned cavalry-infantry raid on Richmond and to deplete the forces stationed in that city by forcing several crossings of the Rapidan River at Morton's Ford and Raccoon Ford. The planned distraction, ending in Union troops retreating back across the river under the cover of darkness was unsuccessful in preventing the Confederate Army from learning about the impending raid on Richmond.

58. *Reserve(s):* Troops held back from battle, but ready to go in when called upon.

59. *Canister:* Ammunition containing numerous marble-sized lead or iron balls that spread like shotgun pellets when fired from a cannon.

60. *Grape:* Ammunition containing several lead or iron balls (fewer in number, and larger than canister) that spread when fired from a cannon.

61. Artillery shell is an iron casing that is timed to explode over a target, showering shrapnel on the enemy.

62. *Forlorn hope* (Dutch *verloren hoop*, "lost heap," adapted as "lost troop"); *enfants perdu* (French, "lost children"): A group of soldiers, selected or volunteering, who take the lead in an assault, essentially a suicide mission.

63. February 9–19, Charlie is marked absent from duty as a result of dysentery.

64. *Haversack:* Soldier's canvas bag used to carry food and supplies, often covered with tar for waterproofing.

65. Disraeli, Benjamin, Earl of Beaconsfield (1804–1881) English literary figure and statesman; although from a Jewish family he was baptized as a Christian at age twelve. He was especially noted for his many novels of political satire. During one of his failed attempts to gain a position in Parliament, he attacked a policy of Irish patriot Daniel O'Connell, who retorted by comparing Disraeli to "the impenitent thief who died on the cross."

66. Farling, Dudley, age 43. Enrolled August 26, 1862, at Albany, N.Y., to serve three years; 147th Regiment; mustered in as first lieutenant and adjutant; as major, December 25, 1863; discharged, October 26, 1864.

67. Sedgwick, John (1813–1864) Graduated West Point 1837, rank 24/50. Before the Civil War he fought in the Seminole War, Mexican War, and was involved in the Indian Wars and the Trail of Tears. Nicknamed "Uncle John," he was well liked by the soldiers he led.

68. *Graybacks:* Fleas or lice, and a derogatory term for Confederate soldiers.

69. Each of the 25 Union states determined its own process for soldiers' voting. Sixteen states permitted solders to vote via absentee ballot. Six states — Indiana, Illinois, and New Jersey being the most prominent and all with Democrat legislatures — did not permit soldiers to vote in the field, but whenever possible in these cases soldiers were granted leave to return home and vote.

70. Kilpatrick, Hugh Judson (1836–1881) Union cavalry general. Led an unsuccessful mission to rescue suffering prisoners of war from the Belle Isle and Libby prison camps during the spring of 1864.

71. Butler, Benjamin Franklin (1818–1893) Union major general of the Army of the James. Though highly criticized for his controversial administration of captured New Orleans in 1862, Butler can be commended for refusing to return fugitive slaves who had come within Union lines, deeming them contraband of war, thus coining the phrase and setting a precedence for the military to ignore the Fugitive Slave Act of 1850.

72. *Copperheads:* Derogatory term for those who opposed Lincoln's policy, abolition, and the war. A Northerner with Southern sympathies was also called a doughface.

73. Schofield, John McAllister (1831–1906) Born in western New York; graduated West Point in 1853, rank 7/52; held several positions throughout his military career including commander of the Army of the Frontier, commander of the Department of the Missouri, commander of the Army of the Ohio and United States Secretary of War.

74. Vicksburg, Mississippi, was the fortress city on the Mississippi River captured by Ulysses S. Grant after a lengthy campaign and siege ending in July 1863. After its fall, the Confederacy was cut in two and the entire Mississippi River came under Union control.

75. Lee's army was entrenched beyond the Rappahannock River.

76. Wadsworth, James S. (1807–1864) Union brigadier general. Educated at Yale and Harvard, Wadsworth was a wealthy and prominent politician and philanthropist from Geneseo, New York. At 56, he was the oldest division commander in the Army of the Potomac, nine years senior to the next eldest divisional commander. He was admired for his concern about the welfare of lower-ranking soldiers. His final encouragement to his men before being shot from his horse mortally wounded: "Steady boys! Go ahead; there isn't danger enough to harm a mouse!"

CHAPTER 6

"I HAVE TRIED MY GUN AND NOW
I SHOULD LIKE TO COME HOME."

MAY 13, 1864

Dear Wife, This the eighth day of Battle[1] and I am as yet unharmed. I pray to God that it may continue so to the end. More than 3/4 of our company are either killed, wounded, or missing. In great haste I write this. O, my wife, my children, my all. God, keep me for them.

With hope in God, I am your Husband,

Chas. F. Biddlecom

———

BIVOUAC ON THE BATTLE FIELD NEAR
SPOTSYLVANIA, VIRGINIA
MAY 16, 1864

Dear Esther,

I am as yet unhurt and we are in hopes the battle is over. There has been no fighting for two days, that is, if this day passes without a fight. It is impossible for me to tell how the action has resulted, whether we are winners or losers. Thereby, I have seen terrible sights such as curdle the blood. But what is strange, I have felt no fear while in action. I pray that I may come safe through all these battles and return to you again as sound as when I left home. I have had some very narrow escapes from bullets and shell.

I saw Smith Crocker and Oly Chilson. They are unhurt. Dillon and Geo Crocker have been missing since the first day. Whether they are killed or prisoners is not known. James Foley[2] is unhurt. Have Father tell his brother Frank so. The division that I am in has been terribly cut up and what is worse we have been repulsed on nearly every move. Our Division General Wadsworth and our brigadier have both been killed. Our colonel was shot dead the first day.[3] Our company is nearly half killed or wounded. What is to become of us is hard to conjecture.

I am down sick with cold and rheumatism. This is the last fight I will ever go into. Keep up good courage and if I am killed, do not feel too badly. I think of you every hour of my life.

Kiss my children for me. I am as ever yours,

Chas. F. Biddlecom

CAMP IN THE FIELD NEAR
SPOTSYLVANIA COURT HOUSE, VIRGINIA
MAY 20, 1864

Dear Esther,

The Rebs have not killed me yet, though, they have tried to several times. Yesterday I was on the skirmish line all day. Just at night, the Rebels charged our lines and drove us out to our pits. We fell back to a grove of pine and fought them out of the pits again. Our new pickets (that were to relieve us) took possession of them and are holding them this morning.

How this campaign is going I cannot tell, but guess we are a little ahead of General Lee. How much longer this series of battles is to last time can only decide. This is the 18th day of the campaign and we have had hot work nearly all the time. Today the Rebel sharpshooters are trying to kill some of us in our fortifications. Both armies are fortified. In fact, I think we must have built as many as 50 miles of rifle pits since commencing the campaign. I am worn out with hard work and fighting.

I threw away my knapsack, blanket, and overcoat, everything except my gun and straps, when we had to run to keep from being captured. We were fairly ambuscaded and had Rebs in front and on each flank. About five of the Johnnies to one of us. So you can see there was no other way, only to get up and dust or go to Richmond captive. I don't fancy being a prisoner, but I am sure that those that were taken the first day have been safer by far than we that escaped.

I came very near being taken last night. The bullets flew around me like a storm of hail. I had a notion once to throw down the old gun and give up, but as good luck seems to be on my side, my comrade in the pit gave them a shot that checked them 'til I had loaded my gun for another shot. We gave them three shots apiece and then run as hard as ever our legs could carry us for the pines. I have tried my gun on the Rebs to my satisfaction and now I should like to come home. But, I suppose Uncle Abe will keep me at this war as long as I can shoot a gun. The Lieutenant is distributing the mail and has just called my name. I hope it is from home.

And it is (dated May 2nd). This is the first mail we have had since leaving Culpeper. I hope we shall get the mail more regular now that communications are established. Mother and the girls need not feel worried about any of my doings. If they will do their duty as well as I am doing mine there will not be any fault found with them. 'Tis not much to brag of, but I am called a good brave soldier by my captain and he is a good judge, being as brave a man as lives. I am very anxious to get home on your account, and the children's. I hope Mother and Laura are satisfied now that I am no coward. I shall try to get home just as soon as this campaign is over. At present, there is no chance of it unless a fellow gets a wound. I don't care about losing a leg yet a while. If I can escape unhurt for another week, I think I shall get home all sound. I have written you twice from the field, so you know by this time where I am. Look in the papers for the Second Brigade of the Fourth Division of the Fifth Corps. Warren[4] commands the corps, Cutler[5] the division, and Colonel Fowler[6] of the 14th, the brigade.

Wadsworth is killed. Rice,[7] our brigade commander, is killed.

Goodbye once more and pray that we may soon meet to part no more this side of the grave.

Chas. F. Biddlecom.

ON THE BATTLEFIELD NEAR
HANOVER JUNCTION, VIRGINIA[8]
MAY 26, 1864

Dear kindred family and friends,

I am still unharmed and I am thankful that God has spared me thus far. For twenty-two days have we been under fire and most every day have we been engaged with the enemy. May 23rd we crossed the North Anna and had a fight with the Rebs. To our brigade belongs the honor of that field. Had it not been for our brigade the Rebs would have the victory. Two brigades of our division, the First and the Third, and part of some other division, broke and ran off the field in great disorder. Finally, it came our turn to try the temper of our Johnny foes. We went in with good style and gave them such a gulling fire that they soon took to their heels for safety. Our commander commanding the brigade, Colonel Hofmann the 56th Pennsylvania, claimed that once more the noble Second Brigade saved the day. I am proud of our regiment, brigade, yes, and company, too. We have lost heavily in officers and men, but we are not discouraged yet. We can fight twenty-two days longer if the job lasts so long. We think we have got Lee "by the tendre" this time and we are going to hang to him until the war is over. The cannons are at work at him now and just in front of us the skirmishers are at work feeling of Johnny's position. Hoping this will find you well and feeling as well as I do. I subscribe myself your son, brother, and husband.

Esther, God has taken care of me so far and I pray that his care and protection may keep me safe through the perils of this campaign and return me safe to you all. Send me some paper, envelopes, four or five stamps, and a half pound of chewing tobacco by mail. My money is all gone, expended and lost to others to procure that indispensable article, tobacco. We have had a wet time this morning and I guess we will not have much fighting today unless the Rebels attack us, which is not very probable.

James Foley is all right, safe and sound. Tell Father and his brother, Frank.

Kiss the babies often.

I am in haste.

Your loving, Charlie

[From Stephen Lapham, Esther's brother, 25th Regiment Michigan Infantry]

> IN THE WOODS THREE MILES FROM THE
> RAILROAD,
> SOUTH 91 MILES FROM ATLANTA, GEORGIA
> MAY 30, 1864

Dear Sister,

It is in a hurry I write you for we have to leave here in a few moments. I know not exactly where I received a letter from you a few days ago and have not had the time to answer 'til now. I was awful glad to hear from you and my wife, and glad you were well. I have just wrote a few lines to Olive. I hope I will get a letter from her in the next mail. It is very irregular about coming and going now days.

They is hard fighting going on within nine miles of here.[9] We were in it three days and two nights. We was relieved last night for a short time to get a little rest. We were so worn out we could hardly come back to here. We have had a great many killed and wounded. Our regiment was very lucky. I don't think out of 200 men we had over 40 killed and wounded. Some of the regiments right with us lost over one third of their men. I feel very thankful myself, for the bullets and shells came as close to me I think as they could without hurting me. I hate the Rebel's cannons, but I can stand the sound of the small bullets pretty well. Our company had two men killed by their shells. I am in hopes this war will end before long. I wouldn't care if our regiment had it its last fight, although I stood it as well as any man could, or any did that was with us. But, if we are called on again, I am with them, if I am able to be.

I feel pretty well now. The boys feel pretty well worn out, all of them. The cannons are roaring considerable. The Rebs are bound to stand it as long as they can. We may have to go into it again in a day or so. I can't write you the particulars, for I have not the time. If I live to get home, I can tell you all about it. I hope Charley is unharmed, but some have to lose their friends in this war. You folks at home are not aware of the number that are used up in it. They are beyond counting almost. I will have to close. Write immediately. Do not be uneasy about me, for if I get killed it will be for our country. I am bound to stand it like a man. Give my love to all inquiring friends.

~ *Stephen*

IN BIVOUAC IN THE FIELD NEAR
HANOVER COURT HOUSE[10]
16 MILES FROM RICHMOND, VIRGINIA
MAY 31, 1864

Dear Esther,

Yours mailed the 20th ins't was received last night and as we are in a position where we can not tell what an hour may produce, whether it will be peaceful or filled with carnage, I will write while there is a lull in the storm. I am unhurt as yet and hope to get through unharmed until we take Richmond. When that is done, I think the government will let the conscripts go home discharged. We are all confident of taking Richmond before the end of June. We gain a little every day so that our lines are becoming more contracted and of course more dense and hard to break through. We have taken many prisoners and they all admit that Lee is outgeneraled and badly whipped.[11] Our loss at first was greater than Lee's, but for the last week or more Grant has been maneuvering. As we have a larger force than Lee, we can hold him in front while a corps of the army marches around the Reb's flank compelling them to fall back to save themselves from capture. Grant will probably work this kind of a game until we get the Rebs in fortifications of Richmond and then the siege will commence ending, as did the siege of Vicksburg. If such is the case, the war will be ended before another winter. Grant is a great general; there is no humbug of a McClellan in his composition.

There was a brisk engagement here last night in which the Rebels lost very heavily. Our artillery had been irritating them all the afternoon with shell and they got mad enough at last to charge the battery. As it happened to be supported by two lines of infantry, instead of taking the battery, Johnny received the grape and canister in double doses. Men that have been on the field say that they lay in heaps.

I would like very much to be exempted from fighting them again, for I must say I have no taste for the business. I don't seem to think of being much scared, but load and fire away as fast as I can, always taking advantage of any little cover that may happen to be in my part of the line. We all do it and I think it owing to our doing so that our loss has been so slight lately. I think from appearances that this division is used as a reserve to strengthen different points in the lines, as the occasion may seem to require. Yesterday afternoon and this morning we are hauling a Dutch regiment of heavy artillery up to the works. They show quite a disposition to run, but we have known them since the second day of this campaign and we calculate that if we are to support them, they will have to stand up to the work.

We are considered by General Warren as being one of his best brigades and we, all of us, think our selves bully in a row, as we are accustomed to call a fight. Hoping that my part of this blood work will soon be over and hoping and praying to God that I may be spared to reach home again unharmed.

Dirty and lousy without a clean shirt for 30 days and only having two opportunity to wash myself you can fancy what sort of an object I am. There is no exception among us. We all fare alike and are all alike dirty and lousy. I want you to keep good courage and think me safe until you hear that I am either killed or wounded. And now kiss the children for me and write as often as possible.

I remain your devoted Husband,

Chas F. Biddlecom

———

FROM SOMEWHERE WITHIN
TEN MILES OF RICHMOND,
VIRGINIA
JUNE 4, 1864

Dear Wife,

I am still alive and unhurt. It does seem to me as though God is taking especial care of me through all the perils of this campaign. Men are hit on all sides of me and I think sometimes that my time has surely come. Our company is dwindling away slowly but surely, one and two at a time, 'til we have now but 18 muskets of the 50 that we left Culpeper with. The men that carried them are killed, wounded, and prisoners, mostly wounded. We know of only three that have been killed and but few of them are severely wounded. We know of but one that has lost a limb. How much longer am I to escape unharmed? I may be hit any moment, for the bullets are humming a death song over my head and an occasional shell howls through the air. It is only the Providence of God that can save us.

Esther, what do the folks at home think of this campaign? Will we succeed in taking Richmond this time or will we have to make another McClellan retreat of it? I can hardly tell anything about how the campaign is going. Only I know this, the Rebs have to give ground. Slowly we are driving them back and all hope and pray that the Fourth of July will find us in the city of Richmond. How I wish the war was ended and I home once more.

Hard tack, pork, beef, coffee, and sugar comprise our fare. I have not had a clean shirt since the campaign commenced, but am as well off as any of the company. I am not any dirtier or lousier than any of the rest. I do believe there is 1000 of them graybacks in my clothes this minute. I have a time killing them every day that I get a chance. My shirt is covered with mites and they are hatching out every second. I can feel them setting out on an exploring expedition up and down and crosswise on my body in search of a place to make a permanent location to raise a family of lice. Now this letter is rather lousy, but a fellow will write of what his mind is filled with and how can mine be otherwise while they are this minute tormenting me? Never mind we are to have some new clothes in a day or two. Those we started with are all tore to rags from hunting Rebels through the brush and woods. All the fighting we have had has been brush whacking, for the Johnnies keep to the woods. Our artillery drive them back from the cleared land into the swamps, and then we go in and hunt them out into the open again.[12] Flanking seems to be Grant's way of doing the job, and we all like the plan. Be hopeful, be cheerful, and trust God for my safe return. Kiss my children for me and tell Father he would not be able to live here over one week at the longest. I am yours,

    C.F. Biddlecom

———•———

147TH REGIMENT NEW YORK STATE VOLUNTEERS
SECOND BRIGADE, FOURTH DIVISION,
FIFTH ARMY CORPS
JUNE 6, 1864

Dear Wife,

The paper, envelops, and tobacco came just a moment since. I am very glad they have arrived for both are very scarce and I may say not to be had for any price.

We moved last night and are today quietly resting to the rear of the whole army. We think our corps is to hold in reserve, but there is no telling. A march of an hour or two would bring us to the front. All seems to be going on well and we all expect it will go on the same way until the city of Richmond is ours. No doubt that it will take weeks, perhaps months, to take Richmond, but its doom is as certain as the rising of the sun. We are drawing the lines slowly, but surely. Even now the inhabitants of Richmond must hear the thunder of our cannon and the battle of our musketry painfully near and coming with slow advance, but with a gradually increasing roar that carries death and ruin to traitors with it.

Our hard fighting is nearly over and now comes the pick and shovel to unearth the miserable wretches that have caused the land to mourn the loss of so many brave sons of God. How fearful are Thy judgments and how sure Thy punishments. Verily the fate of the slave driver is a hard one.

JUNE 7

On picket in the Chickahominy swamp. Gnats and mosquitoes very numerous and hungry. What a wilderness of brush and tangled undergrowth this swamp is. Esther, the green brier (such as grew in Illinois) grow in this swamp and the whole of the swamp is covered with them. From old log to bush, from bush to tree, they run forming a complete network of briers. I am nearly torn to stringlets with them.

We deployed as skirmishers in the open country at the edge of the swamp and then marched by the front into the swamp. Away we went, now to the right, now to the left, over logs, through bushes and briers, until we came to the river. We tore through this labyrinth of almost impenetrable vegetation at least one and half miles. We were in the swamp by nine in the morning (of the seventh) and remained there until six this morning the eighth. We had twenty hours of the hardest fighting I have experienced. Not very deadly to us, but our enemies must reckon their dead by millions.

('tis the mosquitoes I am telling you about. Well, there was some of them down there by the river and they were that large kind such as folks hear tell of, but seldom see.)

Esther, we have drawn some new clothing. We have got washed and changed our dirt and lice for clean skins and cloths that are free from lice. We, all of us, feel first rate and hope ere long to be in Richmond. I think we are done fighting and now comes the sieging or warring out part of the game. You see by what I have written that we have moved our camp again. We marched east and south for seven or eight miles and are now located on the railroad (coming from Richmond to West Point) where it enters the swamps of Chickahominy and we are not more than eight miles from Richmond. I think we must have troops nearer a good deal than we are, for we could hear heavy guns far off in the direction of the Reb lines last night. I think there must have been a fight with our advanced lines and those outer fortifications of Richmond we have heard so much about. I should like to know where they were located, but I have some faint suspicion that the first line of them is or was on the banks of the Rapidan, for we have found fortifications in almost every woods from the Rapidan to this place, and we have built as many as we have found, so that with Johnny's and our digging the country is nicely dug up into dirt banks and rifle pits. Today some of the regiments in our brigade are fortifying and so it has been ever since we left the Wilderness. March all night, fight next day on the skirmish line, and build rifle pits at night. Else, march all day, at night fortify, and then go out in the morning to find what the Rebs have been at. So it has gone so far for 34 days and so it will go until the war is over.

Esther, I am sleepy and I can't write much longer. E.M.R. is a miserable old gouge. The postage on that tobacco should have been but twenty cents on one pound. That is more than the other boys have to pay. Ten cents is all that some of them pay for a pound.

Hoping and trusting in Providence for life and a safe return.

I am as heretofore, the same old Charlie.

———

CAMP OF 147TH NEW YORK VOLUNTEERS REGIMENT
SECOND BRIGADE, FOURTH DIVISION, FIFTH ARMY CORPS
ARMY OF THE POTOMAC
ON THE RAILROAD FROM WEST POINT TO RICHMOND,
CHICKAHOMINY BRIDGE
JUNE 11, 1864

Dear Esther,

Yours of the fifth was received yesterday and I write today in order that you may know that up to this date I am still sound and able to perform my duty with the best of soldiers and of such is this Second Brigade composed. I know you must be anxious about me, but, Esther, do not let anxiety wear on your health. Try and be assured that everything is for the best and remember that God in His infinite mercy is mindful of us all and that not a sparrow falls to the ground without His notice. I am not a good man, I know, but I do trust in God to bring me home again.

We are on the extreme left flank of our army and I think that any fighting is over for the present, unless the Rebs try to flank our left, which is not very probable. There is no news to write that I know of. Everything is peaceful and has been for two days, so far as we hear. We think the siege of Richmond has actually commenced. How long it will last depends in a great measure upon the amount of food the Rebs have stored up, which I judge not to be very large. I think we will be able to eat our hard tack and drink our coffee in Richmond by the Fourth of July. Then, maybe not, for the army thought just so two years ago and missed their calculations. One thing, however, comforts us, i.e. unconditional surrender [13] is our general instead of McClellan, and that is worth 50,000 men to our side. Warren is the man that can carry his corps over more distance than any other general out here, and to him is given the fast work in the marching line. We are always on hand in time and have never yet failed to connect. The idea is "we are going to Richmond this time for sure."

There is but little sickness in our regiment and those that are left are just the lads for a fight, if fighting has to be done. We have got rid of all the cowardly and know now when we go in that every man is true to his company and regiment. Our lieutenant colonel commands the right and a braver man never drew a sword. Our captain is as good as the lieutenant colonel.

Have got new shirt, socks, and pants. Had a good wash and got rid of the lice and feel pretty well, generally. We have had plenty to eat and plenty of appetite to eat it and that makes victuals taste good even if they be coarse. My paper is most gone. I have so many friends to supply and I have subscribed for them a number of letters to relatives with news of those killed or wounded. I will write again in a day or two if I am able. Thank Mother for the few lines she wrote me in your last. Tell her if I have always been a bad son, I will not disgrace my parents now by showing cowardice. Don't show my letters to Ed Brown, or anyone else. If they want to know how things are going down here, let them take a musket and come and see for themselves. I read Laura's letters and should like to hear from some of you very often. Give my kind regards to my family, but don't show my letters. Try and fix some machinery to keep the mosquitoes from eating up the children. I am as ever your devoted,

> *Charlie*

P.S. Hurrah for Frémont and Cochran[14] and an earnest administration of government affairs from March 4, 1865 on through the coming years of prosperity in store for this country!

RAILROAD BRIDGE CHICKAHOMINY RIVER,
VIRGINIA
JUNE 12, 1864

Dear Esther, I write again today. Perhaps it is foolish to write so often, yet what shall I do? I am so lonesome I do not know what to do. I have done nothing but think of home all day. I am homesick, almost homesick enough to cry. I have thought of you all and tried to think that ere long I should see you all again, but alas, how gloomy is the prospect. How many long weeks and perhaps months must pass before the Rebellion is crushed and we poor anxious privates permitted to see home and loved ones again. Many of us will never see home again. In all probability, most of us will be either killed or wounded before the summer is over.

Grant is not generally one of those that stops to count his losses until the campaign is over. We hope the coming strife will be besieging the Rebel strongholds, but I fear Grant will decide to try carrying the Rebel works by charging with the bayonet. If he does, those that have friends in this army may as well reckon them as dead, for thousands will yield up their life in front of the strong fortifications in and around Richmond. This Sunday is almost fearfully quiet. Not a musket shot to be heard and only the half smothered roar of an occasional heavy gun reminds me that we are in the vicinity of the Rebel Army.

From the fifth of May up until one week ago today, with but a few exceptions, we have been under fire so close to the Rebel lines that the sound of humming bullets has become familiar to us. We have almost come to regard them as little as we do the buzzing of flies at home. Now, I do not say it to have you think me brave or careless of life, but the whole company, with the exception of two sentinels, will sleep soundly under whizzing bullets and howling shell, quietly as though at home on "downy beds of ease." Well, the reason of it is that tired nature must never have her nap even though Earth be shook with the thunder of horrible war.

We are having very quiet times at present and in fact have had for the last week. Men are beginning to get sick now that the excitement of battle is cooled off a little. They are thinking over the narrow escapes they have had and counting up those friends that have been killed or wounded in the Battles of the Wilderness, Spots Tavern, Spotsylvania, Hanover Junction, North Anna and those fought this side of the Pamunkey. Sad are the faces and full of grief. Dreary foreboding fills our hearts as we think of what has been done and what is yet left to be done. Gloomy is the prospect before us, for should we win (of which there can be no doubt) awful to think of is the price to be paid for victory. The Duke of Wellington said that next to a battle lost, the saddest thing is a battle won.

Oh, God, how long will thou scourge this poor sin cursed land? When will the measure of our punishment be filled and thy chastening rod be stayed? How many more of the northern men must give their lives a sacrifice to their country ere peace smiles upon our homes again? Who can answer? Somebody is to blame and I think Jeff Davis not the only one. Abraham, thy sins are great and in consequence is the land poverty stricken and filled with mourning for thy deeds. Abraham, poor weak, shady, bedeviled man that though art, the free North is weighing you in the balance of eternal justice and you will be found as dust in the scales. John C. Frémont, the man of more than a single idea, is the one for the country and Abraham, your days of stale jests have nearly run their course. We soldiers think but little of Lincoln and should he be so unlucky as to be nominated at Baltimore, he will be beaten out of sight. I had as soon have Fernando Wood[15] as Lincoln and so we, all of us, feel, with but very few exceptions.

Why does the North submit to so many calls for men? Grant has more men now than he can handle and I believe such is the case with all our generals. Now, in all our fighting I think that every time we have been engaged we have had more men than could be used to advantage, and in some instances we have killed lots of our own men by having two and three lines of battle where a heavy skirmish line was all that could be to any advantage. One thing is very sure; our Division General Colonel Cutler is an old fool and is never around where there is any danger. He limbers off to the rear as soon as the shell begins to fly.

Esther, two of the fellows I tented with last winter deserted the morning we left Culpeper. They wished me to go with them and over the Blue Ridge. It was quite a temptation, for over that route lay freedom, but honor would not let me go. Sometimes since I have thought how much better off they are, so far as ease is concerned, than I am. But never let it be said to my boys that their father was a deserter. No, no. Rather, let my body fill an unmarked grave in the swamps of Chickahominy than that it be said that I was either coward or deserter. I think both of my boys will be brave men if they live to grow up, but I hope it will never be necessary for them to learn the trade of a soldier, for it is a bad thing to know. I already know more of it than I care about and how much more I have yet to learn I can't even guess. Not much I hope.

Esther, there is a limit to all Earthly things and I know there is to my strength. This relaxation of the excitement of active war tells on me worse than the hard work. My mind is beginning to worry again and I fear I shall be sick with the rest of the poor fellows that are having the chronic diarrhea and bilious complaints prevalent in these Old Virginia swamps. If I get sick I hope it will be serious enough to send me to Washington. I don't want to be sick here in one of these field hospitals.

Hoping the war will end with the fall of Richmond and hoping that will fall in a few days. I still keep up good heart and wish this a speedy passage home to my dear ones.

> Chas. F. Biddlecom

Stamps all gone

———

[Charlie's nine-year-old son, Bayard, wrote the following letter.]

> MACEDON, NEW YORK
> JUNE 21, 1864

My dear Father, a one armed soldier boy came here today and Laura bought some paper off him for me and says I cannot make a better use of it than by writing letters on it to you and if I succeed well and you are pleased with my letter I hope you will write me a long one in return.

> Your affectionate son,
> Bayard Biddlecom

———

NEAR PETERSBURG, VIRGINIA[16]
JUNE 21, 1864

Dear Esther,

The sun is fast going down on another day of fighting and I am still unharmed. The bullets have flown thick over our rifle pit all day, but we have not fired a shot in return. Our pit is not on the front line, but back of the front about fifty feet. For that reason we have not fired any. The works of the brigade are in all kinds of shape. In fact, the pits take the form of a fort more than they do that of ordinary pits. Since yesterday we have extended our pit, making it longer, and at the same time we have added to our works a pit to cook in and one for our captain and second lieutenant. The first lieutenant will have to lodge with the company as the men care just enough for him to let him shirk for himself. He is one of those fellows that has an idea that there is not anything known or worth knowing that he is not acquainted with. Well, you know that there is one fellow here about my size that knows a thing or two and there are several more in my fix exactly so that Mr. Lieut. has his hands pretty full most of the time. There is not a man in the company that likes him. Consequently, he has a hard time of it. He is getting of some of his smart things this very moment making fun of a simple sort of fellow, but a pretty good soldier after all.

Well, about our position. Here is the way we are. Pit one is our kitchen. Pit two is captain's quarters. Pit three is our pit. Pit four is the privy. All the companies in the regiment have similar works. 'Tis almost dawn. The Rebels are sending the bullets pretty fast making it very dangerous to be out of the pits. Our men in the front line of pits are answering them very rapidly, though I think their peace of mind is somewhat disturbed for the mortars are commencing to play upon them. We are sending plenty of leaden compliments in return. In fact, I think that we give them full as much as they desire. They have just killed two men. One in the 157th Pennsylvania and the other I don't know where he belongs. This Company has not lost a man since we left Spotsylvania Court House. There is one missing this ten days, but we don't know that he is killed. In fact, we do not know of but two of our company that are killed. Our Colonel is not dead as supposed, but was wounded in the thigh and captured. He is prisoner in Lynchburg.[17]

Down, down goes the sun. Red, blood red, as in keeping with the work we are at, and everything idles until the hot, dry day tomorrow. There has been no rain here for as much as three weeks. The days are pretty hot from 10 o'clock in the morning 'til 4 p.m., but the nights are cool. We generally manage to get plenty of rest every twenty-four hours. Taking everything in to consideration, we are getting along first rate. Last night we drew rations of bread, potatoes, sugar, coffee, and dried apples. I suppose we are getting the potatoes and apples for the good of our health and I am sure it is not a bad plan.

This little company is very healthy. We have but one man sick out of twenty-four men that we draw rations for. Though, where all of the twenty-four men are is more than I know, for we only stack seventeen muskets. We are the largest company in the regiment. Some of the companies stack only six muskets. I hardly think the average of the companies will reach ten able men for the next fight. Pretty hard this, for we left Culpeper with 553 men for the fight. I mean, men with muskets and sixty rounds of ammunition. It is heart rendering to think of. A braver, better lot of fellows never shouldered arms than was the ever glorious, ever to be relied upon, noble 147th when we marched out of camp the forth of May. How few there is left of us to tell the story of the late battles. How I have escaped so many perils is really wonderful and I can only account for it by thinking that God is keeping me to return to my family again.

June 22nd and a bright morning. Johnny Rebs are very much irritated this morning.[18] The bullets are whistling over and around right merrily, whispering in our ears the admonition of, "Keep down heads, for death is in the air." Several bullets have struck our earthwork and two men of the 95th NY have mustered out of the government service and been taken home by the Father of mercies.

Esther, you know that my belief in the salvation of all the human race is strong. Well, it is just as near the realms of light from this little pit of ours as it is from home and should one of these leaden messengers call for me I shall have to go, but my trust in God for protection is great. Extremely lucky has this company been.

[Written in tiny script on a previously used scrap of envelope]

JUNE 22, 1864

Dear Esther, I forgot to write in my letter for the things I want very much, but had it sealed up before I really thought what I was about. I want some more paper and envelopes and some stamps and I want some tobacco. But don't gratify E.M.R. Glen enough to send it through the Macedon office. The other boys get tobacco from home by mail for ten cents per pound postage and I don't believe he is entitled to any more. I would like to have a cotton shirt and a pair of socks, but just see here, the fact is, if you send them through Glen's office, the postage will be more than the things are worth. Have Father try Bud Brigs. I believe he would send them through the same as other Postmasters do. He is used to sending all kinds of stuff through the mail and will be as likely to know what the postage is as any body. If you send a shirt, send a dark colored one, a checked one such as I wore at home.

I must go to Company I pit and see if little Jimmy Foley is all right.

. . .

I have run the risk of getting a hole in my head to find out what I was tolerable certain of before. Foley is unhurt and is well. Have Father send word to his brother Frank.

I wonder if there is one on the face of the earth that would run the risk I have just to inform one man of another man's safety. I hope so, but I doubt it some. Perhaps others are right and I wrong, but our lives are given that we may sacrifice them if necessary for one another's good. But, selfishness is an essential element in almost every soldier's composition sometimes. I think it would be better for me if I had more of it, but it is impossible for me to see a comrade looking at anything I have without giving it to him if I can possibly spare it. That is the way my tobacco and paper and envelopes and postage stamps go, and I suppose it is the way the next will go. I have almost a mind to not have any sent, but then how am I to get along without? That is the question.

Another day is almost gone. The sun is fast going down. This has been a day of almost constant firing and banging away all day long with cannon, mortars, and muskets. Away on our left the big guns have been at it right hard for two or three hours. How on earth the Rebels stand such cannonading is beyond my calculations. Shell from cannon that fairly howl as they swiftly cut the air and shell from the mortars that go gently upward with a milder puff-pish-puff-puff to descend in the Rebel works with an explosion that sends death and bad wounds to scores of the poor

deluded—what shall I call them? They are men the same as I am, there-
fore, men. Foolish to be sure, but yet men, and as such entitled to some
respect— At it again. Away to the left someone is charging. Who, we
can't exactly make out.

. . .

I wonder if I have got to put in two years more of such life as this full of
suffering and not one ray of hope to lighten a poor fellow's heart. Nothing
but sore disappointments and homesickness for the whole time. Oh, my
God, why must it be so? Good morning, I could cry with a will if it would
mend matters. 'Tis too bad, too bad, but let it go. I shall be dead some
time and then, perhaps, my troubles will be over.

NOTES

1. On May 5, after crossing the Rapidan River to start the final offensive against
   Robert E. Lee, the Union army lead by U.S. Grant was intercepted in the
   dense forest of Spotsylvania County, Virginia, by Lee's Confederate army
   in the Battle of the Wilderness. Although Lee was outnumbered, his men
   fought fiercely, using the dense foliage to their advantage. After two horrific
   days of fighting, total casualties on both sides approached 30,000, yet neither
   side could claim any advantage. Instead of retreating, Grant surprised Lee and
   his men by moving around Lee's right flank to continue on toward Richmond
   by way of the crossroads at Spotsylvania Court House. Thus ensued the
   two-week Battle of Spotsylvania Court House, which also concluded with
   no clear victor as Grant, stymied by the Confederates' strong defensive position, disengaged his army, moved around Lee's flank, and carried on toward
   Richmond in the wake of total casualties of over 30,000.

2. Foley, James, age 21. Enlisted at Auburn to serve three years; private 147th
   Regiment NY Company I July 8, 1863; transferred to 91st Infantry Company
   I June 5, 1865.

3. Colonel Frank Miller was incorrectly reported dead, but later found instead
   to have been wounded and captured. (*See note 17 below*)

4. Warren, Gouverneur K. (1830–1882) Graduated West Point 1850, rank 2/44.
   Major general of the Fifth Corps. According to Charlie, Warren was, "ever

present, cool, calculating, heroic, and determined." According to U.S. Grant, he was ". . . a man of intelligence, great earnestness, quick perception . . . he could see every danger at a glance before he had encountered it."

5. Cutler, Lysander (1807–1866) Before the war Cutler was a schoolteacher, businessman, and a brigadier general in the Maine militia. He took command of Wadsworth's division at the Battle of Spotsylvania Court House after Wadsworth was mortally wounded. Considered a rugged and competent officer, he was severely wounded at the Battle of Globe Tavern, resigned from the Army at the end of the war and died as a result of his wounds.

6. Fowler, Edward Brush (1828–1896) Enlisted on April 18, 1861, at Brooklyn, N.Y., as lieutenant-colonel; commissioned into Field & Staff, 84th NY Infantry; severely wounded August 29, 1862, at 2nd Bull Run, Virginia; promoted colonel October 24, 1862, to brigadier general; March 13, 1862, by brevet; mustered out June 6, 1864, at New York, N.Y.

7. Rice, James C. (1829–1864) A self-educated lawyer who rose through the ranks to brigade commander of the Fifth Corps. At the Battle of Spotsylvania Court House he was mortally wounded.

8. The Battle of North Anna (May 23–26) was actually a series of small actions near the North Anna River in central Virginia. Separately known as Telegraph Road Bridge and Jericho Mills (actions on May 23rd), Ox Ford, Quarles Mill, and Hanover Junction (actions on May 24th) and skirmishing on the 25th and 26th that ended in a stalemate, after which Grant ordered another wide movement to the southeast, in the direction of the crossroads at Cold Harbor.

9. This is most likely the Battle of Pickett's Mill, fought May 27, 1864, in the Atlanta Campaign.

10. The Battle of Cold Harbor (May 31–June 12, 1864) was one of the final battles of the Overland Campaign. In his memoirs, Grant wrote, "I have always regretted that the last assault at Cold Harbor was ever made. . . . No advantage whatever was gained to compensate for the heavy losses we sustained."

11. This widely held sentiment that Lee's army was whipped caused Grant to launch the ill-advised assaults at Cold Harbor on June 3, 1864.

12. Throughout the Overland Campaign, after each major battle turned into a stalemate, Grant withdrew and moved around Lee's right flank, hoping to lure him into an open battle, rather than one fought from well-prepared fortifications. The reason Grant kept moving to the right was that his major supply line was waterborne on the Potomac and Pamunkey Rivers.

13. General Ulysses S. Grant's nickname after he demanded the unconditional

surrender of the garrison at Fort Donelson, Tennessee, in February 1862.

14. John C. Frémont and John Cochran (also a minor Union general) ran for President and Vice President in 1864 on the Radical Republican Party ticket, but withdrew from the race in September leaving Lincoln the only Republican candidate.

15. Wood, Fernando (1812–1881) Mayor of New York City in 1854 and again at the start of the war. A Democrat and corrupt Southern sympathizer, he asserted that New York City should become an independent state and secede from the Union.

16. Around this time, Warren's Fifth Corps moved out of the Cold Harbor lines and assumed a blocking position while Grant's army moved toward the James River. Union engineers constructed a pontoon bridge that stretched 2,200 feet across the James to move artillery, wagons, and animals across, while most of the infantry, including Charlie, crossed in boats on June 15–16. Lee was completely deceived by this bold turning movement and soon Union troops were able to attack the undermanned defenses of Petersburg. Grant knew that if Petersburg fell, the critical railroad connections to Richmond would be broken and the capital of the Confederacy would be lost, but a tentative attack by Union forces allowed sufficient time for the Confederate Army to reinforce their defenses strongly enough to prevent a breakthrough and save the city. Grant was forced to start the Siege of Petersburg, which would last through March.

17. From the *Syracuse Standard*: "The 147th (Oswego) regiment took part in the battles of the Wilderness, Virginia., on the 5th and 6th ult., and suffered severe loss. Col. FRANK MILLER, its commandant, was reported killed. Shortly after, a neighbor going to the battle field in search of a missing friend, found a person who claimed that he knew the Colonel, saw him after he was wounded, and placed him while yet living up against a tree upon the battle-field, and showed the very tree where he was placed. It was in the midst of the field that had been burned by the devastating fire in which many of our brave wounded undoubtedly lost their lives, and at the spot designated was found the charred remains of a human being which were fairly supposed to be those of Col. Miller, under which supposition they were gathered up and buried. Thus convinced, the wife and other relatives sorrowed for him as dead, putting on the habiliments of mourning, and appropriate obituaries were published in the home papers. What was the surprise of the afflicted family on Saturday last at receiving a letter from Lieut. Tracy, of this city, dated at Harper's Ferry, June 1st, saying that as a prisoner, he had on the 7th of May seen Col. Miller at Robertson's Tavern, a prisoner and wounded, not dangerously; that the Colonel requested Lieut. T. at the first opportunity, should one occur, to write to his wife and tell her of his condition, fearing

that word might have gone home that he was killed. Lieut. Tracy, in company with Lieut. Birdseye, having escaped from the Rebel prison at Lynchburg, and reached Harper's Ferry, at once attended to the request of Col. M. by writing, which reached them on Saturday morning. The news was almost too good to be credited, and great anxiety existed as to the credibility of its author. The proprietor of this paper happening to be in Oswego, and well acquainted with the parties, gave them assurance of the entire reliability of Lieut. T., and the hearts of the family and a large circle of friends fairly wept for joy, for to them the dead was alive. Although they now know him to be wounded and a prisoner, they trust that he will be in due time returned to them, to again make glad the hearth-stone of home and the social circle of friends."

18. This is likely the Battle of the Jerusalem Plank Road, south of Petersburg. The Fifth Corps was on the northern edge of the battle and not directly engaged.

CHAPTER 7

"I GUESS THIS WAR WILL END."

IN FRONT OF PETERSBURG, VIRGINIA
JUNE 26, 1864

Dear Esther,

I write to let you know that I am still alive and well. I think quite as well as I have ever been at this time of the year. The weather is very warm and our position is not very agreeable. Our heads are just about even with the top of the ground so that we are in a cellar about three feet deep, a bank of earth on one side of us.[1] We have what shade our cotton tent will make, but that is not very much. A fellow will almost cast a shadow under them, the sun shines through so bright. Though, I presume the heat gets tangled some, the same as a "fish net would frost." Have Father tell you the story.

The bullets are making the dirt fly off the top of our pit pretty often today to remind us that it is not safe to go out. Well, we are not anxious about going out. In fact, if the spring was not so far off we would just be contented to stop here as long as we are to serve the government. Don't tell anyone that we (the privates) are patriotic, for it's not so. We are proud, and that in a measure makes us brave, but as for all this newspaper hokum, there is not one grain of truth to two bushels of lies. There are a few men in every company that think enough of their reputation to stand and fight to the last and then there are some more that will fight for fear of being out done by their comrades. As for men fighting from pure love of country, I think them as few as white blackbirds.

We talk of freedom at home and contrast our Washington government with the Richmond government. Well, so far as the white man is concerned, I think about all the real difference is in the different situations in which the two governments are placed, both being just about as mean as the devil can possibly desire. Jeff's subjects are a little more docile than Abe's. Jeff makes sweeping conscriptions. Abe makes great threats and at the same time offers great bounties payable in his greenbacks, which are worth only half their face and are gradually getting worse.

Now all this talk about great Union victories here in this army is bosk. It is more in the newspaper paper accounts than in reality. Grant is a great man for flanking, but as for out outflanking Lee and getting in his rear, there is not room enough on this continent to do it. We go to the left all night and half the next day. Then we start for the front, go about three or four miles, and there is Johnny Reb entrenched as before. We charge and carry one or two of their out lines and then come to a stand still for a week before starting off for the left flank to go through the same program again. It would be all well enough if it did not make so much misery, but I think it rather expensive experimenting.

Now, I would like to have anybody tell me of any important point gained in this six weeks campaign, unless a country filled with mourners and the Washington hospitals with wounded, be of importance. I am willing to suffer as long as there is a need for it and not one moment longer. 'Tis said by some fool officers that we are not paid for thinking. Well, as near as I can sum it up, we are not to work altogether for pay, or at least we were not at the start, whatever may be the case now.

I did have some hope that this war would end this summer, but I think now that this fighting and all this misery about the same as lost for Abraham has been nominated and shortly is in. His election will be the same as was his nomination, a forgone conclusion. That is, unless the Democrats can make run enough to beat him. But, Abe has got the money in his hands and all the contract letting besides, and with what bogus votes he can manufacture in Tenn., Arkansas, Louisiana, N. Carolina, and maybe some other states, he will work his way in. Palsied be my arm if I ever vote for him again. A man that could stand almost over the graves of the thousands of our brave soldiers that have fell in this war, within hearing of the groans of the sick and wounded, and crack his stale jokes, is meaner than Nero fiddling while Rome burned.[2] If Abe is elected this war will be kept along through his second term, for it is getting mighty popular among a certain class in the cities. When you hear of one of these big men in NY giving largely to Sunday Fakes and Christian Commissions, be sure that it is but a tithe of his cheating from the government and he is giving knowing full well that his chance at the public pocket is secured for four or five years to come. Give me a man with a head on his shoulders and then let the head be filled with something better than poor jokes, I don't care if it is filled with cider pumice, I will be satisfied. Give me Frémont or Butler or somebody that knows there is something above and beyond party to live for and I will vote for him. But, Abe, God helping me, never, never shall it be said that I was twice bitten by as small a mouse as he.

Grant will not be allowed to take Richmond and end the war because the contractors will tell Abe that he will lose by not letting Grant take Richmond until after election and then it will be too late to do it this year and this, the fourth year of the war, will pass and the next will go the same. Enough, for once, of this. I mean to get out if I can some way, i.e., if I am not killed. The weather is very hot and sickness will soon be among us. I do not wish to be sick, but if I ever get to Washington, there will end my fighting for I will dead beat the government and thus help the government dead beat the people. That is just what I mean to do.

I am expecting a letter every mail and I think it will be along tonight. Esther, I have been in seven or eight general fights, besides all the little fusses, and have come out safe so far. I guess the charging is done with for a while so that by keeping my head pretty close to the pits, I think I shall get through and come home again. God has certainly protected me and I am grateful for it. Oh, keep me for my wife and children.

Tell Laura to keep away from those contrabands for she will not find it so pleasant as she thinks. I see in the paper that Lieutenant Colonel C. R. Peer is wounded and in Washington.

Ohi Ohi Another man hit. *whiz spat* And another man is badly hurt, if not killed, and I sit and write as though it were nothing and I really wonder at myself, you know, what a horror I always felt when looking at the dead. Well, the same feeling possesses my heart yet. I would hardly look at a dead soldier if it was not for finding out if it was one of our men.

Esther, hoping that these eyes may continue to see the sun rise and set for many a day of peace at home, I wish you all an affectionate good night. Tell Father to keep good courage, for I hope to come home again, sometime.

> *Chas. F. Biddlecom*

> UNION LINES PETERSBURG,
> VIRGINIA
> JUNE 27, 1864

~~My dear son, I am very pleased with your letter and I will write you an answer, too. Bayard, I have no paper except this, your letter, to write on.~~

Dear Esther,

I have been trying to answer Bayard's letter today and I never had as hard work writing a letter in my life. I tell you, it is hard work to write letters to little folks. The trouble is in using words that they can't understand. I wrote to you yesterday, and, in fact, think I must have four or five letters on the road home. I shall write now every time that I can get an opportunity, even if I do not write but a few lines. Our situation is so precarious that I am liable to be hit every day and for this reason I wish to write often. The greatest drawback is that paper is lacking, which you will find out if this ever gets through. Postage is out and this is the last letter to you that I shall send unless I can make another raise on some of my comrades. Paper is also very scarce with us. Tonight 'tis said we are to go to the rear for forty-eight hours. Last night we drew rations of soft bread, sauerkraut, fresh beef, coffee, and sugar. We have drawn potatoes and dried apples on this campaign in abundance. We draw rations every two days.

Hoping for the best and trusting God I remain as heretofore your absent, anxious, homesick husband,

C.F. Biddlecom

[The following correspondence was written to Charlie's son, Bayard, scripted on stationary with this poem, author unknown, on its letterhead.]

"THESE TEARS."

For heroes who in battle fell,
"These tears," nor think that this is all
We shrine their names in Memory's hall
With those who first, at Freedom's call,
    In battle died.
Not those alone whose names are known,
But those whose names no record claim,
    Save where all pride
By sorrow drowned, in shadow bound,
Their memories keep, by those who weep
At bitter cost the loved ones lost.

For heroes who for Freedom die,
"These tears" that from a Nation's eye
Fall freely on them as they lie
With faces turned toward the sky.
    For them no more
Alas ! shall come the roll of drum,
Or stiring fife arouse to strife,
    On sea or shore.
But each year shall disappear,
'Twill with it take, for Freedom's sake,
With added fame each hero's name.

UNION LINES NEAR PETERSBURG,
VIRGINIA
JUNE 27, 1864

My dear Son,

I received your truly good letter last night and to show you that I think a great deal of this first letter of yours I shall send it home in this to have it taken care of so that when I come home we can look at it together. At the same time we will talk over all the things that have taken place since I left home to fight the battles of our country in order to keep the country free so that my two little boys will not have to live in a country where the rich man oppresses the poor man as they do in some countries and as they will in this country if this Rebellion is not put down. 'Tis for you, Stafford, little Emma, and such little folks that all this toil and bloodshed is to benefit most. Bayard, you must in all ways respect the soldiers that come home wounded and remember how much they have suffered, and are suffering, for such as you. Bayard, I hope this fighting will be over before a great while so that I can come home. Won't we have good times, you and Stafford and little Emma and me, playing? I expect Grandmother will scold us for making a great noise, but we shall have to make some racket to let them know how glad we all are to see each other again. Mother writes to me that you go to Sabbath school. I am glad to hear it and glad to hear that you are learning so fast. Do you ever go fishing this summer? If you do, you must write to me and tell me what you catch. We will go sometimes when I come home and we go to live by ourselves again. Don't you think we will take a great deal of comfort when that time comes?

Bayard, you must be a very good boy and learn as much as you can this summer. Mother writes to me that Stafford is growing strong and is able to go to the Grocery alone and call on his Grandfather for candy and peanuts, and that Emma is full of fun all the time. How I wish I was there with you. What a dust we four would raise playing. You must kiss Mother and the two little ones for me. Aunt Laura tells me some funny stories about you children. She says Stafford preaches to you about playing Sundays and that Emma can't be kept in place at all, and lots of other things I liked very much to read. Do you ever see any of the little boys that live in the Hook and won't Mother let you go up to the Hook some day and see them? What do you do out of school? Do you help Grandfather in the garden or anything like that? I hope you do. I hope you do not run away this summer, but always ask your mother to let you go. Bayard, the sheet is almost full and I have no more paper, so I shall have to stop. Accept this, my dear boy, from your affectionate father,

    C. F. Biddlecom

Dear Esther,

The paper and envelopes came last night and although I mailed a letter home last night, still it seems as though I ought to write every day now while I have the opportunity. The time may come soon when we shall be on the move and then I shall not have opportunity to send letters home even if I write, which will be very doubtful. The air today is full of death. Every instant a bullet goes whirring overhead reminding me that there is no safety outside of the pits. There is an artillery duel going on today and the shot and shell from both Rebel and Union batteries pass directly over our heads. The sound is not very disagreeable after getting used to it. That is, when we know they are passing overhead. But, it may be very unpleasant should Johnny Reb conclude to depress his gun and shorten the fuse of the shell and try to drive us out of our pits. They seem to have been very considerate towards us so far, contenting themselves with filling the air with bullets and foregoing the shell. Well, I suppose they have been somewhat troubled with bullets, too. Our boys have a fashion of paying off with the same kind of currency so that we must be about even so far as popping at each other's heads is concerned.

One thing about it that I don't like and that is laying in the back line of works where we get the full benefit of all the bullets, but have no chance to shoot back again. We did not go to the rear last night, but are to be relieved for 72 hours tonight at 10 o'clock. We shall go far enough to be out of shell range, I hope, though do not fully expect it. Anyway, the fact of it is that we would hardly know what to do with ourselves if we were not in danger of being killed every time we poked our heads above the top of the ground.

"Wo, oh, whoo, wooo" goes a shell just to our right. "Wang," and the fragments fill the air with dust as they strike the earth. Woe to the luckless soldier that is in the way for a bad wound is almost a sure consequence. We do not lose many men for all the Rebel shelling from the fact that their artillery is not properly handled. Our artillery always gets the advantage of them and I think that is one of the reasons why we do not get more of their shell.

. . .

Well, I have taken a little rest during which time the Rebs have had another trial at shelling and have been speedily dried up. So, as usual, I don't think the Rebs have hurt any of us today. The boys are beginning to be very cautious about how they expose themselves now that the excitement of the fight is over and do not venture as they did a day or two ago.

. . .

June 29th 2 p.m. We were relieved from the front last night about 11 o'clock and we are now lying off taking it very easy. We are within range of the Rebel cannon, but are so screened by the woods that I hardly think the Johnnies know where we are. We are to have a rest of three days and then relieve the First Brigade that came up and relieved us. We are fixing up for a regular siege and may be here a month, quite likely three months. Well, never mind if we are three months taking Petersburg, it will be the same as three months taking Richmond. For Lee's supplies are cut off the same as though we were immediately under the inner fortifications.[3] Richmond, and where we are now, Lee will have a hard time breaking through. We are south and west of him at last, so that he is, in fact, isolated from the rest of the Confederacy, cut off except from the country north of Richmond, and that can't afford him a week's food for his army. I don't think he dare try a raid toward the north, for we can put a force ahead of him before he can move far. He will have to foot it every mile and transport his stores by wagon trains. So far as I can see, Grant has the best of Lee this time and if the army keeps as healthy as it is at this time we shall eventually compel Lee either to fight his way to the southward or surrender. I think it will be an impossibility for him to break through our lines. He has tried several times to do it, but so far has failed and his army has suffered terribly in trying to carry our works. This charging is getting played out. Men will not charge now as well as they did when the campaign commenced.

We are living first rate, got pickled cabbage, sauerkraut, potatoes, and dried apples just often enough to keep us wishing for more. We have the same rations of bread, meat, coffee, and sugar as before, and we get a ration of beans about as often as is healthful for us. When we were in the Chickahominy swamp we were dosed with quinine and whiskey and since we have been over here we have had one ration of whiskey served out. I pray that it may be the last that will ever be issued to soldiers as long as the world stands. Several men were killed by the Rebs. The whiskey made them so brave that they exposed themselves to Rebel fire. Of course, some of them had to pay the penalty of getting tight in a tight place and are now snugly stowed away under ground to await the resurrection reveille, for their ears are forever closed to all earthly bugle calls.

Esther. I am so glad to hear that Stafford is getting along so well that I hardly know how to express it. Emma must have grown beyond my knowledge. Do you think I would know her if I were to see her in any place except home? That is, unless you were with her? I don't believe I would. She must have changed very much since I left home. What did Father do with the flock of sheep? Did he sell them all, or has he got all except the ten he sold to Herrendeen? I see by the papers that wool is very high. I think eighty to ninety cents per lb. I wish I could be at home through this hot weather, especially through strawberry and cherry time. Yes darn it, all the time. I hate this life worse than a cat does hot soap. If I ever get out I will stuff my old uniform with straw and stand it up in one corner to look at when I feel out of humor just to remind me that home with its little cares and troubles is not the worst place in the world for a man to enjoy life.

I shall write again in a day or two if I am spared life and limb. I know you will be glad to hear from me often. Whether you want to hear or not,

I think you will have to bear the infliction of at least two letters every week, as lonely as I am situated at present. James Foley has come through safe so far. I have just this moment seen him. Smith Crocker is sick and in hospital. Chilson is in hospital with dropsy. Both of the boys have been first-rate soldiers. I don't believe any other town has furnished any better men for the army than Farmington. *Doo-yoo-boom.* Away in the distance our big guns are pouring it out to Johnny's lines. So it will go for a month to come and how much longer I don't know.

Hurrah for Frémont and Cochran[4]

> *Goodbye my Esther,*
> *Chas. F. Biddlecom*

(What does Bayard think of the letter I wrote to him?)

———

147TH REGIMENT NY VOLUNTEERS
UNION LINES SOUTH OF PETERSBURG,
VIRGINIA
JULY 1, 1864

Dear Esther,

This is our third day out of the pits. Tonight we are to go back again for another three days of misery and 24 hours of that time I shall be in the skirmish pits, but there is no more danger there than there is in the front line of rifle pits, or as some call it, the breastwork. We have had it very fine these three days. Yesterday, the last day of June, was regular muster day and we mustered accordingly. We have pay due us for four months service and as we are all out of money we should like very much to see the paymaster (the one that pays in greenbacks — the one that pays in hard coin is just outside of our works and generally when a man gets paid off by him he is mustered out of the service and out of the world at the same moment). We have pay for two months at $13 and two months at $16 per month making $58 due from the government. 'Tis not much, but we would like to have some of the money, if not all of it, as soon as the government can pay it.

We shall be out of the pits again the night of the 4th if everything remains as it is at present. But we are anticipating a big dance the 4th[5] and an effort to take the city. Now, as I never was much of an admirer of dancing, and as I very much dislike dancing to the ball of a musket, I should like above all things the privilege of being absent at the time that dance comes off; but I am considered an excellent dancer in this kind of shindig and for that reason there will be no chance of escaping this one. So, let it be then. For of one thing I am sure and that is that all you can have of a cut is the skin and all the government can have of a soldier is his life.

One thing they can't deprive me of and that is the conscience of having done my whole duty to the country and that is something which the government has not done towards the conscripts, nor do they ever intend to deal fairly by us. If they did, we should be home the latter part of the month. For if the next draft is for but one year, then it will be very mean to keep us longer than one year in the service. But the government has long since lost all sense of justice and shame on them for so utterly forgetting the lessons taught them by the founders of the nation. History has no parallel to the meanness of this administration.

Now here is one instance: There was a young man in this regiment that was arrested last fall for desertion, not from this regiment, nor do I know that the officer that arrested him pretended to know from what regiment he deserted. He was sent here hand cuffed and treated in all respects as a felon. He denied the charge of ever deserting, and denied ever belonging to the army. He demanded a trial, but it was not granted. Instead he was put on duty. He would not do duty at first, but was punished and made to do duty. Well, muster day came; he was not mustered for pay and clothing was denied to him. So it went on from bad to worse until this campaign commenced. Now he fills a grave, and not a soldier's grave, though he died fighting for a government that had blackened his name and character forever. The muster rolls of this regiment are the documents that will forever bear false witness against him, for opposite his name ———— the word *deserter*. This is one of the inevitable results of the suspension of the habeas corpus.[6] Better suspend a poor devil by the neck at once, than treat him as this poor fellow has been treated. This case is but one of the thousands like it.

Now, do you or any of your folks think I am going to vote for Abe Lincoln? No. I will see him where Parson Brownlow[7] sends all his enemies first and I will see this country ground to impalpable dust. I could go on and give lots of cases just similar to this if I thought it worthwhile, but it is not. I am well convinced in my own mind and there is no use trying to talk Abe Lincoln to me. With the habeas corpus suspended the people have no liberties left. To be accused is enough to procure an arrest and when a man is arrested he has no chance at all. If I were out of this army as before, I would not come as a drafted man. I would steal something and go to state prison for ten years. I never would enlist again while Lincoln is in office and I am not different from the rest of the boys. They all feel just as I do and are becoming disgusted with the war. We have been told so many lies that we do not know who is telling the truth. I mistrust that our armies are getting the worst of it in some places and I think we are destined to fail here. Still, I hope not. For success is the only way to get things done and I can't bear the thought of staying in the army for two years and eighteen days yet to come.

Esther if I am not killed before the night of the third, I shall write again. Hoping and trusting in God for safety, I keep up a good heart when danger is ahead. I must not hold back now after going through so much danger. I have won a character as a soldier that I think something of. Our folks never gave me credit for being much of a man when I was at home. Now that I have won the confidence and respect of my officers, I must try and keep it while I stay in the army, that my boys may have it to say that Father was not an absolute failure in all things. If a shiftless and luck twisted, good for nothing in common life, he was at least a brave and good soldier.

Affectionately your husband, CFB

———•———

THE U.S. CHRISTIAN COMMISSION
SENDS THIS AS THE SOLDIER'S MESSENGER TO HIS HOME.
LET IT HASTEN TO THOSE WHO WAIT FOR TIDINGS.
"GOD IS LOVE."

UNION LINES SOUTH EAST OF
PETERSBURG, VIRGINIA
JULY 2, 1864

Dear Esther,

The shirt and socks came last night and with them came a letter from you dated the 25th of June. Accept my thanks for the clothes, especially the shirt, and also, for the letter. We are in the front line of works again, but things are changed somewhat since we were here before. The First Brigade entered into agreement with the Rebels to stop firing on each other unless advances are made by either one army or the other. So we are having very quiet times and there is no danger of getting hit if a fellow pokes his head above the breastworks. Both sides take a look at each other once in a while and seem to regard the other just (to me it seems) as though they wished every musket was broken, each bayonet lost, every cannon spiked,[8] and all the swords and spears made into plowshares and pruning hooks, and that they were at home studying the arts of peace, instead of being here practicing the devilish science of war.

Everything (in our medial front) is as peaceful as one could wish. The citizens have been hoeing their corn today right between our lines and the Rebel lines, while away to our right the cannons are at work pounding away at a fearful rate. Well, it suits me to have a truce for a while and if it could ripen into a mutual feeling of friendship and peace, I am sure I should not find the least bit of fault with the arrangement.

When you see anything in the papers praising the Army of the Potomac for its pluck and courage, just set it down as the worst kind of exaggeration, for it is as false as can be (i.e. if there is such a thing as degrees of falsity). The facts are that this army is worn out, discouraged, demoralized, and cannot be successfully handled to fight at this time. One reason of this is that we have lost terribly much of the army that started on the campaign. From the best information I can get the losses are at least seventy percent of the original numbers.[9] Another is that the men are wary of the wonderful lies that have been told us through the medium of regimental and company commanders. Probably the most patent of reasons is that we have not been as successful as we anticipated we should be when we commenced the campaign, nor have we been as successful as we ought to have been considering our losses.

The privates in the Northern Army are apt to think for themselves now and from that thinking they are making up their verdicts and it is reading: First, that this administration is a failure. Second, that the war is prosecuted more for the aggrandizement of contractors than it is for the putting down of the Rebellion. Third, one that we are still deliberating, is or is not General Grant another humbug of the McClellan type? Perhaps these verdicts may be all of them erroneous, but the first two are settled and let Grant beware western laurels turn into Virginia willows. This army has had so many miserable failures on account of bad generals that another failure will result in its total ruin. Grant is skiving hard, but if he has not a more than Napoleon ability, he can never cope with this R. E. Lee in such a country as this Virginia. The only thing that can whip Lee is starvation, and in order to keep him in Richmond we have got to maintain a line of at least one hundred miles.[10] In other words, about 400 miles of men standing shoulder to shoulder or out he goes to some other hole in the wall to cause us an infinite deal of trouble to take him out of it again.

As long as he can keep his army in the field, he will not starve, for the people are heart and soul in the rebellion and will sacrifice everything but the bare necessaries of life in order to feed his army. This talking about the Rebs starving is unfounded. Victuals I have seen compared favorably with our troops, though their rations are different from ours. They have hoecake instead of our horrid hard tack and though they won't swap bread with us, they have swapped bacon for our fresh beef. I would like to trade with them every time. Coffee and sugar they do not draw, but pure spring water appears to agree with them first rate. Most of their clothing is of more durable material than the clothing we are getting. I have seen some of the very best of Austrian grey uniforms, pants, jackets, caps, and hats of the same material on their privates. I have not seen a bare footed one among them. They have all been well shod. Probably you would like to know how I find out so much. Well, we get in front of the North Carolina troops and we have first rate times trading. They are the same troops in front of us here that were at the Chickahominy. This is the reason we are not fighting all the time.

The mail is going.

  Goodbye.

  Chas. F. Biddlecom

U.S. SANITARY COMMISSION[11] OFFICE,
244 F STREET
WASHINGTON, D.C.

UNION LINES PETERSBURG, VA
JULY 5, 1864

Dear Esther,

We came out of the pits again last night all safe and sound and we are laying off at our ease again for three days more. The campaign is substantially at an end and we shall probably remain where we are for months. We hear that the paymaster is not coming up for two months more, so I want you to send me some money, about $5.00. The fact is this campaign has broke us all down financially. Most of the boys had sent their money home as soon as paid off, expecting to be paid again. When they were out and no paymaster came, they just went in on the beg and borrow and they soon fixed me out. The money expended for tobacco is a dead loss, but no matter, I must try and live here some way and if Uncle Sam won't give me money I must get it some other way. Tobacco is as cheap here as it is at home, so is paper and envelopes. I guess that I can get along for two months more with five dollars. I tell you what it is, I don't like to ask for a cent from home but I must have a better supply of tobacco and I must have more variety of food than we are getting, or else sickness is sure to mark me for the hospital. If we get paid in six months it is more than I anticipate. Well, the longer they keep it the more will be saved, but it is not much at about 20 cts. per day in gold.

Oh, Damn such a country. There. That is the first time I have sworn in a long time, especially in writing, but the fact is my patience is exhausted. I expected when I left home that the war would be over before this time, but our hopes are all dashed to the ground and it is hard to conjecture when it will end, but probably not for six months, if even then. I suppose that the turnover in the treasury is the reason our pay is stopped back. All's well that ends well and if I get away from here in a year more with the loss of a leg or an arm, I shall think all has ended well better than I even hope for at present.

So, Ira B. Lapham[12] has served out his time and been mustered out of the Federal service and into the peaceful service of Him who said love thy neighbor as thy self and do good to those that disappoint you, and a thousand other commands that would seem to forbid the killing of men in war, as well in any in other manner, especially this, "vengeance is mine and I will repay saith the, Lord." Esther, I am a Quaker so far as war is concerned and were I out of this the enticements would have to be stronger than have ever been offered yet to get me into it again. The three stars[13] that glisten on the shoulders of General Grant would be not inducement even if I had the necessary ability to command the combined armies of the Union.

Our 4th of July passed very quietly and the same night we left the pits and came back here in the woods where we are resting and cleaning up our rusty arms and accouterments. I tell you what, sixty days of campaigning for Grant has taken off the shine and our battered and rusty guns, torn uniforms, and hackneyed faces are all the signs that tell of service rendered the country. I wish they would appreciate it enough to pay us, but those that endure the most hardships and make the best fight are the ones last to be remembered. Maybe the day will come when General Warren will remember whom it was that saved the Fifth Corps at the North Anna and kept his stars secure. For if we, the Second Brigade, Fourth Division, had done as the rest of the troops did, General Warren would have had the pleasure of enjoying private life at this time. Again, the other day when he charged the Rebel lines,[14] if the other brigades had acted their part as well as our brigade did, we would have had Petersburg and Johnny Reb at our mercy. But he, Warren, fails to give us any credit for our good conduct. Well, he must look wild for it won't take much more like treatment to fix us for running every time we are carried into a fight. No pay, no praise, nothing fair in our treatment, and see how long he can depend on us. Those that think we have not done our utmost had better come and try a campaign.

How does the folks like the removal of Secretary Chase?[15] I suppose they are all Lincoln and Johnson. Yet, I wonder if Chase was not getting too popular and Lincoln must kill him the same as he undertook to do with Frémont and some more that could be named.

Kiss the children for me and write soon.

Affectionately yours,
Chas. F. Biddlecom

———

ENCAMPMENT OF THE SECOND BRIGADE
NO NEARER PETERSBURG, VIRGINIA
THAN WE WERE TWO WEEKS AGO
JULY 9, 1864

Dear Esther,

I once more settle myself for the purpose of sending you a few lines to keep you advised of my continued safety and good health. If Johnny Reb will just behave himself and not commence his shelling, I shall have a good time writing. The morning is quiet and cool and the breeze feels refreshing after having such hot, sultry weather as it has been for several days. Everything is very dry. There has been no rain to speak of since we left the North Anna, and what is strangest of all is that the rains that are commonly very heavy in Virginia have been very light for a long time back. So much so that everything is as dry as powder and all that is necessary for a conflagration is one spark of fire.

This is our fifth day out of the pits and I understand we are to be out one more, making six days out before we go in again. Last night just before six o'clock the Rebs undertook to carry Burnside's pits at the point bayonet, but they made a failure and suffered severely. They did not get four or five rods from their pits before our men opened up on them from two lines of works. At the same time they were under the concentrated fire of thirty or forty pieces of artillery, some of them heavy pieces. That did not prevent the Rebs from throwing quite a shower of shell into the woods where we are encamped. I do not hear that any of our brigade were hit. The night passed quietly enough and everything is still this morning. Though, the ground bell of the season will likely enough open in ten minutes. Then again, it may be quiet for a week. There is no telling anything about how things are to go until ten minutes beforehand.

O, how I do wish it was over and poor Charlie was home again. When, oh, when will that time come? When will I be able to lay me down to sleep without hearing the sound of cannon and small arms ringing in my ears? Esther, if ever there was a lot of men misused it is the conscripts that came out last fall. Only see what a law they have fixed up to draft men with now, taking them for one year and giving them the same bounties that we received, yet taking them into the service a year later and sending them home a year sooner than we poor devils. It seems as if the congress owed us a grudge and has found every means to torment us some way or another. Every time I think of it I have to grind my teeth together to keep from cursing the whole concern. Some of the boys are confident that the law is such as to make it certain that we are to be discharged at the end of the year, but I have seen nothing that I can derive any comfort from.

How I wish it was the law that I could come home at the end of my first year. I should then have but nineteen days to serve and if they got me in a fight in that time they would be smarter than I am. That is all there is about that.

July 10th and a quiet Sabbath. At this time, for the first time in a long time, there is not a gun to be heard. 'Tis the calm that proceeds, instead of follows, the storm. For may be in an hour the air will be filled with shell. Somehow in the afternoon both armies are the most excitable, owing, I presume, to fact that the hot sun and these tormenting flies have produced a kind of crossness that sets them to going.

The same brigade of North Carolina troops[16] that this brigade flogged on the North Anna are holding the Rebel works in front of us, and they are the same that were in front of us at the Chickahominy railroad bridge. We have got so well acquainted with each other that our pickets get water from the same spring and some of them have even been over and taken supper with our pickets. Probably you will see some account of that supper in the Tribune. We have entered into an agreement with them that if either party is advancing the first volley shall be fired in the air as a warning to the others to lay low behind the pits. Rather a queer bargain to enter into you will say but, Esther, between the majorities of both armies there is no real enmity. This is so especially with the conscripts on both sides because of the fact that we are here through compulsion and fight each of them more to satisfy pride than because there is any feeling of ill will between. The time has been when I would shoot one of them on sight, but I thank God that I have got over that kind of feeling and have only a pity for them, as well as for any poor fellow that carries a knapsack, box, and gun in either army.

I drew a new blouse today and I wish I could send my old coat home, for I think a great deal of it as I have worn it throughout the campaign. I should like to save it as a souvenir of the hard fought battles of the

Wilderness, Laurel Hill, Spotsylvania, North Anna, and Petersburg. I should like to keep it with all its dust, samples of different soil from Culpeper to this place. 'Tis not much of a coat now, the skirts torn and ragged, and it is sadly ripped under the arms. Still, as I look at it as it hangs on the butt of my musket, I think more of it than I ever did of any article of dress I ever owned in my life before. Sadly, like everything else I suppose, it will, as Mother says sometimes, "go the way of all earthly things." That is, to dust and faith. The old coat's journey will not be a long one, for the sun and dust have already turned its dark blue to a dingy kind of nondescript mud color. Isn't this lots to say just about an old coat?

Well, I have just room to write you all lots of comfort. Kiss the children for me and tell Bayard to write whenever he is in the mood.

 Chas. Biddlecom

P.S. James Foley is well. He showed me a letter from Frank in which he told James that he thought I was lying when I was sending him word that James was well. So, you see how a fellow gets paid for his trouble some times?

[The following letter was written by Ben F. McVeigh from Springfield, Il.]

JULY 10, 1864

Charles, My Dear Sir,

Your very acceptable letter of the 28th mailed at Washington July 4th is just received. Never was we gladder to hear from anyone than we was from you. I had intended to have rote to your wife today to see if we could get any news from you. I was afraid you had met with some mishap. I have always bin watching the First Army Corps movements as I thought you was in it. I have put your whole address in my daybook for I will send you a journal accasionaly. As for news we have nothing but war news.

The health of the country is good. We are building a new schoolhouse, 24 x 38 feet. The Methodists have bin trying to build a church all summer but something always turns up. Finally they turned Andrew out of the community and got in some Rochester brethren. Our bridge is about to fall down. I was about to make an effort to move it down between me and Cantrell, but the best mare I ever had died. She would have sold quick for $200. But then this Devil's war may drag me from home and it will be of no use.

You speak of Old Abe, we are on a stand still a waiting for the signs of the times. There is one thing serten, I am not going to vote for a man I know will put me in the army. If there is any posable chance for Frémont I will vote for him but the sight looks dull. I hear now there has bin strong talk of the Democrats splitting and hitching on to Frémont. If it is so he will run in. Otherwise I think the Democrats will elect their man. If they nominate Grant he is the President.

We have sad news from the 114th Regiment Illinois Volunteers. Our boys are all in it. They met with a sad defeat. Milton Woodruff[17] is killed. Joseph Natt is prisoner—but one consolation, Joseph can stand as much starving as anybody. I will enclose you a letter cut from the journal with some insight of how things is managed to get us all killed off. All their killed and wounded was left in the Rebs hands. I will change the subject.

Since I received your letter there has bin several in to hear it read. Net Woodruff was over. She wanted to take it home. I told her I would fetch it to meeting this afternoon. I think your letter will make several votes for Frémont. I find most men will vote with the soldiers. I have no questions to ask, you gave me all the information I could ask for.

With our kindest wishes we remain to hear from you often as ever,

Your friend,

B.F. McVeigh

UNION LINES PETERSBURG, VIRGINIA
IN THE REAR LINE OF PITS
147TH NEW YORK VOLUNTEERS
JULY 13, 1864

Yours mailed the seventh was read night before last and should have been answered yesterday, but the weather was so hot and the flies so troublesome that it did seem to be almost impossible to write. 'Tis cooler this afternoon and there is a fine breeze blowing that keeps the flies quiet, so I have concluded to let you know that I still survive the perils of the siege (for siege it is at last). We were seven days out of the pits and this has been our second day back in. Things have changed some since we were here before.

When we came in night before last we found six mortars planted in rear of our brigade all ready to open when the time shall come for bombarding in earnest. Last night the Third Delaware Infantry came up from the rear with picks and shovels and threw a batter for four rifled cannon right in our front. We have a mortar battery in rear that pitches shells over our heads into the Rebel lines and a battery of rifled guns to knock anything the Rebels may get up by a direct fire in front. The shells from the mortars are thrown at an elevation of forty-five degrees with very small charges of powder. Their flight is quite slow, requiring at least twenty seconds for one to fly 600 yards. Their motion is so slow that they can be seen in the daytime by standing in the right position and keeping a good lookout. At night, their course can be tracked by the burning of the fuse.

Last night we were treated to a show of fire works, quite interesting to us, but I thought at the time that while it was fun for us, it was death, death, and broken homes for the boys and girls of the Rebel families. What was strangest of all was that though the Rebs were suffering from the effects of our shell, they did not possess the means of replying to our fire with any effect. They threw some shell over us, but I do not think they hit a man. The Reb sharp shooters off to our right continue to pop away day and night, but our works are built high enough so that they rarely hit any of our men. We are only about a half mile from the town of Petersburg and our guns can send shell and shot into every nook and corner of the town. Our forces are throwing up forts on all sides of where we lay and in a few days the works will be so far completed that the bombarding will go on as usual. Well, if it has got to come off, why, the sooner the better. I had rather have it come on and be over than to lay here dreading it. We have got our work in good shape for the coming storm of iron and lead. So far I have taken my even chances with the rest of the boys and have come out all right. I guess now, when the chances for safety are much more than they were in the field, that I shall come through. Something in my heart tells me that I shall see you again.

James Foley I saw this morning. He was looking well. Father can tell his brother and Frank can do as he likes about believing it.

I will write again soon, if I am spared. Tell my two boys their father thinks of them every hour. Home, home, my dear, old home, how I long for thy blessings.

> *Affectionately,*
> *Your Charlie*

———

UNION LINES NEAR PETERSBURG VIRGINIA
JULY 16, 1864
CAMP 147TH NY VOL IN THE WOODS NEAR
THE RR BRIDGE

Dear Esther,

I expected a letter from home last night but did not get one. I think it will come tonight. If it doesn't I suspect the Rebs have gotten it somewhere out the route through Maryland. Everything remains as usual along the lines. The daily routine is in artillery duel, morning and evening. The middle of the day being very hot, I presume both sides are willing to lay still. In fact, both sides are well whipped and for my part I have come to conclusion that it was a drawn game, the losses and gains on one side balancing those of the other so nearly that neither can draw any permanent advantage. That the campaign is not as successful as it ought to have been is a fact patent to all of us.

Argue against it as best we may, still the solemn fate comes home to us that we are checked, that flanking is played out, and the enemy is still in our front and strongly fortified, as has been the case all the way from the Wilderness to this place. Grant has failed in finding the end of their line and consequently there is no other way except to storm their forts or carry it by regular siege. The first is a very dubious undertaking and the last, a job requiring a deal of patience and hard work. The prosecution of a successful siege is liable to have many drawbacks. One of which appears to be that while we are trying to take the little, insignificant city of Petersburg, the Rebs are active threatening Washington and Baltimore.[18] The loss of either place would end the war, for European nations would then give the South an armed recognition at the same time saying to the North, "We can not long suffer the affairs of the world to longer suffer the interruption incident to your war for an idea." For it is nothing else at this time but a war for an idea and that not a very plain one. As I have written before, pride makes us fight as private soldiers and pride keeps the administration supplied with the men and means to keep up the war.

For what? Surely, it is not for the Union, the Constitution, and the enforcement of the laws. For first, after all this killing of men on both sides there never can be any more union of feeling between the North and South, the Constitution thus being violated by those sworn to protect it. As for the laws, we have so far proven that we are impotent to enforce them. Hence, it is nothing but a war for an idea, and that is *Pride* to be sure. The ever lasting Darkey is dragged into the whirlpool of politics and through him is the cry sent up that this is a war for freedom on the one side and slavery on the other. Well, 'tis true in a certain sense, and in another it is false. I wonder, if it were true that this was a war in which was to be decided the freedom or slavery of the whites of the northern states, whether it would require large bounties and at last a Conscription Act to fill up our armies. I guess not. Were it for the freedom of the white men, they would fight very differently from what they do now. I say that this army is an army of cowards from the fact that the principles that we commenced fighting for have been lost sight of and we are no longer fighting to maintain inviolate the Union and Constitution.

Now, lest any should take me for a Union Saver, I will just say that I don't care a (——) for the Union and think it not worth the life of one man, even the poorest devil of a soldier known. To me, I fight because I am too proud to be called a coward, not that I think all my fighting will do any good to the human family. I am not a freedom shrieker[19] for I don't howl, "Down with the southern aristocrat and up with Sambo and Dinah, though it cost the last dollar and the last drop of blood!" (Now, mind I say the last dollar and put it before the last drop of blood, just as do the shoddy freedom shriekers.) I don't think it will pay to fill both North and South with white women mourning for those lost in this war so that Miss Lucy and Master Sambo[20] may kick up their long heals and jog for a freedom which they are incapacitated (I was going to say, by nature) to truly appreciate.

So, I am no freedom shrieker. I am a peace man.

I would like to have an armistice for just one week during which time the private soldiers of each army should have the privilege of meeting in mass convention, undisturbed by any commissioned numbskull of an officer or any Civil office higher than a Justice of the Peace. In the week's time I believe we should end this war and restore the Union and agree to live together in harmony under the old Constitution. I think it is generally the case that between the private soldiers in all wars there is thought to be no point at it. Whatever may have been the case when this war broke out, of this I am sure, the privates of both armies are pretty well convinced that the war has continued long enough and that it is time to end it.

Now, let Abraham conscript 500,000 men and send them into this service and I believe they will mutiny and run him out of Washington and I for one will (treason here) say that it is but the legitimate fruits of his snail administration. Sorry am I that there ever was such a law as is this Conscription Act passed. Not because I fell a victim to it, but because without the $300 clause in, it is oppressive. And without any restricting clause, it gives too much chance to a poor, weak minded man to sweep the country of everything able to bear arms. I think now that Abe will call out 1,000,000 men before another spring (that is, if he succeeds in being elected next November) and they will be offered up a sacrifice on the altar of Freedom *in a horn* (that's what they call it, I believe, when a poor fellow is shot). To Hell with the devilish twaddle about freedom and let's fight with what men we have got and either whip or get whipped and not take the last man there is in the North and then fail at last.

I wonder how a soldier's family of say wife and six children are to live on $16 per month, and not get that when it is due, and have wheat $2.50 per bushel, pork at $.25 per lb. and everything at starvation prices. There is no use talking, something will have to be done, and that soon, or this army is gone to ever lasting smash. When you hear men say they wish Lee would burn Washington and take Lincoln prisoner, even those that voted for him (in 1860), you may be sure that something is wrong in high places. I have written just as thousands feel today because I was lonesome and wanted something to do. Besides, there is nothing so good for the health as good grovel.

Write as often as you can and keep good courage. I shall be home in two more years, if not sooner shot. That, I believe, is the law.

Kiss my babies for me and remember that my thoughts are with you very often.

   C.F.B

(Have you sent any money yet?)

With Charley and Lewis in the wide pits as representatives of Company A on the picket line. Rebs distant about 15 rods. "All quiet along the lines . . ."

UNION LINES NEAR PETERSBURG,
VIRGINIA
147TH NEW YORK VOLUNTEERS
IN FRONT LINE OF WORKS
JULY 19, 1864

For the first time in one month there is no firing to be heard and for the first time in six weeks it rains and comes down real old fashioned like. One of the moderate kind of rain, such as comes down gently saturating everything not positively impervious to water. Not like one of those thunderstorms that come swiftly down just to give Old Mother Earth a douche, nearly washing off her dear old face for the day. This rain comes just right to suit everybody except the Second Corps and I should not wonder that they find some fault with it. They are encamped on earth that has been ground to impalpable dust to a depth of four inches and as it is clay land they will have soon a bed of mortar to sleep in. Dear Esther, your letter enclosing this sheet of paper, five postage stamps and $5.00 was thankfully received last night. The one containing six quids of tobacco came night before last and was thankfully received. Two nights ago I received a letter from Ben McVeigh, which I will send you with this.

Night before last a Rebel major and six privates came into our lines and told a yarn that Johnny Reb intended to charge the line where we were lying to see if they could break through. He said Johnny Reb had been reinforced and was coming down on us with four lines of bullets. Well, our generals were not long in filling two lines of works with men, besides sending up two more lines of battle with orders for them to entrench themselves, which they did. Everything was done with dispatch and Johnny, instead of catching us napping would have caught the biggest kind of a flogging and lost his own works in the bargain. For we should have made a counter charge and followed them into their works. At 3 o'clock a.m.

we were given orders to fresh cap our guns, fix our bayonets, and stand ready to give Johnny fits. The night wore away and daylight came, but Johnny let his discretion, not his valor, govern his actions and just laid still. It was well for him that he did, for we had four lines in the works and at least one more good line of battery one-hundred rods back, all packed and ready to come up.

It started raining—too hard to write on the skirmish line.

. . .

July 20th

Have had my breakfast and been to the sutler and tried to get some things with this $5.00 you sent, but it is no go. So, I shall have to go without tobacco, write letters with a pencil, and do as best I can without them. Nothing but greenbacks are good for anything here. I am well for all that I know, but I am dreadfully disappointed about the money. If you send me any money, send Abe's greenback plasters.

Your affectionate husband,

Chas. F. Biddlecom

UNION LINES NEAR PETERSBURG, VIRGINIA
147TH IN CAMP IN THE WOODS
JULY 23, 1864

Dear Esther,

Yours of the 17th was received last night. I am glad that you have been up to Farmington to see the neighbors. So, Mrs. Roberts is in a way to present Andy with another heir. I wonder if there is any limit to a full blooded Quaker's breeding propensities. If there is, I should like to know the number.

Es, how I should like now to be with you, but no, there is no such thing as a poor devil of a private having any of his desires gratified. I hope this coming draft will be the last that the country will be called upon to fill.

And I wish (but I dare not write it, for it is treasonable) that the people of the North would say to Abraham Lincoln, "You have spent enough of the money and wasted too much of what is more precious than (not gold, for that is an article out of the question) greenbacks, (which will soon sell for .26 cents a bushel, the same as potatoes) the lives of our northern men." I should be very glad and nothing would please me better than to have the men north say, "No, Abraham, you can't have another man of us." They say that misery loves company, but I am not mean enough yet to want to see men forced away from home and family and brought here to suffer and die for the miserable pittance of $16 per month payable in green-backed trash. Especially as I am fully convinced that whatever might be done by other men, Abraham and his advisers are not going to conquer the South this year, nor next. Nor do I believe that this halting, slipshod policy will ever result in a final victory. On the contrary, I can see my country going, going, going slowly but surely down to that bottomless pit of anarchy and ruin that so surely follows in the tracks of war, conducted as this has been without any definite end in view. For this talking about suppressing a rebellion and at the same time trampling underfoot lives and Constitution, the same that the Rebels are said to have violated. What then is the use of my firing into the carcasses of the d——d, rotten Confederates? Let Abraham draft 500,000 more men and he will find when election time comes that he has made 500,000 votes for his opponents. Go at it, Abe. Thank God your days are numbered and instead of cracking jokes over the grave of the nation, your weak head will be exercised in thinking how to eke out a sustenance and pay the taxes that your own folly has laid on your back. Excuse me, Es, I never will write any thing but news and won't cuss Abe any more.

I am well better than I wish. It would be a comfort to be a little sick for a few days so as to have a little rest, but I am distressingly healthy. I never was singly healthy or stronger than I am now.

UNION LINES PETERSBURG, VIRGINIA
JULY 27, 1864

Dear Wife,

Yours mailed the 21st came to sight last night and found me very tired and quite sick.[21] I felt some better this morning, but rather expect another pull down this afternoon. My complaint is of a bilious type, I believe it is something like ague and fever, and is somewhat intermittent. I have felt better mornings and then been very sick at night. For three days I have not kept any food on my stomach more than an hour or two before up it comes. I have eaten a crust of bread and drank a little coffee this morning and am in hopes it will stay down. I am excused from duty today and shall do my best to get well, but greatly fear that I am to have a run of the fever before I get well again. Don't be alarmed, for my constitution withstands a heavy fit of sickness.

Yesterday, I saw Henry Cline and Josiah Francisco, otherwise known as Di Cisco. Also saw Allen Cooper, cousin of Ed Brown, and two other fellows that used to belong to the Old 28th. A few days ago I was accidently found out by a man from Farmington. T'was no other than the notorious Peter Wagoner, Nate Aldrich's hired man, the same one that had the scrape with the Stafford girl. I think you will know what I mean without my writing more. I had a letter from Geo Peckham the other night. He is back in the Lincoln Hospital in Washington. He had been out only eight days, was returned to us most dead, weighing only 140 pounds. Well, if he had hard times, what have we had?

There has been a great deal of pick and shovel work done here and the works are, as yet, only just commenced. This campaign is to be one of picks and shovels, I conclude from what I see. The works are very extensive and it is getting to be very hard work for the Rebs to hit any of us. We were at work yesterday digging what is known in the military as a covert way, which is nothing more than a sunken road. This one is about ten feet wide and four feet deep, with the earth taken from the road piled up on the side next to the Rebs. A fellow might walk out with his gull and promenade up and down this road without being in any great danger of being hurt. I wish I could make a drawing of these works, but as I have not the distance and angles necessary to make a draft I can't make anything that would convey to you anything like a definite idea of what they are like.

So, Father would come here in a minute if called out? Well, he would wish himself home again in less than half a minute. If old Mr. Roberts wants to try government stock, I am sure his chance is good, and likely to be better. I am sure there is enough government stock in market. I wonder if Father don't think me getting disloyal. If so, I beg live to say that such is not the case, but at the same time I am not an admirer of Abraham's policy, nor do I see how the country is to furnish 500,000 more men without the business of the country suffering very severely. It looks to me as though at this time, in the midst of harvest and when the ground is being prepared for the fall sowing, that to take the men from their farms is almost like taking the bread out of the nation's mouth. I fear that the Army, however large, will never be able to wipe out this rebellion, and be it known that I am opposed to sacrificing the last dollar and the last man, as those that stay home are. I object to this new Conscription Act, for I think it gives the President too much power over the militia forces. I think the folks at home will think as I do if they could only see what I see.

Look for instance at the poor man with wife and five or six children (which is about the average number for a poor devil at the age of 40) forced away from home to serve his country for $16 per month (and get that very irregular), at the same time flour is quoted at $15 per barrel, potatoes $1.00 per bushel, corn $1.40, and pork from $40 to $47 per barrel. His monthly pay will not feed his family with the coarsest food that is wholesome, let alone clothe them. There is rent to pay, fuel to buy, and all to come out of $16 payable in a currency that is not worth half its face. At the same time every article of prime necessity, of food and clothing, are up to starvation prices and going up all the time. While a soldier's pay remains the same, the price of labor at home generally corresponds very nearly with the price of farm produce. If produce is high, labor is correspondingly high. If produce is low, labor corresponds at a low price. With a man in the army there is two things that are fixed. First, that he must serve until shot or discharged. Second, that some time within six or eight months after his miserable pittance of $16.00 is due he will perhaps get it. But what has become of this family during all this time? Where are they? Starved to death, begging, or in the almshouse. I think there should be exemptions in a conscription law again. I believe there should be such a thing as a money exemption from this fact: there are men in the country that are worth easily more to the country at home than they could be here, especially as privates. In fact, I believe that any man in business that employs a number of hands at a fair compensation per day is of more benefit to the country at large than he would be here.

Now, as for being a patriot, I claim that a man can be one and be an earnest advocate of peace at the same time, even should there have to be some things given to the South, even though she should come back under treaty stipulations instead of throwing herself at Abraham's feet. Now, if I were a Southern man, I should dreadfully hate to see an unconditional surrender. I don't believe we can ever compel them to come to the rest of Abe's *terms*. Esther, this is the last scrap of paper I have and if you want to hear from me, you will have to send some more.

UNION LINES PETERSBURG, VIRGINIA
JULY 30, 1864

Yours of the 24th came to hand this morning. Accept my thanks for the letter and the $5.00 greenback. I will try and see if I can't keep myself in paper, envelopes and tobacco. We were up and dressed for a fight again this morning, but were not engaged, being too far on the left to render aid to Burnside's darkies. They made a charge and took a pile of dirt that had been a Reb fort no longer than yesterday. Burnside had mined the fort and placed about twenty tons of powder under it and then the careless devil went and put fire to the powder and blew Johnny Reb skyward, fort and all together. So, I think the nigs did not have much of a job to take the fort. Well, it was all fighting and sufficed to kill off a few good men.[22] Things will finally settle down into quiet for a week, or so, to be followed by another campaign with the pick and shovel, for perhaps a month.

I don't think this war will ever end by fighting. This forenoon we had the most terrific cannonade since the campaign commenced. No doubt many Rebs were killed and wounded. We were not engaged. Our brigade has been very lucky lately. Some of the old regiments of the brigade, some of those that joined us since we left Culpeper, have suffered some owing to being too reckless. Probably they will learn to respect a bullet after a few more of them have paid the penalty of being too careless of themselves. I respect a brave man and despise a coward as much as any man can, but there is a difference between poking one's head in danger when there is no use of it and going into a fight and doing one's duty coolly and courageously. I think the man that gets hit, when by keeping himself down he could escape, is the veriest fool in the world.

My health is not first rate just at present. I am suffering with a tickling in my throat and considerable cough. My bilious complaint, I think, is cured. In just two years from yesterday and today, if living and well, I shall be on my way home. I don't expect to be discharged as long as the government can hold me. As for this war ending, I have not the least idea that time will ever come, at least while the North are as foolish as to furnish men and means. Whip the Rebs into submission? Fudge. I judge they are made of the same kind of stuff as our Northern soldiers, and for that reason there is no such thing as conquering them. As long as there is one on each side left, the war will go on. We were in hopes that Greeley's mission to Niagara[23] would result in something being done that would ultimately lead to peace, but we have seen our hopes nipped in the bud again for the ten thousandth time.

UNION LINES PETERSBURG, VIRGINIA
AUGUST 1, 1864

(Our fool of a lieutenant has been acting so while I have been writing this that I could hardly think. Hope you will make it out)

Dear Esther,

Yesterday afternoon we were marched from our old camp near the railroad that runs from Petersburg to Norfolk along the right of the line held by the Fifth Corps, joined Burnside's left flank distant something less than one mile from the point in Burnside's center where he mined the Rebel fort. After blowing it, two regiments of confederate infantry, and sixteen cannons skywards, Burnside made a charge with his darkies, or rather the nigs charged and took the debris of the fort and then made a dash for Johnny's second line. They were repulsed and driven back to the ruins of the fort where they stood their ground for some two or three hours and were then charged out of it and into their own works, losing very heavily. Darkey done well as long as the white officers stayed with them, but their officers were either drunk, or else, d—d dumb. A good deal of both, I guess. What officers did stay with their sable commands[24] acted like fools and would not let the Africans shoot at the Rebs. They even went so far as to make the men take the caps off their guns and unfix their bayonets. All this was caused, as we understand, by the Rebs coming down with their arms reversed, making the officers think they were going to surrender. When the Rebs got within short range, they turned their musket muzzles forward and gave the blacks a withering volley and then charged with the bayonet. Of course, the blacks run. There never was (were) men born that could stand such a charge. I don't want to kill another Reb, but I wish it had been our brigade there instead of those nigs. We would have poured the lead into them instead of standing there like a pack of deadheads. No officers in our brigade could have kept us from firing and if ever we had fired one shot, there would have went into the Johnnies' faces such a torrent of lead that human nature would have been unable to stand under it.

We were near being sent there and although I still have the trembles every time I think of a fight, I must say that just such a chance as the nigs had is what our brigade would like, i.e. if we have got to fight. If there is such a thing as hardship and danger it is reserved for our brigade. When we came here to Petersburg they were the first to find the Rebs, skirmished them into their first line of works, charged them out the first and into their second line.[25] Had the First brigade of our division done their duty and not acted like cowards, as they have done several times this campaign, we should have taken their second and last line of defenses, Petersburg and all. The ever glorious 147th has been nearer to and stayed longer under fire than any regiment in this army corps. For this we are more relied upon in a difficult position than any other. There, that is bragging enough for this time.

I started to tell you where we are. Well, we are on picket again, out of the pits and away from the front, off to the left and rear of the army doing picket duty to prevent Johnny Reb from any of his flank movements. The way it has been several times before, we go in and win the ground, then build the defenses to hold it until some other troops are sent to garrison them. We are put to picketing for a few days, then sent to hunt the Rebs out of the woods again and fortify a line under their guns. Well, we are the lads that can do all that kind of work.

But about that picket line, I have not told you about that yet. Well, it is in the pinewoods near where we were when we were guarding those bridges when we first came here from the other side of the James River. How long we are to stay here I do not know, but I presume for several days as the brigade is all out and our colonel is laying out camp somewhere near here. The First brigade is out further down on, or near, the bridges where we were away towards the James River. I suppose our division must be picketing as much as six or eight miles of line and as we are under pretty strict orders, I presume there is some danger of the Rebs getting on our flank and in our rear. We are to act as skirmishers and hold them back until the forces can be got in shape to meet them. Then you know, our supply trains are back well to the rear and we have to look out for raiding parties of Reb cavalry so that our time is likely to be pretty well filled with duty, but it is better than the dust and heat of the entrenchments. Not only that, but we are out of range of the Rebel shot and shell and that is quite soothing to a fellows nerves.

My health will improve out here very fast for we are out of the smoke and out of the noise and clamor of camp. Besides that, we are away from the rumors of all kinds of evil to our forces on one side and of wonderful victories gained by us on the other side, just as the different manufacturers of news happen to fall. As a general thing there is not one grain of truth in ten wagon loads of the stuff they get. Most of the news in the papers from this year is manufactured on the railroad where the boys get their water. 'Tis there where most all the politics is talked and 'tis there where the military movements are figured out. Now let me say, as foolish as you may think it in me for saying so, there is more good sound sense in that railroad cut than is to be found around our Division Headquarters just as there are more (or what would make more) good generals than there are officers in our division. Most any d——d fool can be an officer, but it takes a smart man to fill the place of private.

Es, I guess this war will end. Maybe not this fall, but before another spring anyway. Old Abe will have to make peace, for the army are getting sick of such work. By and by there will come along a man like Oliver Cromwell to pitch Abe outdoors, bag and baggage, and I hope there will come some such man, if he can't be gotten out without. But, I think Abraham has gashed his political throat 'til there is no use trying save his life. The army will vote against him four to one and by the time he forces 500,000 more into the army his political death and damnation will be accomplished beyond the hope of Salvation.

Tell Bayard to write to me and tell Stafford Papa can see just how he looks and guess pretty well how he acts. Emma, I should not know.

Isn't that too bad? Does Father ever say when he thinks I will be home? I should like to have someone's opinion about it, even if it was ever so wild. The old conscripts are laying up a fearful grist of revenge to be meted out to the government if they ever get a chance. *Let it slide.* Only think, they hold us for three years and make a new law drafting for one year, yet still hold on to us for the full term. I could shoot the getter up of that conscript law with a better heart than I ever did a Reb, for the lawmaker is an all mighty <u>sight meaner</u>!

Kiss my children for me. Tell my parents I have not forgotten them, and good night to you all. I must be going (to supper).

   C.F. Biddlecom

———

    PICKET RESERVE, PICKET LINE TO THE
    LEFT AND REAR OF UNION LINES
    PETERSBURG, VIRGINIA
    AUGUST 6, 1864

Dear Esther,

Yours mailed the first of August came to sight last night and as I am on picket (the quietest place I have found since we left the Chickahominy) I will write you while out here. We are out about one mile from camp and the nearest Rebels are over towards Petersburg where we left them confronted by Burnside's nigs. There is just as much musketry firing over there as has been for most of the two months past. I suppose we are three or four miles to the left and rear of our old place in the pits and I hope we may be left here as long as there is any need of having troops here. The duty is pretty severe, but not very dangerous. That is, we are on post just half of the time and this is what is called hard duty, but 'tis better than laying in the pits. I believe I shan't write any more about war in this letter.

Seems to me that Gates diarrhea yielded to medicine so easily that he was able to resume his business within twelve hours after receiving medical advice and medicine. Oi, bah! What a baby! Don't Mother think him rather much of an infant sometimes? He should have a taste of what we get bellies full of: a morsel of hardship, a crop full of hard tack and raw pork, washed down with copious draughts of strong coffee. If that is not sufficient, why we have the dulcet notes of war to still his nerves and lull him to sleep.

Bayard must be getting to be a pretty good fisherman to catch ten fish out of Mud Creek. I hope he will remember his scripture lessons better than I ever did. If he does not, he might as well omit them altogether. Of all the verses that I learned when a Sunday school scholar I can't repeat one. I always thought more of having a good swim in the outlet than I did of learning anything unless it was Deviltry. Well, I don't know but I am just as good a man and just as brave a soldier as I should have been if I remembered all those verses. You write that Stafford goes to school. Does he learn and are you quite sure that his health is good enough to warrant you in letting him go? I fear he is hardly strong enough to go to school. How much does he weigh? How much does Emma weigh? Stafford's picnics must be grand affairs. Does his grandfather think and make as much of him as ever? Poor Mother, how I pity her. She has had so many painful attacks of erysipelas.[26] I used to have it but of late have not been troubled with it.

Well, Esther, ere this you know that the dangerous point in the siege of Petersburg has passed and from present indications I think we of the Second Brigade have a further lease on life. I hope it will so happen that we will never be in another fight. Esther, did you ever have to do the advising and writing for half a dozen? If you have, you know how I am fixed. I have just wrote an English letter for a French man and just to hear him talk you would think I had done him an everlasting favor. His wife is English. I get to see some queer letters from wives to their husbands in the army, for how can I answer a letter without seeing it? This woman is smart as a whip. I should judge from the letter she writes that she composes and spells well, but the writing is somewhat blind and if I had not served a pretty good apprenticeship at reading just such, it would be hard work to make out some of the writing I am called upon to read. Well, it is somewhat vexatious to be bothered with other's correspondence, but as it is an act of benevolence, I suppose that I shall receive my reward "after many days."

I have a letter from George Peckham. He is transferred to the Veteran Reserve Corps, or what used to be the Invalid Corps. Wagoner was over to see me a little while ago. We have come to the conclusion to vote the Chicago nominee for president rather than to vote for Lincoln and the further continuance of the war, being satisfied that the emancipation of slavery is not to be brought about by fighting, and believing as we do that a peace is not attainable that will be honorable and lasting, believing furthermore that slavery has already received such wounds that it never can recover from them so as to be the controlling power it once was, and that it will, before many years die a peaceful death. And again, we believe that to waste more blood and treasure in this war will be productive of more evil to the white race than it will be of good to the black race. Recognizing the old established rule of the *greatest good to the greatest number*, we think that the obligations we owe to God, our whole country, our fellow man, and especially our fellow soldiers, and to our consciences, require that we should vote for peace. Though, at the same time we will fight on, and fight ever, if it cannot be obtained without.

Now, if there is any fault to be found with that doctrine let us hear it. I wish Laura would carefully examine the state of affairs and see if she does not come to the same conclusion as I have, that is: to support Lincoln is suicidal and is the last thing that is desirable. I think from the temper of the Rebels we meet on picket that a very advantageous peace can be made and one that will result in the final overthrow of the institution of slavery. Only Abraham must not ask too much at one time. If a treaty can be made that will bring about the abolition of slavery in fifty years, or even twice that time, is it not better to make it than it is to go on making the earth desolate, filling the country with mourning for lost kindred? Answer in reason. Answer, for I wish to know the temper of folks at home.

I think Laura owes me a letter. I am your,

> *Charlie*

———•———

PETERSBURG, VIRGINIA
AUGUST 12, 1864

Dear Esther,

Yours of the third was duly received and should have been answered several days since — that is, two or three days ago. I was on picket when I received it and calculated to have answered it before we came in, but the weather was so hot and I felt so tired and dull it seemed to be a great task to write. We were on post two days and two nights without relief and as we were up the greater portion of the night, I was so sleepy that I should have slept like a log if it had not been for flies so thick that we almost breathe them. At any rate, I ask pardon for not writing from the picket line. I almost always like to write from the picket line. Everything is so quiet out there that a fellow knows of a certainty that the four hours he is not out as vedette[27] are his own and he is not able to be disturbed.

Es, we are in the same camp as when I wrote last and have got it all fixed up in fine style and will probably have to leave it in a few days, for we never stay long after camp is nicely fixed and policed (military for cleaned). Rumor is busy finding out a place for this poor, hacked about brigade to be sent to. Well, you should not wonder if we were out of this in a day or two or if we are here 'til next year this time. I shall not be much disappointed. There is no signs of the paymaster yet. Wonder if Old Abe knows that the machine he runs is fast going to the Devil for the want of oiling. Soldiers won't fight without pay and rations.

. . .

Sunday, August 14 We were withdrawn from the picket this morning and have all our traps packed for a long march. We have moved about two miles and are laying off in a deserted camp of the Second Corps. Where we are about to go is beyond a guess. If it is into a fight, may God protect me as I believe He has done heretofore. I will conjecture nothing for fear that I may be wrong. If everything goes smoothly with me I shall write again soon. Until then, I must defer answering your letter in detail.

I remember leaving a letter for my parents in case I were killed. I wrote two, one I destroyed and the other I left. I can't tell what I wrote and as I directed it not to be opened unless I am killed; it will be time then for you to know. Be assured that there is nothing in it that will injure you. I can only hope that this move will be as all our last moves have been, for the better.

Esther, I must bid you goodbye and if this is the last time I write to you, be sure that Charlie fell doing his duty, aye, more than his duty to his poor, sin cursed country and its weak administration.

Kisses for you and the children. Your affectionate husband,

    Chas. F. Biddlecom

I saw Sampson Fry, Smith Crocker, and Leote Chilson Sunday the 7th. They were well and felt well. James Foley is all right. Have Father tell his brother Frank.

———

FROM THE WELDON RAILROAD
AND THE VAUGHN PIKE

This morning they tell us the Second Corps have the south side of Danville Railroad. We have the Reb's flank turned and are closing in on them on the back side of Petersburg. We are within one mile of the doomed city with our left flank. This rotten Confederacy is tottering. Ere another month is past I do believe the Rebs will be smashed to atoms. Everything is going well and now I can hope for a return home.

I wonder how gold is selling about these days.[28] Down, down it must go. We will have an end of this. Every man from the least to the greatest means business. Harsh, but very effective.

Shot, shell, bullets, and for a finish, the long slim three-cornered awl

pointed thing whose cognomen is "bagnet" (bayonet). Grant won't be
denied. Meade, his lieutenant, and Warren, the ever present, cool, calculating, heroic, and determined, are at work pounding to powder the
Rebel forces south side of the Appomattox. Butler is north of them yet a
little while. We have them sure and certain as death. God preserve me to
help finish the work. Though, I regard the glory gained by fighting worth
but little as a generality, in this special case I will not give (if I come safe
through it) my experience for the best farm in Macedon. Especially if I
must be called a coward as are the sulkers.

We soldiers will have things our own way in politics when we get
home. I suppose it will be of a great avail for one of the Pettit Coat
Gentry, Home Guard, Fishing Pole Brigade, and members of the corps
of "*I would like to goes,* but Father is getting old and it would bring his
grey hairs in sorrow to the grave and Mother is so nervous, I am sure she
would mourn to her death if any thing should happen to me, besides, the
business requires my very constant attention and more than all, I am not
sound in health and would not live three months if I were in their army."
To ask us to vote for them after this . . . men will be put in office that
have a record of deeds done and not those that have wonderful professions
and only desire to be elected to show the community that they are great
men. Woe be to them.

The sacred heroes whose characters are carved in their flesh with the
horrid missiles of war will be very apt to say to them, "go to the D——l
you cursed sneak and let's have some one legged or one armed old war
horse that has been tried by fire and found true as the needle for the
pole." Lord, how I pity such fellows as our Brother Gates. He will have
to provide himself with a double eyeglass of extra ordinary power if he
hopes to gain office anything above postmaster.

Well this is a queer letter, but then a fellow has to write something to
fill up the sheet and get the stamp's worth out of government for carrying
it. I have received a letter from Laura but none from you very lately. Write
and let me know if you get the $50.00 I sent you.

We are expecting the Rebs to come down and see us soon, for they will try to get out somewhere. Woe to them if they come here.

Be of good cheer for the end is at hand. Kiss my babies for me and when you answer this tell me all about them. Laura says Emma has grown so she goes out to tea alone and like all the rest of the Biddlecoms, is a great talker.,

Good day Ester, I must go cook my dinner.

> *Chas F Biddlecom*

———•———

> PETERSBURG AND WELDON RAILROAD,
> VIRGINIA
> AUGUST 21, 1864

Dear Esther,

For the last four days we have been having rather exciting times. We have broken lines of communication between the Rebels and they are determined to drive us off and open the line again. They have tried our part of the line twice and failed each time. 'Tis now about three o'clock and we are anticipating another attack in a few minutes. The Rebels suffered terribly in killed and wounded this morning. Our brigade captured four stand of colors, some 500 or 600 prisoners, besides the wounded Rebels. We did not lose a man in two day's fighting. We did not see but one man hit in the brigade, and he killed by the premature explosion of one of our own shell. Everything seems to be going well all along the line and I begin to think we are doing something towards ending the war. Though, the least mistake will sometimes result in a defeat.[29]

This is the ninth day since breaking camp where I wrote to you last. The first afternoon we were on the skirmish line and a hotter place I never saw in my experience of war. Still, our company came out without loss. Company K lost one killed and two wounded. The second day towards dark the Rebs came down on our breastworks and tried to drive us out, but they took a whipping and then gave it up. Yesterday passed off quiet. We move in our lines to the left and threw up other and stronger lines of works. This morning the Rebs tried us the second time and got the biggest kind of licking. What is to come yet, God only knows.

I think Foley is all sound, yet I will go and see. I got a letter from you this morning with twenty-one postage stamps in it. I will try and write again soon. Praying to God and hoping that my prayers will be heard. I hope to be returned to you safe and sound ere many months. I don't see but that I fight just as hard and do as well as I did before I ceased to think of Abe Lincoln as a second Washington. I should no doubt fight as hard as ever, but it will be for the continuation of the Union and the Old Constitution, not for what Abe cares to proclaim every few days.

Kiss the children for me and tell my parents and sisters that I think of them very often. Should everything go smooth with me I will answer Laura's letter in a day or two. I may not be able to write for several days to come and perhaps never, but we will hope for the best.

Colonel Hofmann of the 56th PA Volunteers commands our brigade and Lieutenant Colonel Harney commands the regiment, Second Brigade, Fourth Division, Third Corps.

I am as ever your loving husband,

Chas. F. Biddlecom, Co. A 147th

P.S. Foley is all right, have Father tell Frank.

WELDON RAILROAD NEAR REAMS STATION, VIRGINIA

AUGUST 1864

Dear Esther,

I will write you a few lines today to let you know that I am all right. Yesterday I received two papers, the Express and the Ambassador, and only a day or two before that a letter from you. I shall not be able to write you very long letters, but will write as often as possible. I see by the NY and Washington papers some other troops are getting the praise for doing things in the fight last Sunday that they had no hand in. The battle last Sunday and for that matter, Saturday too, was won by the hard fighting of the Fourth Division, Fifth Corps. Our brigade done the heft of the fighting and we ought to have the praise due us, for that is all we are getting in the way of pay for our services. 'Tis not fair to be robbed of what is our just due.

Esther, we were in a very critical position and part of the troops to right and to the left of us broke and ran away (fell back they call it to be polite), reporting to the batteries in our rear that the Rebs had our whole line. The batteries then opened fire on us with shell. One shell killed and wounded six of our men. Another went through the pit not six feet from where I was laying, trying to flatten so as not to get my back scratched with the shell as they passed. Now, there was never a Reb within fifty rods of our line, nor could they get any nearer, for we poured the lead out to them in regular hail storm style.[30]

Sunday the Second Brigade gave Johnny Reb a sound thrashing. 'Tis hard to think of, but at last I know that my rifle has not been fired without doing some harm in some way. Johnny Reb had taken cover in a ditch and when ordered to come in prisoner, he started to run away into the woods where our third line of troops lay hidden. I fired at him; he came down, and was afterwards brought in on a stretcher. He was a Rebel captain. He died in a little while after being brought in. I am sorry that his actions rendered it necessary for one to fire at him. My nerves were in just the right way, my blood was up and my former experience with a rifle was too good to let a Rebel get away. He has done fighting.

I have the old throat disorder come back again. I am afraid it will be a hard thing to care for here in the foggy weather. Should I get sent to the hospital, I shall try to come home on furlough. There is no such thing as a discharge in this army. I must say goodbye. I am ever thine,

Chas. F. Biddlecom

P.S. send me a pair of suspenders and a half dollar, if you have it to spare. Government owes us six months pay.

———·———

FIFTH CORPS, SECOND DIVISION, THIRD BRIGADE
SECOND DIVISION HOSPITAL NEAR THE JERUSALEM
PLANK ROAD NEAR PETERSBURG, VIRGINIA
SEPTEMBER 2, 1864

Dear Esther,

After all my checkered experience I find the last check filled with a hospital.[31] I came here this morning by order of the surgeon, sick but not dying, with some kind of throat complaint. I think the same that I had when I came home from the army before. How long I shall stay here or where I shall go, whether to the front again or to some general hospital, I can't conjecture. I think I have seen the last of the front for some time to come. My throat is very sore outside and inside. The outside is all blistered with oil and the inside is as rough as a grater. How or when it will be cured is not known to these doctors. I am not going to get well too easy if I can help it. Having done duty all summer without having called on them for any assistance, I mean more to take my ease at the hospital a while. If I get to Washington, I never will come back to the front again, i.e., as long as there is an invalid corps. Don't write me until you hear from me again. Don't worry for I shall do very well. I am your husband,

    Chas. F. Biddlecom

"Head down in the saddle" must be our motto these days for we poor, tired privates do not have an hour's peace out of twenty-four. The twenty-three and a fraction are occupied in shifting position or packing up and falling in to go, which is as bad as a march.

———·———

CAMP OF THE 147TH
ONE MILE EASTWARD OF WARREN'S ROAD AT
THE OLD YELLOW BRICK HOUSE[32]
(THAT IS PART OF THE HISTORY OF THIS CAMPAIGN)
THIRD BRIGADE, THIRD DIVISION, FIFTH CORPS
SEPTEMBER 17, 1864

Dear Es,

I received a letter from you this morning mailed the 12th inst. and was very glad to hear from home again. I expected to get it yesterday morning, but was not much disappointed, for I knew my letter from the hospital would cause some delay. I am very glad to know that you are, all of you, well and enjoying the comforts of home. My health is tolerable fair with the exception of a nasty sore neck caused by the cinchona oil I put on to cure a soreness on the inside, and the dilapidated condition of my left shoe, which has a bad fit of the out (being out at the toe, and out at the side, and the sole ripped from heal to toe and so far down on the side that when I walk it goes slip-flip-slap). I may say that I am getting on very well for one of my age, strength, constitution, and disposition.

You see by the heading to this (which, by the by, is near the middle of the first page) that we have had another change in the corps by which we have changed from the Second to the Third Division. Our Division General is Crawford,[33] all else remains the same except the badge, which will be a red disk with a blue cross. We lost in the transfer two regiment of Delaware troops and a battalion of Pennsylvania troops (the 157th), but are to have two regiments in their place. As we are now, the brigade is composed of the 147th, 76th, and 95th New York Volunteers, and the 56th Pennsylvania Volunteers. Our brigade is on the reserve. We have to be in a constant state of readiness to "dig out" to any point on the line that the Johnny Reb see fit to pitch in to.

Now, some folks might think being reserve was a nice thing, but they should just have a trial of it. If their general is anything like our gallant Hofmann, that is, as tireless as a wagon wheel and as vigilant as ever was a cat in pursuit of mice, then they would soon yelp out as we do, "Take us up to the front pits and let us remain there!" But, by the by, it is just because we have stayed in the pits and held them in the hour of peril that we have been sent to the rear as a reserve brigade. D—n this being too reliable. If we had ran once or twice it would have been easier for us now, but running is not in our composition. So, we are now called Warren's pets and if all Warren's pets have as much hard work to do as we, then the Old Nick catch Warren and all his pets. I had rather not belong to his pets, as most all of these pets are either killed, wounded, or captured in the course of time. No, I don't belong to the *Enfants Perdu* and have still a hope to escape all the casualties of war and return to you safe and sound when Grant's 60, 70, 80, 90, 100 days more, or less, shall have come and gone and this "Cruel War" is ended (by fighting, of course, and I am afraid that will be when the current of Mud Creek flows toward Bristoe and some other wonderful thing happens).

Rumor says that Johnny Reb captured two regiments of cavalry and the 2,500 beef cattle they were guarding near City Point yesterday.[34] If such is the case, the Rebs will be able to stand it a month or two longer, and not only that, but we shall be short our beef ration, and that would be terrible very! The beef is so good, so fat, and so tender. That is, if you call nail rods and India rubber tender. I am not sure, but I guess the beef will kill more Rebs than we shall with bullets. If it don't, their stomachs are capable of digesting even pig lead and tin scraps. However, I hope the Second Corps will succeed in making the Rebs leave some of the cattle behind them. Not for the meat, but just to keep them from driving them off to pasture beyond their lines, for I think a month or two good pasturing would make the beef tolerable.

The convention at Chicago[35] was a soulless affair and I can't go it, not a bit of it. I was in hopes that better things would turn up, but there is no hope in that quarter without some misfortune to our army. Little Mc will have a poor show, but without more telling victories Abe's chance will be slim, for the disaffected Republicans will cast to Frémont. This, and the McClellan vote, may carry the election to the House of Representatives and in that case Lincoln will be the next President. In spite of it, I don't like Lincoln at all, but I shall have to go with him or none, as he is the one most available.[36]

Tell the folks at home not to be so sanguine about this war ending soon, for things are not as favorable as the government would have them think. There is a great deal that has to be done yet before the war can end. Just tell them to look all over and see what has been done by this army since the fourth of May and if they can get any great encouragement of the review they are welcome to it, and I must say, they are easily satisfied. Tell them to keep their temper and not get too excited, for everything in this life works for good to someone and this war may be a benefit to some, but just who has not as yet developed in our vision. End it will, of course, but how or when, God in his infinite wisdom only knows.

There is nothing in the world so nice as a quiet little nook in some verdant prairie, especially after all the confusion and every other thing that is incident to soldering in this grand Army of the Potomac. No news in these diggings. Write to me who has enlisted in Farmington that I know and when you see Cack's folks tell them I am sorry if I offended them in my last letter. I think it no more than fair for them to write and ask an explanation. You may say the same to Andy Roberts for all that I care. I guess everybody's heart is as hollow as mine. I would not use a stamp, as mean as they have been about writing.

Kisses for you all and my affectionate regards to my parents and sisters.

Chas. F. Biddlecom

—·—

147TH NY VOLUNTEERS
IN THE FRONT LINE OF WORKS NORTH OF
WARREN'S HEADQUARTERS
OLD YELLOW BRICK HOUSE
PETERSBURG AND WELDON RAILROAD, VIRGINIA
SEPTEMBER 28, 1864

Dear Esther,

I read your letter mailed the 22nd last night and will write this morning for we know not what the day may bring.[37] We may have a fight, but the probabilities are against it. Off on the right, away beyond Petersburg, the sounds have been continuous for two days past, but everything is quiet in that quarter this morning.[38] It may be the quiet that precedes the coming storm and if it should break here on the Noble Old Fifth Corps, I trust we may be able to stand the shock. Everything indicates a big fight, but I can hardly think we will be engaged unless the Rebs try to drive us from this position. It looks like madness for them to undertake anything of that kind. We all think the hard fighting will be done down in Butler's front, but as I said before, there is nothing certain about it.

The paymaster is here at last. We have received our pay rolls and will be paid off today. I shall send you fifty dollars either in this or the next letter and you must make yourself and the children comfortable for the winter. I would send more, but I don't know when I shall get any more pay, maybe not for six or eight months. Be sure and have the children warmly clad for the winter and take good care that they don't catch colds that will make them sick all winter. Now is the time that they are most likely to get colds and it will be hard to cure them before spring. Put on their flannel, if they have not them on already. You must take care of those you have at home and not have too much solicitude for me. It won't help my cause a bit and only makes you feel bad for nothing. I know you can't keep from thinking, but all the bad feelings you have will not bring me home a moment quicker.

Esther, think this—that my lot is not the hardest there is to bear. Say, for instance, Dave Bowman's. Only think, if he gets himself clear of the Canada authorities, he will be despised by everybody where he lives. I should not wonder if his old mother went crazy over it (i.e., if it cost Silas anything like $2000, for there is nothing that can touch the old lady's heart so quick as the lop of the cash). I would like to be out of this, but not at the expense of my honor, for I have but little and any heavy drafts on it would use it up. If I can live this out and keep what honor I now have, I shall feel that there is one green spot in my life that Bayard and Stafford can look at without being ashamed to own that they were my sons. I do not expect to have much but a good name to leave to them and for that very reason I had rather be killed here with my face to the foe than come home to live the remainder of my life, be it long or short, abhorred by myself and hated by every good man, as I should be if I acted as the miserable dodgers that are running to Canada.

Well, as fast as the real earnest souled Union men have passed out, Horatio the Miserable Mean[39] has filled their places with his "faithful friends" and a more worthless set are not to be found in the army than are the officers of the 95th. Only a little while ago, a lieutenant and the Major had a fight and the lieutenant was dismissed. Both were full of whiskey at the time. Three or four nights since, the whole crew of them was drunk again and a fight was the result. Of such as these has Seymour been making officers. We have some of the same stress in this regiment and let me say that where there is a drunken brute of an officer, that same man is a Democrat and a supporter of little Mc. There are some very good men that support Mc, but by far the larger part are poor, miserable devils that are not worth the uniforms that cover them. We have some officers in this regiment that deserve (according to the Articles of War) a dishonorable dismissal from the army. Let the poor, miserable, Copperhead crew talk of having their freedom of speech abridged. The very fact that we have such officers in the army gives the lie to all such accusations. For I have heard them call Lincoln all the names that their evil minds could invent and they are not molested. Some of them deserved to have their speech stopped with a rope, but Abraham is wonderful in his mercy and so they will escape a hanging and live on to curse our (the private soldiers') existence until whiskey makes an end of them by killing them or getting them before a court martial or under charges for drunkenness and disorderly conduct and then they will have to travail.

I am afraid the Democrats are going to carry the state of New York in the next election and God help the poor private soldier from NY if they do. Seymour has been accused of placing hindrances in the way of the Union and the government of Lincoln and the officers that he has commissioned is as great a stumbling block as he ever threw in the fray, yet whatever he may do in the future and that will be all that devilish ingenuity can invent. How I wish I could have the privilege of showing to some of our well meaning, but sadly deluded privates the consequences that are sure to follow if McClellan is elected. But, it will not do to stir up strife and contention here at this time when it is requisite to success that we, all of us, act together as brothers. The most that I have said to any has been this, "I would not fight for one thing and vote for another thing directly opposite." And with this I have left them.

Tell Father that the Union must use every endeavor to get out all the votes on election day and if there is any weak kneed brother, to try and nurse him up and keep him alive until after the 8th of November, for be sure of one thing, you will want every vote now in Farmington. I know of many that voted for Lincoln (in 1860) that will vote the Copperhead ticket this election. There are the Bowermans and Plum and several more that will slip in snake tickets unless they are tended to, and that at once. If I were there, I could shame them into voting Lincoln or else staying at home, which is better than voting for Mc. Just have Father put Elwood Smith after Plum.

How long, oh, how long must I stay here? Twelve months have dragged their weary length along and I am still kept from home and family. Must it be that twenty-two months more have got to pass away before I can come home? Oh, horrors of horrors. How can I think of it and not be sick at heart? Well, let the good people of New York elect a Union governor and then I will try for a commission. I think I could get one now by lying and voting the Copperhead ticket, but, it won't do, oh, no. I can't say it, but I should expect to be killed the first fight I went into if I did, and I think I should deserve it.

The paper and pencil have not arrived. Something is getting wrong with the mail, I am thinking. Still, I shall trust this $50 with it knowing very well that if I keep it, I shall spend it and when it is gone, I shall be worse off than I shall be if I don't have it. I do but expect to be paid off in the field again. One of the boys in the Pioneer Corps[40] is very certain of going home, all hands, before election. That will be the only way Abe can get our votes. For we feel that the government has dealt out unfairly by us and there is but few of us that will so far forget the injury done is to us by those that inflated it, although it would be better for us to do so. This kissing the rod that a fellow get a lick with is not in a soldier's nature to put up with patiently.

Well, I must finish and hope that this will go through all safe and sound. Let Caleb alone a little while and maybe I will be there to settle with him. How are the folks getting along? I wish you would write to McVeigh's folks once in a while. I am sure they think a good deal of us both and we may live at the same neighborhood with them again some time, for I shall go west as soon as I can after getting home. I can't waste any more time pounding stone farms in New York. Kiss my babies for me and tell Bayard that he must write me a letter as soon as he can. I wish I were with you all tonight as I was one year ago.

> *Chas. F. Biddlecom*

—·—

OCTOBER 4, 1864
147TH NY VOLS
BACK INSIDE THE OLD LINE OF WORKS NEAR
THE OLD YELLOW BRICK HOUSE
WARREN ROAD, WELDON RAILROAD, VIRGINIA

Dear Esther,

Yours mailed the 29th was received this morning and though I wrote to you yesterday I still think I must improve this opportunity to write again.

Everything is on the move, no rest for men nor beast, night or day, all the time. I really believe our generals expect us to perform more labor than it is possible for flesh and blood to perform.

We moved back here after dark last night. The rumor is that Warren thought this a very important point and that in as much as there was to be but a small force left, he must have those that could be relied on. So, back comes the Third Brigade, Third Division, and I presume that we shall stay here for some time. Unless the Rebels pitch on we shall not have any fighting to do and if they do pitch on, the poor rascals will rue the day they ever undertook to break through the lines at this point.

Things look now as though our good behavior was to reap us a reward and that for all of our hardships we were to have a little rest. Our staying in the rifle pits the 19th of August after every other brigade had left, and our action of the 21st of August, has given us a name that we are very proud of. I am glad that our folks are proud of me for once. 'Tis so seldom that I have been able to do anything that meets with their approval. I am sure I have done everything possible for me to do as a soldier to make an honorable name as a private soldier, well knowing that should I live I should have my reward. If not in the applause of others, still I should have the approval of my own conscience, and that would be something that I would be destitute of if I had paid three hundred dollars or succeeded in making out a case of physical disability.

I am feeling first rate. My neck is well, my cough is no worse, and I hope some better. I am fleshing up some and do not look so poor as I did when I came home before. I have great hopes of getting home soon, maybe by the first of next month, but doubtful as soon as that. That I shall come home by New Year's Day, I have hardly a doubt.

Say, I must tell you the news. 'Tis this, General Warren asked General Crawford if he had any troops in these works (our works east and north of the Yellow Brick House) that he could rely upon in case of emergency. Crawford said he did not know and that all his men left here were recruits. Warren told him to send for Hofmann's brigade, that they could be relied upon. Now, is it not a big thing to belong to such a regiment and brigade as this is? Just to think that out of the whole Fifth Corps we should be the brigade most depended upon. Well, maybe being Warren's pets will be of some good to us after all.

We get the papers here every day and this morning we have more good news from Sheridan.[41] "Push along, keep moving," is all they say now a day. The Rebels are getting hard knocks every day and I hardly think the Rebels can hold Petersburg more than a week or ten days longer. We have seen the inside of their rifle pits and forts at last and now they must get, or be surrounded.

> Goodbye,
> Chas. F. Biddlecom

———

CAMP 147TH NY VOLUNTEERS
YELLOW HOUSE, VIRGINIA
OCTOBER 8, 1864

Dear Esther,

Yours mailed the third is received. The money I sent you was to make yourself and the children comfortable for the winter and I want it used for that purpose. The way prices are at present there is no more of it than you will want to clothe yourself and the children properly. Do not let the children go without the necessary clothes to keep them warm. Get Bayard a cap or hat and don't let him go with a straw hat for the sake of saving a little money. Money used in buying good warm clothing is put to much better use than in buying medicines to cure colds and fevers caused by going poorly clad. Get shoes for yourself and the children. Be comfortable first and then save what is left. You will find that there is nothing to be gained in the long run by going poorly clad to save a few dollars. Of course, you will not be extravagant, I know well enough, so use the money. I will send more, but don't know when I shall be paid again. If the next payday comes, it will be in about a month. I suppose that if I had sent you $10.00 more you would then wish to save all that with the fifty and then wish for some more to try and skinch along with.

It is important that I live and keep my health. My stomach does not take kindly to the rations we get at all times and I must have something else, even if it cost some cash. I owed a dollar bill to the sutler and after paying that and sending you the $50 out of the $90 I received, I am left full as short as I care about being. If I get paid the first of November I will send you $20.00 every two months while I am in the service, and more if I can. Perhaps I have been more extravagant than I ought to have been, but it is very hard to eat salt pork, hard tack, and fresh beef weeks and months together when a fellow can get anything else, especially when he thinks of home and knows that his family is living on the good things of this life. I don't put this in as a plea of justification for not sending more money home, for I don't think any is necessary. Do you?

I have this day cast my votes for Lincoln and voted the state ticket as far down as for prison inspector. A Mr. J.L. Lake is here from Oswego and of him I procured the necessary papers. The whole of them are consigned to the care of Joab S. Biddlecom, to be passed over to the Board of Elections the eighth of next month. Mr. Lake will take the envelope to Washington and it will be forwarded from there to Macedon by mail. No news at this point of any monument. I got your letter with the fine comb, but the pencil has not arrived. I will write again in two or three days if circumstances permit. Goodbye,

> *Your Charlie*

YELLOW HOUSE, VIRGINIA
OCTOBER 14, 1864

Dear Esther, yours of the eighth came last night and though I was glad to hear from you, still your letter has filled my mind with anxiety. I greatly fear the dysentery will attack some of you and from what you write I conclude the disease is of a very fatal character. You must be very careful of yourself and of the children. Be sure and keep them warm and do not allow them to be exposed to sudden changes of weather for it produces the worst consequences, especially in cases of dysentery. Now, I wish you to be very careful of Stafford. Don't let him play too hard as to tire himself out and he will not be near as apt to have the dysentery. You did not tell me what ailed Father. Has he got the dysentery? I am very anxious about you all. I fear the worst. What would become of us all if he should die? I dread to think of it and yet I can't help but fear the worst while I hope on like ever for the best.

I think it is my nature to be ever hoping for the good that is to come and to that very cause I attribute my fortunate escape. For while in the middle of danger with the very air filled with death, I have never lost that presence of mind so necessary to a soldier in action. I have thought sometimes that those that were badly frightened took so much pains to get out of danger that they run more risk than they would if they had kept their position and trusted Him who takes notice of all mankind. There has always been a settled belief in my heart that God would care for me in the hour of danger. I am far from being a good man. In fact, I know that I am a very wicked man, but for a long time I have striven to live a more consistent life. As yet, I have made but poor progress. It taxes my mind continually and I hope the day may come when I can say to myself, "Charlie, some of your faults are corrected."

Everything goes smoothly forward and every hour gives us advantages over the Rebels. Our brigade is camped a little to the right of Fort Wadsworth. I think we will be left here as a garrison for the right flank of the fort for some time, perhaps as long as there is any need of having troops in this quarter. When we move away from these lines the fate of the Confederacy will be decided and it is not necessary to speculate on what that fate will be. Any day from this time on may witness the execution of that masterly stroke that Grant is surely to give that will be crushing in its effect. The time is near at hand and Grant is not one of those that will be denied. The Rebels are very uneasy and, I may say, almost despairing. The hand of death is upon them, even now its fingers are closing slowly and there is no relaxing the grim grasp.

I think the month of November will surely witness the dissolution of this miserable confederacy. There is but one cause that keeps the Rebels going and that is the hope that the coming election will result disastrously to Lincoln and the Union. Though, even that will not save them, for Grant and Lincoln are determined to have an end of this. Even the election of McClellan[42] would spur the administration to a more persistent effort, if it were possible, than is being made at present. If McClellan is elected, we will have to assault the Rebels instead of waiting 'til starvation compels them to come out and fight.

There is a terrible rumbling away to the right. 'Tis not like the sound of cannon, but more like the sounds of exploding mines such as if Burnside was there. There has been three or four of them at different times this morning. Maybe we should hear that Fort Darling[43] has gone skyward and that the Rebs are closely shut up in Richmond.

This is my first day in camp in four days. Last night I came in from a three days trip to the picket line. Everything was all quiet, not a shot fired in our front and I may say that we had a fine time of it. Our regiment is now to do all the skirmishing for the brigade. We are to have the Spencer rifle,[44] a gun that has a magazine and shoots seven times without reloading. The seven loads can be fired while a fellow would count to a dozen and it can be refilled in less time than it takes to load one of our Enfield rifles.[45] We are able to fill the air with a storm of lead with the Enfield and when we get the Spencer we will be the worst snip the Rebs ever came in contact with. We are in no worse fix than when we were before, for we always have had the skirmishing to do and now we shall be rid of some other duties that we have had to take our share of heretofore.

I am tired and sleepy and can't write as I wish to. I will write again in a few days if I can get the opportunity. Be very careful of your health at all times and especially now that the dysentery is about. Kiss my children for me and may God take care of us all. Your affectionate husband,

   Charlie

——•——

Dear Esther,

I will write you a few lines this morning to let you know that I am still alive and have not forgotten you. Everything is as quiet as one could wish and as far as we can see, is likely to remain so for some time to come. I hardly think this brigade will ever be engaged in a fight with the Rebs again. We are occupying a position that is not assailable and the Rebel position is too strong to be attempted by the force on this part of the line. I presume we shall stay here as long as the war lasts and I look upon the war as virtually ended now. Though, there may yet be more bombarding and picket firing, we have come to regard it as of no account from the fact that it amounts to just nothing at all in the way of killing men.

  Our pickets and the Rebel pickets, where they are close enough together to hurt each other, made an agreement to shoot high first and before the second shot gets along the men are all stowed away in their pits. Then they crack away 'til they are tired out and not one gets hurt. The bombarding is pretty much the same in its results, for both sides have bomb cover and though shell and Old Virginia yellow dirt may fly nobody is hurt, or what is almost the same thing, probably not two men will be hurt in a week's bombing. This heavy artillery fighting is not more dangerous than the 4th of July celebrations, for they never are within range of muskets 'til after the infantry and engineers have built forts for them. Then all they do is fling shell at long ranges. Captain Dempsey[46] and I were talking this morning. He regards the war as ended, and he is a pretty good judge. At least, I have found his predictions come true in almost every case. We are some five or six miles from the extreme left and there is where the next fight will come off. That is, if there is to be another fight in this quarter, which I don't believe. Jeff Davis is on a trip south.[47] We think he has shipped, just as ships are sometimes cleared for the South and a market. In other words, we think he is off for Europe the first chance he gets to safely run the blockade.

Jingo, how my belly aches. 'Tis crying dinner and a quart of coffee that would kill a fellow anywhere, but in the army. I shall have to heed the call. I take it you are well, as usual, from the fact that I have not received a letter from you very lately. I presume I shall get a letter from you tonight or tomorrow morning. I guess it is contrary to the Quaker discipline to write letters any other day than Sunday, for I observe your letters are all written Sunday and Sunday night. That is the reason I get them so regularly.

Esther, I have great hopes that I shall see home once more, and that within 60 days. A drafted man's time is out as soon as the Rebellion is crushed. We shall all get our discharge as soon as the necessary routine can be gone through when it is evident that the war is finished. Keep good courage a little while longer and it will be all over. I could get a furlough now, but I had rather wait a while and see if I can get a discharge. With great love for you all I am your husband,

C.F. Biddlecom

———

CAMP 147TH NEW YORK VOLUNTEERS
YELLOW HOUSE, VIRGINIA
OCTOBER 22, 1864

Dear Esther,

Yours of the 17th was thankfully received yesterday. I mailed a letter to you the same day, but will write again today, for it is probable that I shall have plenty of time to write. We have been here one week tomorrow and have had the easiest time since we left Culpeper. I think we will have easy times as long as the war lasts. We may possibly get into another fight, but I doubt it very much. Night before last we received the news of Sheridan's last victory in Shenandoah Valley,[48] and last night the details were received. Such shouting as filled the pinewoods in this portion of Old Virginia is a sure indication of good pluck in the soldiers of the Army of the Potomac.

But, I must mention one thing. We have in our brigade a regiment of Copperheads from the river counties and the City of New York. They were as silent as the grave over the news of the victory. So much for the friends of Little Mac. From what I see of the 95th Regiment of New York Volunteers (so they are called, but bounty jumpers would be a name more fitting) I can but come to the conclusion that a Union defeat would (unless they happened to be in the fight) be more acceptable to them than a Union victory. Now, this same 95th Regiment has done good fighting in this war, but the officers that come out of it have been killed, wounded, and used up with hardships 'til there is scarce one of the old stock of officers.

'tis most pesky cold and windy here. The air feels as if it had whittled over a snow bank somewhere away up north. You need not pity me so very much because I have to sleep on the ground, for I get good, comfortable rests on my bed of bean poles and would not sleep in a soft bed if I had the chance. A plank is as good as I want and that is not quite equal to the poles. I sleep warm enough. As for rheumatism, that has been rained on, sweated out, and marched day and night 'til I think it has left in disgust at the miserable treatment it has received. I think it is time to quit. Write to Dan's wife and tell her to keep a courageous heart and all will come out right in the end, which is not far off.

Good night my Esther.

Charles F. Biddlecom

CAMP 147TH NY VOLUNTEERS
BETWEEN FORT HAYES AND FORT HOWARD
UNION LINE EAST OF YELLOW HOUSE
PETERSBURG AND WELDON RAILROAD, VIRGINIA
OCTOBER 26, 1864

Dear wife,

I have seated myself with my back against an old pine stump with a piece of board, a part of the cover of a cracker box, for a table, for the purpose of writing a letter to you. It may be the last. We will hope for the best while I anticipate the worst. We are on the eve of a great battle and one that I think will be decisive. What part we are to have we can't even conjecture, but I presume that we will have a position in the front lines where there is plenty of lead hunting up subjects for the grave. Such is generally the luck that attends us. I wish it were otherwise, but I think there is some terrible work laid out for us to do.

If we escape, I shall be very thankful. But if we are to go in, I hope the fight will end the war. If it takes a week or a month, I want to have an end of this life. If there is any more fighting for me let it come. If it is decreed that I am to be killed, why a few weeks or months in camp will make but little difference to me and if it is set down for me to come safe out, why, the sooner I shall be home. All that is left for me to do is "trust in God and keep my powder dry." I have come out of so many terrible places that I have some hope in my being saved to come home again.

Esther, if in the coming battle death should single me out, console yourself by believing that I meet the summons like a good soldier. "Hope on, hope ever" 'tis all we have to keep us from complete wretchedness. While we hope for the best, let us trust in Him whose care is over all. I always think of General Rice's words as we were going into the Battle of Laurel Hill on the eighth of May, "Steady, my brave men. God takes care of us all!" I have thought of his words every time we have been under fire since and even in the hottest of the fight, my heart has not failed me and my nerves have been steady. As my eye has glanced for an instant along the old Enfield, I have thought that to those few words of our General was due the victory of the eighth of May and perhaps the good behavior of our brigade in the difficult positions we have been in. I, for one, have certainly been a better soldier than I should have been if I did not remember General Rice's words.

Esther, my wife, what would I give to be through with this horrible job. Heaven knows how bad I dislike the killing of man even though they are Rebels. Oh, how I long for home once more. I think of you and the children very, very often. Yes, I may say constantly. I suppose a year has made a great change in the children. I can only think of them as I left them.

Sad and lonely is my heart as I write and my thoughts, my hopes and wishes are all with you, my dear ones.

Kisses for you all and hope in a union soon.

I am as ever, your Charlie

———•———

147TH REGIMENT NY VOLUNTEERS
BACK IN CAMP AGAIN BETWEEN FORT HAYES
AND FORT HOWARD
UNION LINE EAST OF YELLOW HOUSE, VIRGINIA
OCTOBER 29, 1864

Dear Esther,

We are back in our old camp again after a two days hard marching, one day out and one day back. We were not engaged with the enemy, but our regiment has lost one man, and he the one of all the regiment that we could least afford to lose. The lieutenant colonel of our regiment is missing. He is either killed or captured, probably killed. Lieutenant Colonel Harney[49] was too brave a man to be captured without making a great effort to get away. Rumor has it that he volunteered to lead a Division of the Second Corps in a charge on the Rebel forces and was killed in front of the charging column. Further than that, we do not know.

We, the 147th, deployed (if you know what that is) as flankers for the left flank of our brigade, which was on the left of the Fifth Corps troops. We were endeavoring to form a junction with the Second Corps, which was on the left of the whole army that made the move to the left of the line. What we were to do I can't tell, unless it was to go out and get the Second Corps threshed. Anyway, the Second took a sound flogging, all owing to General Hancock[50] trying to do the whole job before we of the Fifth Corps could aid him. Had he waited a half hour, all would have been well with him, but his dash got him whipped. It is not the first time.[51] So much for a man being jealous of another. I am sorry it happened so, for had everything operated as was intended it would have saved us the trouble of going out there again. Now, after everything gets quiet again, Warren will take the Fifth Corps and go and take the Danville Road without help, just as we did the Weldon R.R. after the Second and Sixth Corps were threshed trying to do the same job. Well, we are the lads that can do it. Rough as the work will be, we shall hurt the Rebs more than we get hurt. Though, that is but poor pay for the valuable men that we shall lose.

Our little Captain McKinlock has command of the 147th. He is brave and knows the men he is to handle. He is capable and the men in the regiment know it. Everything will go well, so far as the commanding officer is concerned. We were placed in several very honorable positions while out on this move and from what we hear we will be positioned such in the future. One position we had was to keep stragglers from running to the rear. We done it so much to the satisfaction of General Warren that were saved from going back out on picket. The next was to skirmish a body of timber to drive out all the skulkers[52] from the Second Corps. We made a clean sweep of it, taking about forty prisoners, which we turned over to the Fifth Corps Provost Guard. How long before the next fight will come off is quite uncertain but not before another ten or fifteen days have passed. I am now going over to the 111th Regiment. They lay on our right about three quarters of a mile distant. Frank Foley[53] is on picket, so I shall not see him. I will close by saying that I am trying to be truly thankful to the

Disposer of all things for my safe return to camp. I will write again as
soon as I get rested a little. *Yours forever, Charlie*

———

UNION LINES WEST OF THE WELDON RAILROAD,
VIRGINIA
THIRD BRIGADE, THIRD DIVISION, FIFTH CORPS
ACTING AS RESERVE AND FLANKER TO THE
FIFTH CORPS
OCTOBER 30, 1864

Dear Wife,

The army is out on another campaign and of course we are in the mess.
As usual, we are detached from our division (the Third) and are temporar-
ily attached to the Second Division. We have the responsible position of
protecting the right flank of that part of the army operating west of the
Weldon Railroad. We broke camp October 30th and moved up to the right
flank, which we guarded from early in the morning 'til some time after
noon and then we were trotted around to the center to be ready in case
of need to reinforce any part of the line the Rebs might attack.

We laid down in line ready to move at a moment's notice and remained
so for an hour or two. Then we were cantered off to the left on a double
quick to act as a support for a charging column that was to charge for some
house. What one I don't know, for when we got to the point of operations
it was quite dark. The charge did not come off as we calculated. So, we
were left as bait for the Rebs, to entice them to charge us whence we were
to fall back and draw them into a trap. Well, everything was fixed all nice
by daylight, the trap set with our brigade as the bait, but the Johnnies,
instead of fighting blindly, concluded it would be better to try and see what
was the nature of things in our position by chucking shell into our little
low pits. Well, all right. We fell back as per arrangement and Johnny Reb
charged, but came no further than our pits. The calculation was that they
would follow on after us and then two lines of battle that were all ready
on our right flank were to swing in behind them and force them on to a

force of ours that was in the pits that our First Division had taken from the Rebs the day before. The lines run as this:

We done our part according to program, but the other part failed I suppose. But it was no fault of ours. We reformed our lines inside, or rather, out the back side of the pits taken from the Rebs and in five minutes we were on the double quick for the right flank to keep the Rebs from outflanking and gobbling up the 15th Heavy Artillery, a Dutch regiment from NY City (and the sooner the Rebs take them the better it will be for our brigade, the lager beer drinking, and sauerkraut eating, cowardly scamps). We had to gallop down a road (engulfed by a Rebel battery) a distance of three-quarters of a mile. The air was more than vocal with the whiz of fragments of "Rotten Bulls" and the spherical case was rattling into the wood like hail on a barn roof. However, we were the boys to send on an errand of salvation to the Dutch and we came through without having a man struck, which I think was truly a miracle. We were in time and the Dutch were saved. We are now on the right of the First Division and have good works. We have the Vaughn Turnpike over which the Rebs have been wagoning supplies since we took the Weldon Railroad.

NOTES

1. Over thirty miles of elaborate trenches were dug from the eastern outskirts of Richmond to around the eastern and southern outskirts of Petersburg. A barren no man's land separated the two lines, sometimes only by a matter of yards.

2. Lincoln's reputation as a jokester was as endearing to some as it was offensive to others.

3. Charlie underestimated the resolve and ability of the Confederate Army. Grant's attacks in late June, the Battle of Jerusalem Plank Road and the Wilson-Kautz Cavalry Raid, damaged two of the five railroads supplying the area and extended the line of siege further west, but both railroads were back in operation within a few weeks.

4. Frémont and Cochran were nominated for President and Vice President by the Radical Republicans (an abolitionist party) at the Cleveland Convention in May of 1864, but withdrew from the campaign by September 1864, leaving Lincoln as the Republican candidate.

5. This was a battlefield rumor. Nothing was planned for July 4th.

6. *Habeas corpus*: The legal right of a person in free society not to be punished or detained without a fair trial. At the start of the war, Lincoln suspended the writ of habeas corpus "to suppress the insurrection existing in the United States."

7. *Brownlow's Paper,* a Whig/Republican newspaper published in Jonesborough, Tennessee, by William G. Brownlow, was notorious for printing blunt truths and denouncing opinions contrary to his own, regardless of the truth or possible impact.

8. *Spiking a cannon:* Disabling a cannon before it is captured by the enemy by driving a soft nail down the touch hole, making it impossible to ignite the gunpowder.

9. Grant began the Overland Campaign with about 118,000 men and suffered about 55,000 casualties, or 46 percent. This does not include the men whose three-year enlistments expired and left the army. A steady stream of reinforcements brought numbers back up to 125,000 by spring 1865. By comparison, Lee began with 64,000 men and lost half of them, but had fewer replacements. The Confederate Army attempted to hold Richmond and Petersburg with no more than 50,000 men.

10. Despite Charlie's pessimism, only about 30 miles of entrenchments were required to contain Lee's Army.

11. The United States Sanitary Commission, created in 1861, was a federally-chartered private relief agency created to coordinate the work of mostly female

volunteers who wanted to contribute to the Union war effort. Its purpose was to teach disease prevention and to supplement the government's provision of the basic needs of soldiers including food, supplies, medical care, assistance receiving benefits, etc. It was the pre-cursor to the American Red Cross.

12. Lapham, Ira Beal, age 32. Enlisted at Macedon, N.Y., on December 30, 1863; Ninth New York Heavy Artillery, Company C; severely wounded in the left foot at the Battle of Monocacy, Maryland; on July 9, 1864, his foot was amputated and he died at Alexandria, Virginia, on June 17, 1864.

13. Grant was the first lieutenant general (three stars) in the U.S. Army since George Washington.

14. The Battle of the Jerusalem Plank Road or First Battle of the Weldon Railroad, June 21–24, 1864, resulted in a slight Union gain of ground at a cost of nearly 4,000 mainly Union troops killed, wounded, and captured.

15. Chase, Salmon P. (1808–1873) Coined the Free Soil Party slogan: "Free Soil. Free Labor. Free Men," among other catchy, anti-slavery phrases. As a prominent member of the Republican Party, he served as the Secretary of the Treasury during the Civil War at which time he directed the establishment of a national system of paper currency. In June of 1864, Lincoln accepted his resignation and appointed him Chief Justice of the Supreme Court, a position he held until his death in 1873.

16. This could be Scales's Brigade, commanded at the time by Colonel William L. Lowrance.

17. Woodruff, Milton; resident of Springfield, Illinois. Enlisted on August 5, 1863, as corporal; September 9, 1862, mustered in 114th Regiment IL Infantry Company G; killed June 10, 1864, at Brice's Crossroads, Mississippi.

18. Robert E. Lee detached his Second Corps, commanded by Lieutenant General Jubal Early, and sent them on a large raid through the Shenandoah Valley and Maryland, eventually reaching the defensive perimeter of Washington, D.C. William T. Sherman's capture of Atlanta, along with Farragut's victory at Mobile Bay (the last major Confederate port open on the Gulf of Mexico), and the eventual defeat of Early in the Shenandoah Valley, positively influenced Lincoln's favor in the upcoming November election.

19. *Freedom shrieker:* A derogatory term, used for "fanatics" considered too vocal about anti-slavery opinions.

20. Sambo, Dinah, and Lucy were degraded, negatively stereotyped characters popular in minstrel shows performed at taverns, theaters, and circuses by blackface performers (white people corking their faces to portray blacks).

21. Absent from duty July 26–27. Diarrhea.

22. Battle of the Crater: On July 30, 1864, Generals Meade, and Burnside

attempted to execute a plan devised by the coal miners in the 48th Pennsylvania Volunteer Infantry to break through the Confederate line surrounding Petersburg. After weeks of undermining a confederate fort and filling the tunnel with explosives, it was blown skyward leaving a crater twenty-five to thirty feet deep and one hundred to one-hundred fifty feet in diameter. The saddest aspect of the Crater was that a black regiment of soldiers (Edward Ferrero's division) were well trained in how to maneuver around the edge of the crater, but at the last minute Meade got political cold feet about the ramifications that might occur if too many of those blacks leading the charge were killed. So, he and Grant ordered Burnside to substitute a white division. General James Ledlie's was chosen by lot and they were sent in without training. The black troops came in on the heels of the whites and all were trapped helplessly in the pit of the crater, but the Confederate troops paid particular attention to shooting down black soldiers. (The claim is often made that Confederate policy was to "take no black prisoners"). The failed attack resulted in significant Union casualties.

23. On July 18, Horace Greeley of the *New York Tribune* and John Hay, Abraham Lincoln's private secretary, met in Niagara Falls, Canada, with Clement Clay and James Holcombe, agents of the Confederacy. They presented a letter from Lincoln describing emancipation as a prior condition for any peace negotiations, causing the conference to collapse. Lincoln was publicly criticized when papers claimed that it was he who had sabotaged the chance for peace and mentioned nothing about the conditions he proposed.

24. *Sable commands:* A reference to black soldiers.

25. Major General Gouverneur K. Warren's Fifth Corps first attacked Petersburg on June 18, 1864, at the southern end of the Confederate line (the Dimmock line). The First Division (Brigadier General Charles Griffin) saw some heavy action at a point called Rive's Salient (where the famous Colonel Joshua Lawrence Chamberlain was severely wounded), but the Second and Third Division (Charlie's) saw little combat.

26. *Erysipelas:* An acute streptococcus bacteria skin infection.

27. *Vedette:* Sentry or picket on horseback.

28. The price of gold rose and fell with the public's confidence in military actions.

29. The Battle of Globe Tavern, also known as the Second Battle of the Weldon Railroad or the Battle of Yellow House, fought August 18–21, 1864, was the second attempt by the Union Army to sever the Weldon Railroad and cut the Confederate supply line. G.K. Warren's Fifth Corps destroyed miles of track and withstood strong attacks from Confederate troops under P.G.T. Beauregard and A.P. Hill. It was the first Union victory in the Richmond-

Petersburg Campaign, forcing Confederates to carry their supplies 30 miles by wagon to bypass the Union line.

30. Colonel J. William Hofmann's brigade began the battle in the center of the division line on Thursday, August 18, with the 147th NY deployed forward as skirmishers. The brigade was soon sent into action on their right to provide assistance to the division of Brigadier General Romeyn B. Ayres, which was being hit hard by the Confederate division of Major General Henry Heth. Charlie's division commander, Lysander Cutler, wrote in his after action report: "I at once sent to him my Second Brigade, Colonel Hofmann, who rendered him, as I am informed by General Ayres, very valuable aid, enabling him to hold his ground at a critical moment and to repulse the enemy. . . . I wish to urge upon the general the great anxiety I have to see Colonel Hofmann, commanding Second Brigade, suitably rewarded for his very faithful and gallant services. Since this campaign commenced the brigade has captured eight battle-flags and large numbers of prisoners." Hofmann's brigade was also attacked by the Confederates on Friday, August 19 (which Charlie somehow remembers as Saturday) and Sunday. In both cases the attacks were repulsed with heavy losses.

31. Charlie was marked absent from duty September 1, 2, 3, and 4, then returned to duty, before being absent from again on September 10 and 11, due to bronchitis.

32. Modern historians refer to this as Globe Tavern.

33. Crawford, Samuel W. (1829–1892) Though he was trained and served primarily as a medical doctor, Crawford learned to take command and fill a combat leadership role with some success. Author of *Genesis of the Civil War: The Story of Sumter 1860–1861.*

34. The Beefsteak Raid was a Confederate cavalry raid that took place September 14–17, 1864. Confederate leader Major General Wade Hampton led a force of 3,000 troopers on a 100-mile ride behind enemy lines to steal 2,468 cattle, eleven wagons full of supplies, and 304 prisoners, and herd them into Confederate lines.

35. The 1864 Democratic National Convention was held in Chicago on August 29–31, 1864, to nominate a candidate for President. The Democratic Party, fragmented between moderate Peace Democrats, proposing a negotiated peace (for Horatio Seymour); Radical Peace Democrats (Copperheads), proposing an immediate end to the war without naming a victor (for Thomas Seymour); and War Democrats, (for McClellan) ultimately nominated pro-war General George B. McClellan for President and anti-war Representative George H. Pendleton for Vice President.

36. This is the first time that Charlie reluctantly mentions his support of Lincoln.

37. From the Muster Rolls: Absent from Duty September 23–28th. Boil. Returned to duty.

38. The Battle of Peebles' Farm, also known as Poplar Spring Church, fought September 30–October 2, 1864, brought the Union closer to their goal of cutting supply lines in to Petersburg.

39. Seymour, Horatio (1810–1886) A wealthy Moderate Democrat politician known for his upstanding reputation and for dedicating his life to serving New York and the Union. He served as Governor of New York 1853–55, and 1863–65; opposed the 1863 draft because it favored the rich and was accused of encouraging the workingman riots that resulted from the draft with his famous speech which began, "My friends . . ."

40. *Pioneer Corps:* Also known as the Engineer Corps; built bridges, railroads, and to cut roads through forests, just as civilian pioneers had.

41. The Battle of Opequon or the Third Battle of Winchester on September 19, 1864, is considered an important turning point of Philip Sheridan's Shenandoah Valley Campaign. Several key commanders on both sides were lost, as well as approximately 8,300 men. Another Union victory boosted public opinion of Abe Lincoln.

42. McClellan, George B. (1826–1885) Nicknamed Young Napoleon or Little Mac. Graduated West Point in 1846, rank 2/59. Organizer and first commanding general of the Army of the Potomac, McClellan was well respected for his intelligent organizational and tactical plans and loved by his soldiers, but criticized for his overly cautious and indecisive leadership in battle.

43. Fort Darling was a powerful Rebel fort overlooking the James River blocking the route to Richmond.

44. One Confederate called the Spencer rifle, "that tarnation Yankee rifle they load on Sunday and shoot all week."

45. The Enfield rifle was basically the British equivalent of the more famous Springfield rifle. Both were "rifled muskets," single shot weapons, loaded from the muzzle, limiting the soldier to an effective firing rate of two or three shots per minute.

46. Dempsey, Joseph, age 40. Enlisted September 5, 1862, at Oswego, N.Y.; captain of 147th NY Infantry Volunteers Company K; for a term of three years. Five foot six inches tall with dark hair. Born in Ireland. The *Regimental Descriptive Book* states that he died on August 19, 1864. Charlie indicates otherwise. Other records show that he was wounded at Five Forks, Virginia,

and mustered out with his company on June 7, 1865, at Washington, D.C. His gravestone says he died in 1902.

47. On September 25, Jefferson Davis traveled to Georgia to confer with General John Bell Hood about his upcoming Franklin-Nashville campaign.

48. The Third Battle of Winchester was won by Sheridan on October 19, 1864.

49. Harney, George; age 28. Enrolled at Oswego, N.Y., to serve three years; mustered in as captain 147th Regiment NY Company B on August 30, 1862; major on March 1, 1863; lieutenant-colonel on December 25, 1863; captured in action October 27, 1864, at Hatcher's Run, Virginia; paroled, no date; mustered out with regiment June 7, 1865, Washington, D.C. In the Battle of Gettysburg, it was Major Harney who bravely held the 147th Regiment in position until they finally received the missed order to retreat.

50. Hancock, Winfield Scott (*a.k.a.* Hancock the Superb) (1824–1886) A career United States Army officer who served with distinction for four decades. Still suffering from wounds incurred at the Battle of Gettysburg, his defeat at First Hatcher's Run was the final impetus for his leaving the field.

51. Fought October 27–28, 1864, the Battle of the Boydton Plank Road (also known as Burgess Mill or First Hatcher's Run) was an attempt to cut the South Side Railroad, a critical supply line to Petersburg. Union troops numbering over 30,000 men withdrew from Petersburg lines and marched west, but were forced into a retreat. Confederates retained control of the railroad for the rest of the winter.

52. *Skulker:* A soldier who hides from work out of cowardice or laziness.

53. Foley, Frank, age 38. Enlisted at Manchester, N.Y., as private 111 Regiment NY Infantry Company A; mustered out June 4, 1865, Alexandria, Maryland.

CHAPTER 8

COMFORTABLE WINTER QUARTERS

OCTOBER 31, 1864

Dear Wife, I have just this moment received yours of the 23rd. I got the papers last night. T'was glad to get them and still more glad to get the letter. I have not much more to say. One thing, the tickets I voted first will come through all safe and in time. Those that Father sent I threw in the fire because I did not at the time think them of any use to me. What turn has Stafford taken that you think him liable for sudden death? Tell me all about it, will you? I must stop. I am very tired and nerves are unsteady. I can't half write.

> *Charles*

> CAMP OF THE 147TH
> BETWEEN FORT HAYS AND
> FORT HOWARD EAST OF THE
> YELLOW HOUSE, VIRGINIA
> NOVEMBER 4, 1864

Dear Esther,

Yours of the third inst. came to hand last night. I was looking for it and should have been disappointed had it failed to arrive. Laura's letter has not made its appearance yet, so I do not know whether I have any cause to be wrathy or not. What has caused the delay of her letter I cannot imagine for the tickets have been here a day or two, perhaps three days. I think my tickets that I gave in charge of Mr. John L. Leake of Oswego will reach Macedon in time for election.[1] Mr. L. is a very strong administration man and he came here on purpose to receive the Lincoln votes and forward them to different individuals to which they were directed. If those tickets that I sent by him fail, then I shall fail to vote at this election. I should be sorry to lose my votes, but unless Leake has lost the envelope, all will be right. At any rate, it is too late for me to think of sending a new package home at this late day.

Was George Turner wounded or taken prisoner that caused him to lay all day and all night on the field? How come he was stripped of boots and the rest of his dunnage.² Was he a Copperhead? If he was I am not sorry for him nor should I be sorry if they literally skinned him.

We have got our winter huts built and have moved in. Whatever projects we may undertake we shall come back here to make our camp for the winter, unless the Rebs evacuate Petersburg, which is not likely they will do. I am very sanguine in the belief that this war will end by the first of January and if Lincoln is elected next Tuesday, I shall expect to see some very prominent signs of peace before the first day of December. But should there not be any signs of peace by the first day of January, we, the drafted men in this army, mean to see if Congress will do something for us so as to make our term of service correspond with that of those called into service under the amended law. Or, in other words, we mean to try and get discharged. We have in this regiment some officers that are in favor of our being discharged from the service (not because we are not good soldiers) on the ground that our being held in the service after the fact of the last call for men for one year is unjust. I think Congress cannot help seeing the injustice done us and we are expecting that in the event of the war's continuance, we will be mustered out of service or given an opportunity to enlist in such regiments and branch of service as we wish. I don't desire a furlough unless it is positively certain that the war is to continue through another campaign. If it is likely to and everything else fails, then I am going in for a commission somewhere, if not a white one, then a black one. For serve as a private another year is what I don't mean to do. Goodbye my Esther,

Chas. F. Biddlecom

———

CAMP 147TH NY VOLUNTEERS
(OR WHAT IS TERMED "COMFORTABLE WINTER QUARTERS")
BETWEEN FORTS HAYS AND HOWARD, EAST OF YELLOW HOUSE
PETERSBURG, VIRGINIA
WELDON RAILROAD
NOVEMBER 8, 1864
ELECTION DAY

Today is to be decided (by the people) the election. Whether this war so far is success or failure, whether there is enough of the Old Union and the Old Principle of liberty of the past left to pay for fighting, to firmly establish the one and maintain inviolate forever the other, and by so doing cement anew the foundation and bind together more firmly the super structure of a nation of free men, or whether we shall abandon all that has been gained by abandoning the war for freedom, for equal rights and honest laws, since the landing of the Pilgrims.

Today is to be decided the future of American civilization. Whether it shall go on, on, on and upward 'til man in his glorious achievements shall have made himself (what he is calculated by Deity to be) but a little lower than the angels, or shall a policy be inaugurated that has for its object that total abandonment of all those rights and privileges without which man is but a brute, a policy that will bring down on us the scorn of all good men of whatever nation may rise from the ruins of what was once Proud America.

There is no middle policy left for us now. We have but one chance to choose. First, of Lincoln and the universal rights of man, let it cost of blood and treasure what it may to maintain them. Or, McClellan and another compromise with the Devil by which man is degraded and brought a little nearer to the Devil in everything.

'Tis night and I am writing by the faint lights of a miserable, poor candle and while I write I am wondering what the verdict is. Whether the nation is to live and prosper or go down the side of time to oblivion a miserable wreck, her name and place on Earth only known and marked in future ages by a few doubtful records and the debris of ruined cities. By adopting General McPendlton³ and Vallandigham Chicago Copperhead as our representative of principle, we turn our backs toward God and that which is right and look the Devil in the face and at the same time make a long, very long stride toward everlasting perdition (I don't mean an orthodox hell exactly, though I am not quite sure that we should deserve anything more mild). If Lincoln is elected today the war with Johnny Reb is but child's play, for they will see that there is a spirit in the free men of the North that will not be defeated, a spirit that is bound to win. And what is still better, it will show to the world that the Spirit of Seventy-Six still lives (today) and that the Fires of Liberty burn as bright as in days past and that we the people of the North and West are bound to live and be as heretofore the Universal Yankee Nation, in spite of Jeff Davis and all rest of his crew at home and his friends abroad. Now, I have rung the charge on this particular one thing and that is this, I think it altogether best for us poor soldiers that Abe be elected President and I believe he has this, the eighth day of November, 1864, been elected President for four years from the forth day of March, 1865.

. . .

Dear Esther, I am on guard this the ninth day of November and it is 4 o'clock p.m. I could not finish my letter last night in time for the mail. The first lieutenant would not give me a minute's time 'til after I had fixed the rafters and ridgepole of his cabin. After that I was tired and nervous and could not write. I am trying to make a finish of it this afternoon. Last night I received two papers, the Ambassador and a Palmyra paper, and also, a little bundle of cloth straps with a hard bunch sewed to them. I don't know what they are for, but I think in case I get played with a bullet in the leg or arm I could stop up the hole with one of them. What did you intend them for? Are they what the surgeon call compress bandages? Esther, I wish you would prohibit Laura from reading my very poor letters to anyone. The letters that I write are not intended for publication and I do not wish the learned ladies of Macedon to find out what a poor grammarian I am, nor what a soft head I am. I still have a little pride left. Humiliating as soldiering is, I am not quite devoid of all sensibility. So Esther, just say to her that Charlie dislikes the plan of having his inferior productions published to any except the family and I wish it understood that Mr. Addison Gates is not to know anything that I write. My sister, Sarah, I think has entirely forgotten me. Well, I am sure I can't help it, but I do some times think of her. So, Father thinks I had better get a furlough this winter unless I can get discharged. All right. Perhaps I shall do so. We have built quarters for the winter and I suppose our fighting for this year is over unless the Rebels make the attack. If the Union cause triumphed at the poles yesterday, our work is ended, for we are all very confident there will be an effort made by the South to come home to the Union again. Jeff Davis is not the only man in the South and there are those that are quite willing to come back again without asking any terms that we cannot grant with honor to our alms. I think Abraham is all right and I think the first days of January will see me in Macedon once more an a civilian again, too.

Esther, take good are of yourself and the children and I am sure all will go well with you. I trust God will spare me my life a while longer.

Love your affectionate, Charlie

CAMP THIRD BRIGADE THIRD DIVISION FIFTH ARMY CORPS
UNION LINES BETWEEN FORT HAYES AND FORT HOWARD
EAST OF YELLOW HOUSE VIRGINIA
NOVEMBER 12, 1864

Dear Esther,

Yours of the seventh came last night and, of course, I must answer it this morning. Now, before I forget it, I want to tell you how to fix postage stamps so they won't be stuck fast to your letters. When you send them get a piece of tin foil such as fine cut tobacco is put up in. Do them up in it, take care, keep the gummed sides apart, and have the foil next to the gum. By so doing you will save me a world of trouble getting them loose from the paper. I have to steam them sometimes and have spoiled quite a number getting them off.

Well, 'tis a good thing to have a wife that is thought so much of by people that even her scapegoat of a husband comes in for a small share of their thoughts. Well, I am much obliged to Mr. Tedman for his regards, even though it is all on your account. I should have liked it very much if I could have been at home for two or three weeks before election. I think I could have influenced some votes, but do not think I could have affected much just at the last minute. Certainly, not enough to have paid for coming home. Had I been home I should not have fought anyone. I can get all I want of that kind of victuals here. I have had my belly full of it several times this last summer. Tell Mother that I don't believe in fist knocking; when I fight, I want arms. So there would not have been any missing on my account, even if I had come home.

I don't care much about not being home to election as long as I can send my ballots home and have them count the same as they would were I there and cast them myself. Last night we got the news of how election had gone in enough of the states to make it very certain that Abraham is to hold over for four years longer. I saw, too, that the assemblyman for Western District of Wayne was elected, so I presume the Union ticket was triumphant in Macedon. We feel to thank the people of the North and West for this victory over the Copperheaded traitors that desired to, and meant to, give us a stab in the back by putting McPendleton over us. We could have got along with McClellan well enough, but his general's stars are all the Chicago traitors cared anything for. Mc's name carried with it a certain amount of strength that was all the Democracy cared for. Mc was the cat's paw with which they hoped to poke the chestnuts out of the fire with. Mc's politics were nothing to them; Pendleton was the representative of their policy. Well, let the whole crew go to the Devil together. Let McClellan change his base and make a masterly retreat for Salt River and the marshes that border on that dismal stream.[4] Let him put the Copperheads to ditching as he did the Union Army in the swamps of Chickahominy and if he has as good success killing off Copperheads as he did Union soldiers, there will not be any worth mentioning in four years more.

Well, after all, the election of Lincoln is not much in itself, but the principles established are of the greatest importance. First of all is the decision of the people: that they would maintain their nationality and that the foundation stone, the central base of our government as established by the Fathers of the Nation, should still remain where the builders laid it. That we would still remember that all mankind were created equal with certain inalienable rights among which are life, liberty, and the pursuit of happiness. Far, far beyond and above the mere election of Lincoln is the proclamation of the free men of the North and West to the whole world that we still are free and we mean that America shall yet be free, free to all of whatever kindred tongue or color. And that freedom shall extend over the whole nation, though it cost rivers of blood to firmly establish it. The verdict of the people is that there shall be no compromise with, no cringing to, no bowing down to, traitors in arms. But that we, the nation, can and will triumph over all treason, over all rebellion, and live on, on through the centuries as the greatest nation of Earth. Greatest nation because we shall be the most righteous people on Earth, for we will be like above Ben Adam.[5] We will love the Lord by loving our fellow man and our name on the Registers shall lead all the rest. (Get Laura to explain this to you.)

Now, how would it have been if Abraham had been beaten? The nations of Europe would have scoffed at us and asked, "Where now are your boasted free institutions? Where is your representative government? Gone, all gone. And you are on the downhill to ruin, and here goes for giving you a kick to help finish what your traitor son, Jeff Davis, has commenced." Before another ten years had passed the English flag would float over many a state that at this moment look up to Old Glory as she floats on high and is proud that her sons have fought and died to make her the emblem of our National Union and liberty.

I wonder if we soldiers are appreciated now. I wonder if we need any Chicago platform sympathy after the election just passed. I wonder if a blue uniform is a disgrace to a man. I wonder if we are a lot of thieves and robbers now. Who is sick now? We Blue Coats or the Butternut[6] Gentry that have Jeff for their king? Who needs sympathy most? We poor soldiers? Or the d——d and doubly d——d Copperheaded traitors? May God have mercy on their miserable "state and condition" as Southerland Gardner would say. Enough of this Methodist ministering.

And you need not let this letter be read to the Old Maids of Macedon for I don't wish them to know anything of me. For to them I am nothing but a rear rank private in the One hundred and forty-seventh. Let them get their information from Captain Mumford or some other blockhead in shoulder straps. My little light does not amount to much and if I have a mind to put it under a peck measure, or perhaps a top thimble, it would be better I should do it. Now, if you don't quit I shall commence my letters, "I now take my pen in hand" and write them out of one of these two shilling letter writers. I know that you and the family can appreciate what I write and will make all necessary allowances for mistakes of all kinds. I do not write to gain the good will of any of the folks in Macedon, nor do I think they care enough for me to make my letters any way interesting to them.

Everything goes on finely and today, Sunday the 12th, we are enjoying ourselves in our shanties. Generals Crawford and Hofmann have just been inspecting our camp. Who did Dar Catkamier marry? Tell me, will you? I am well and expect to come home to stay some time in January, if not before. Kiss the children for me and know by this that I am still your,

  Charlie

CAMP OF THE THIRD BRIGADE THIRD
DIVISION FIFTH ARMY CORPS
UNION LINES TO THE LEFT OF
PETERSBURG AND TO THE RIGHT OF
THE YELLOW HOUSE, VIRGINIA
NOVEMBER 20, 1864

Dear Esther,

Yours of last Sunday was in camp last Friday night, but as I was on picket, I did not get it 'til I came into camp last night. When we go out as pickets, we stay three days. We were relieved last night and shall not go out again for two or three weeks, i.e., if nothing unusual occurs. Everything was quiet in our front, so we had a pleasant enough time. Though the last 24 hours were rather wet, still we managed to get along without suffering any to speak of. We got off in a good time, for it has rained all the time since we left the picket line and it is quite cold today. So much so that the boys that relieved us must suffer considerably. We have had and are still having lots of work to do fixing up for the winter. I am in hopes that this week will see the end of shanty building and then we shall have easy times again until the spring campaign opens (i.e., if there is another campaign, which I think doubtful).

Esther, write to McVeigh's folks for I can get no time to write by daylight. We get candles only occasionally and those we save to cook and eat by when we are out all day at work and have to cook after dark. Say to them that I have not forgotten them and I will write a long letter to Ben just as soon as the hurry is over.

There has been a great quantity of water fallen for the last sixty hours and I conclude that active operations (in the army) have come to a standstill and will hardly commence again before spring comes. This is a queer climate. When once it gets a little wet the rain will continue to pour down for days and weeks together. Down falls the rain just as easy as if raining were the natural condition of the weather. Mud, mud, over shoe, (and there is a general order against a private wearing boots) half way to the knee and in places, a** deep. Just a good mortar for daubing a shanty or making a mud fireplace, just such as we four (Horace Jones,[5] Don Ferdinand,[8] Booth, Fifth Sergeant, and C.F. Vanvilliez,[9] and I) have for our home for the winter and I hope for the war. When I think of last summer's campaign, of the fighting, the marching, and the digging fortifications, I am sick of living and I really think I should go crazy did I know for a certainty that I had to serve another summer.

I suppose you would like to know something of our house, so I will draw you a plan of it.

All built of pine logs, six logs high and covered with four pieces of shelter tent. The bunks are wide enough to accommodate two men. Our bunk is a double-decked concern. The Deacon (Jones) and Don Ferdinand occupy the lower deck and the sergeant and C.F.V. sleep on the upper deck. I sleep backside, as usual, and the bed is just as soft as can be made from Virginia pine. Our coverlets, comforts, quilts, sheets, and blankets are all comprised in two army blankets and two rubber blankets. For pillows, our knapsacks do duty. Now, this bed is not as suggestive of ease as some I have slept on. Still, I must say that I can do some fast sleeping on it and wake up in the morning as fresh as a daisy and I think I should were it (the bed) a pile of rails, cord wood, or a coil of chain.

Send me three or four large sized needles and some good linen thread, some that is strong enough for fish line. I want to see if I can keep my pants buttoned up. I have done nothing but hunt buttons and thread for the last month and they are now as bad off for buttons as an old bachelor's shirt. If you have a pair of socks for me, please, send them along.

———

CAMP OF THE 147TH NEW YORK VOLUNTEERS
UNION LINES TO THE LEFT OF PETERSBURG
AND RIGHT OF YELLOW HOUSE, VIRGINIA
DECEMBER 2, 1864

Dear Esther,

'Tis time to write home again, so here is at it to see if I can write something that will interest you enough to pay for the paper and ink I shall use, to say nothing of the time it will take to write it. Thanksgiving Day has come again and found me a private soldier in the Federal Army. Well, I am thankful that I am alive this day and I should be thankful were there no day set apart for the express purpose of being observed as a day of thanksgiving and prayer to Him "from whom blessings flow."

Esther, I suppose you all had good victuals for dinner and enjoyed yourselves first rate. Perhaps Elder Lamb preached and prayed and you all listened to him. But, did he tell you how much you had to thank God for? Did he tell you that in addition to life, health, and bountiful harvests there was yet another great blessing to be thankful for, one that is to be ever enduring, one that is far above all the victories won by our army since the war commenced? I mean the great victory of November 8, 1864. For fear that he did not, I will preach a Thanksgiving sermon of my own. I think I will get along very well without a text, but in order to have it (the sermon) according to the regulation pattern I will take for my text a line from an old hymn: Praise God from whom all blessings flow. Praise God for the glorious achievements of our army. Praise Him for sustaining the American Nation through the perilous days of her infancy. Aye, thank God for the men of the Revolution whose hearts were filled with a love for justice that conquered the many adverse circumstances of Revolutionary days and finally triumphed over the oppression of the parent nation and established our American Union on the broad foundation of the Declaration of Independence and gave us for the charter of our manhood the Constitution of the United States. Yes, the charter of our manhood, for it is the charter of our freedom, and man without freedom is a brute.

Thank God for all this, but above all let us thank God that the Spirit that triumphed in ancient days is still alive. That from 1776 down through the years of trial and difficulty, on past the war of 1812, in the years of our prosperity and even to this day, the old Spirit of Liberty lives and, though often hidden under the black mantle of southern slavery, has again manifested its power in this year of trial, as it were, by fire. It has been with us in the calm, in the field when the fighting was hottest, and in the trenches by night, even the same as it was with our ancestors at Lexington, Bunker Hill, Saratoga, in the winter camp at Valley Forge, and in the trenches of York Town. Thank God those at home in the North and West have not forgotten the example set them by noble sires, but have been to the poles and with their ballots given to the world an example of unity of nation built by and given them by the "Fathers." Let the civilized people of Earth thank God for the election of 1864. Let them in company of the noble men of our armies and those still left at home thank God.

THIRD BRIGADE THIRD DIVISION
FIFTH ARMY CORPS
147TH NY VOLUNTEERS COMPANY A
DECEMBER 6, 1864

Dear Esther,

We have been driven out of our nice, winter quarters to accommodate the Sixth Corps. We moved yesterday afternoon and are now located outside of the rear line, some two miles back of where we were quartered. The weather is at present very fine. Though, there is the unmistakable smell of a storm. We are just laying off here in an old apple orchard, on a dry, sandy knoll, waiting for orders to do something. What it will be is only a matter of speculation, perhaps a dash for Weldon. Many think we are to take a trip to the Carolinas or Georgia to cooperate with Sherman.[10] I presume all our guessing will be at fault and we shall go to some point not thought of by any of us. Privates and officers will speculate about the future movements, let the prospects be what they may, and often the wildest seeming conjectures will turn out to be the nearest right.

There is something in the wind that smells very much like a fight, where or when is another thing. Well, I have hoped that our fighting was over and that before this corps would be in a position where there was a row in front, there would be something done for peace, but it looks like anything but easy times this winter, or, in fact, for as long as there is any fighting to be done. 'Tis a bad thing to be too reliable. Our regiment has a reputation for standing fire that is anything but enviable, especially when we want to have a rest. I sometimes think that we will be rushed in as long as there is but a man of us left. 'Tis nothing but the 147th and 76th New York, the rest of the brigade without those two regiments is not worth the rations the men eat. The three Pennsylvania regiments are assumed to run and leave us to fight it out alone, and they have done it some half dozen times this last summer. The 147th is the last to turn their backs to the foe and the first to rally for another trial, is the talk in the brigade, in the division, in the corps, and, in fact, in the Army of the Potomac. Wherever known our reputation is notorious. Johnny Rebs know our tar bucket hats and had as soon meet the Devil as the 147th. Well, 'tis all very fine to talk about, but to make the name cost us many a good man and no doubt it will cost us dear to keep it.

Some regiments come here and stay their time out hardly knowing what it means to fight. Other regiments, like ours, never escape a battle. The sound of shell and bullet are familiar to our ears, far more so than are more pleasant sounds. We can live on hard tack and coffee, with now

and then a ration of pork to grease our throats, while other troops laze off
and eat soft bread and Sanitary Commission stuff and so have diarrhea
and are kept from fighting.

Oh, how much I wish the government would draft a million men and
send them down here so that we could give them a taste of what war is. I
want the men that are drawn, not 1,000 to 1,500 dollar representatives. I
want men that have something or someone at home they think enough of
so that a sense of pride will keep them from deserting. Of the representative soldiers sent to this army more than one half of them are worse than
nothing. Lots of them have purposely been taken prisoner. Others have
deserted and are by this time in Canada. Many that came from NY City
have found their way back to that sink of pollution by way of Richmond,
Wilmington, or the Bermudas.

There is another game that the cowardly sons of bitches are playing.
'Tis this, they desert while on picket, go over to the Rebel pickets, trade
uniforms with them, then go down the lines in front of some other Union
corps, come in, give themselves up, tell a good story, get paroled, take the
oath of allegiance, and make for the north. As evidence of this we have
the fact that over 250 men claiming to have belonged to Company B 41st
North Carolina Infantry have come in front of the Second Corps. Now,
101 men makes a company of infantry in our army, and 'tis not to be supposed that the companies in the Rebel army are any larger than ours. So,
you see that there must be a screw loose somewhere. I think a large portion of those Rebel deserters belong to the Fifth and North Army Corps.
Though, there are also a great many Rebs deserting and coming to our
lines and lots more of them deserting and going home to the swamps of
the Carolinas and to the mountains of Old Virginia.

Now, at the same time the mercenary whelps that have been sent us
are going, going, going, I, for one, shall be glad when they are gone. They
must look wild, or some of them will get buttonholes shot in their jackets.
Now, if the North has no more men to send us, for Heaven's sake, let them

say so and not try to fill their quotas by sending us such a miserable lot of trash as those that came this fall. Let's have the draft and make the solid men of the north come out here and fight for the government and in situations under which they gained their wealth. Their farms are no better than mine was. Their families are no dearer to them than mine are to me. So, just let them come. This sending niggers, Irish, and Dutch from Amsterdam, Rotterdam Dutch, and God d——d Dutch, is played out.

. . .

'Tis after dinner and the speculations as to our destination are as numerous as ever, and it all points down the coast to some point in Georgia. How long it will be before we know what is to be done no one seems to know, or care. All I care is this, if I have got to do any more fighting, the sooner it comes, the sooner it will be over. God will take care of us all and we shall not die unless it is His will, even though the air be thick with leaden death. I will write again in a day or two. By that time, probably I shall know more of the move that is to come (i.e. if we make a move). Hoping ever for the end of the war to come.

> *I am your affectionate,*
> *Charlie*

—•—

CAMP 147TH NY VOLUNTEERS
REAR LINE SOUTH EAST OF PETERSBURG, VIRGINIA
DECEMBER 20, 1864

Dear Wife,

Your letter enclosing the five dollar greenback came to hand two or three days ago, but I have been very busy building cabins to live in and consequently have not written as promptly this time as usual. We did not get our old quarters back again, but are building new ones. We are located down the Jerusalem Plank Road, some six miles south of Petersburg and one mile east of the Plank Road. Our business is to guard the rear and live comfortable until spring, unless something turns up so that Warren is wanted for some fancy job, like our last raid. In that case, the Fifth Corps will have to be trotted out.

We, none of us, have any great love for the Sixth Corps. Last winter we had to give them our quarters at Rappahannock Station and Kelly's Ford. When we again turned out for them this winter, we concluded that we would burn our cabins if we are molested again. 'Tis not fair for us to have to be turned out of house and home every time there comes a corps to this army. If the Sixth Corps wanted the position, why did they not take it and hold it? Last time, when they tried taking the Weldon Railroad and got whipped, and the Second Corps with them at that, we took the railroad and fortified the line, and by all fair rules should have been left to hold the line as long as it was of any importance. However, the Fifth Corps is too good fighting stock to be left in an easy place, so out we had to go. Well, they are welcome to the position, quarters and all, if they will only let us alone for the winter.

By the last accounts, Sherman has Savannah, Thomas has given Hood a dressing, and Stoneman and Burbridge are tormenting Breckenridge in East Tennessee.[11, 12] There is lots more good news, all which you will see in the papers. Seemingly, there is but little armed rebellion outside Richmond and Petersburg. Well, when Sherman has finished his Georgia Campaign we will try and fix this nest of Rebels here in and around Petersburg.

I have great hope that the war will terminate this winter. I can't see for my life how or where the Rebs are to fight another campaign. They will not be able to keep a force outside of Richmond and we will only just fight them enough in defense to keep them from enjoying much sleep night or day. One hundred thousand good soldiers, in addition to those now here, would end the war, so far as fighting is concerned, in one or two days, and the fighting would not be very severe at that. The rest of the work would be watching them starve into submission.

I will write again as soon as the shanty is finished. Until then, you will have to be content with this. I received a letter from Cousin Emma and will answer her letter in a day or two. I think of trying for a furlough in January.

Kiss the Children for me.

Your husband, Charlie

———

[Charlie is marked absent on the Company Muster Rolls of December 31, 1864]

CAMP 147TH NY VOLUNTEERS
SOUTH EAST OF PETERSBURG, VIRGINIA
JANUARY 9, 1865

Dear Wife,

Yours of the third came to hand yesterday and from it I learned that you were anxiously looking for a letter from me. I knew you would be looking for it. I did the best I could and wrote as soon as possible, but henceforth I hope to be able to do better. The work is getting pretty well along. Even if we have to drill some, there will be time between the forenoon and afternoon that I can devote to writing.

There is no news in this division and the most that I can say is that my health is first rate. In fact, I can't remember a time when it was any better. I am fat as a pig and think I must weigh very nearly, if not quite, one hundred and fifty pounds. I feel first rate and have a good appetite. I wish I may come home feeling as well as I do now.

I have not seen anybody from Macedon or Farmington, except Father Wagoner, since we came back from the raid. I remember seeing young Wayne and a boy by the name of Norman. I think it may be possible for me to go over to the Sixth Corps this week and if I do I will try and see Young Whitbeck and perhaps some more of the Macedon boys. I don't understand why Mrs. Whitbeck should desire her son to get acquainted me. Surely, she must have received some very exalted opinion of me, better than I deserve. I am not the most desirable acquaintance her son could make and what little good I could do him would be but a slight compensation for the soil I might do him. Now, how it happens that Palmer does not get enough to eat is more than I can see. Insofar, we have plenty most of the time and what I call plenty these days ought to satisfy anybody.

So you think Emma a smart child. Does any body else think so? Well, I think it quite likely she is smart and full of mischief, too. And Stafford, what of him? Does he grow any and tell me, is he stronger than he was when I left home and will he be likely to grow to be a man? Tell me all about the children and the folks at home. I don't know that I care anything particular for Mrs. Dr. Whitbeck or Mrs. Elder Lamb. So, Es, write more about the children, and not so much of Aunt Lamb's troubles.

About Palmer and his not getting enough to eat, if he gets along without having to eat cold lard, or have a piece of three cornered steel rammed into his bowels, then he, nor his mother, ought to complain. Rather, they should thank God that he is permitted to do the duty of a soldier in the army unharmed by the deadly bullet or the glittering bayonet. Judge for the fuss the old women make over their sons. 'Tis that constant worrying of fathers and mothers at home that make so many cowardly sneaks here. Just let them think that there is One over all that cares for the soldiers, and will continue this protection, even through the dangers of battle. Not a sparrow falls without His notice.

CAMP THIRD DIVISION THIRD BRIGADE
FIFTH CORPS
WINTER QUARTERS OF THE
147TH NEW YORK VOLUNTEERS
SOUTH EAST OF PETERSBURG, AWAY IN DIXIE
SUNDAY, JANUARY 22, 1865

Dear Wife,

Your letter of the 17th inst. was received this morning. It came a welcome messenger from the dear ones at home. From the regularity with which you write I know when to expect them and it is very seldom that I am disappointed, probably not once when you are a dozen times. Everything goes on after the same old routine like a horse grinding bark in a mill. There will be no change until we take the field again in the spring. Then, if we are to have another campaign we shall have enough excitement. Our mule shed is not finished yet. We have about two days work to do on it to finish it. The shed is in the form of a letter L (50 x 50).

Yesterday was raining and cold. Today the weather is milder and very foggy. All last week I was saying to myself, "When Sunday comes I will take a walk over to the Second Division and hunt up Leote Chilson and Smith Crocker," but the rain of yesterday filled the brooks and swamp holes brim full so that this morning I concluded to wait a week. I shall take the first opportunity that offers to visit the Sixth Cavalry.

Now about a furlough, I presume from what Lieutenant Berry told me the other day that I can get a furlough about the middle of February and shall shape my actions accordingly. There has been issued an order from Brigadier giving furloughs to all soldiers in the brigade that have been with their regiments and companies since the campaign commenced. As I have been present in every engagement with my company, there will be no difficulty in the way of getting one. You remark that having to return to the front again will take away the pleasure of the visit. Well, what if it does? Can't a poor devil have a chance to try a change of bitter? So long as there is an abundance of gall and vinegar to gulp down, why may I not vary the dose a little and have for once a change? I am sure of this — that we poor soldiers are not over fed with sweetness. So, if I should have the opportunity to mix a fifteen-day furlough with all these long months of hard service, I think I shall do it. I guess you had rather have me come home, even if I did not stay more than two hours, than to have me go into the next campaign and get killed and never come home again. You see, this soldiering is rather uncertain business. We may have a fight in a week or two, possibly as hard a fight as any we ever had. Though, the signs do not look like it. In fact, everything indicates (to me) the close of the war before the end of March. I should not be the least surprised if tomorrow, or the next day after, or any day, the news comes to us that the war had closed. Still, for all that, I have before now been disappointed. I don't mean to get too sanguine in the belief that the war is to end without another fight, so that if I should be called on to go into another battle, I would be undone by disappointment. I think it best to be always ready, especially in times like these, and then I am never at a loss what to do. My musket is always in good shooting order and my cartridges dry. Five minutes is sufficient for me to get ready to move, and I mean to be on hand every time as long as I am in the army.

So the House is getting too small for you and Laura. Well, that is a trifle state of affairs. Where has gone her great heart full of patriotism? Why, less than a year ago nothing but Harpers Ferry or Hilton Head and a school of picaninnies was sufficient to satisfy her longing desire to do something very benevolent for mankind in general, and the sable portion in particular. Now, if there is anything in the world that is trying to my feelings, it's having anything to do with folks that are governed by impulse, instead of fixed principles. Don't let what Laura says in her peevishness have any durable affect on your feelings. 'Tis not worth minding. And, if mother is vexed at this, tell her for me that Charlie is not the foolish boy he once was, a year in the army has learned him a few things. One thing is to speak plainly and honestly what I do speak, but at the same time do it calmly and after a due consideration. The army is a very good school for hot heads such as I was, and if they are apt scholars, they can learn much that is very useful.

I am too much influenced by the impulse of the moment myself and I know that mother and Laura are twice as bad as I am. Sarah is not like any one of us. She grooms her speech, if not by principle, at least by a proper regard for the feelings for others. And Father, the stiff upper lip, the firm and unwavering, straight forwards step, tells very plainly what his character is. There is not the least bit of danger of his thinking the house too small, or that providing you a home while I am in the army, too hard. He has for a foundation something far better than impulse, 'tis a fixed principle that would support him on the cross or at the stake if it was tried, to the bitter end.

I think I begin to have a better insight of men than I used to and it is quite time that I did. Many things that I once thought harsh and unjust I have come to see better knowledge of and to see them altogether in a different light. I have come to the conclusion that they were not very far out of the way after all. Other things, actions and words, that at the time I looked upon as almost Divine in their benevolence, I have found to be only momentary in their existence, realizing that they were produced by impulse and not founded on, or even regulated by, any fixed and determined principle. Give me for a friend in these trying times the one that took my hand when I left home to join the army, and bid me go do my duty like a man, and at the same time assured me that my family should be taken care of. Tears and deep drawn sighs are very good for outward show, but, after all, they are not as satisfactory (to me at least) as the firm, unshaken lip and steady speech of him who bid me, "Go."

Now, if Bayard grows up such a wild devil as I was, I will put him in the army or navy as sure as shooting and I reckon that will bring him to his understanding. At any rate, I think the service has done me good. 'Tis a first rate place for thinking over one's folly. No place on Earth equals the picket for reliving the varied experience of one's boyhood and early manhood. During the midnight watch every sound is hushed and the very air seems stilled. While the picket watches think, think, think, 'tis all he can do to keep Old Lonesome away. Then, when the bullets fly and sundry erratic fragments of shell are seeking a fellow's life and he has to lay low in the pits to keep his light from being snuffed out, then is a good opportunity to reckon up and balance accounts with the world in general and a fellow's near relatives and family in particular. Many, many, many a time have I thought of the careless word or deed never recalled or amended and during those midnight hours would I have given almost life itself to have the opportunity of making amends for them. Not through fear of what is beyond this life, but in order that after my flesh had turned to dust, and my bones to traces of white lime, those that knew me in life could say, "Charlie is gone, and though his life was full of inconsistencies, still he was a good hearted fellow, and if he did not amount to much as man, still he done no one any harm."

NOTES

1. Nineteen of the twenty-five Union states allowed soldiers to vote by absentee ballot, but all states allowed soldiers to vote if they showed up in person.

2. *Dunnage:* baggage or equipment

3. *General McPendlton:* Portmanteau of General George B. McClellan and George H. Pendleton, his running mate.

4. This is a reference to McClellan's conduct in the Peninsula Campaign of 1862. Hit hard by Robert E. Lee in what became known as the Seven Days Battles, McClellan abandoned his plans to attack Richmond and ordered a retreat toward the James River. He euphemized that he was merely "changing his base" of supply. His flight to the safety of a boat while men were still in battle was a source of public ridicule, especially during his 1864 Presidential election campaign.

5. *Ben Adam:* Hebrew, *Son of Adam*, also *son of man*, implying a righteous man

6. *Butternut:* Refers to the orange shade of Confederate soldiers' homespun and dyed clothing.

7. Jones, Horace, (*a.k.a.* The Deacon) age 18. Enlisted August 5, 1862; Oswego, N.Y., to serve three years; mustered in private 147th Regiment NY Company A, September 23, 1862; mustered out with company June 7, 1865, Washington, D.C.

8. Ferdinand, Don; mustered in as private 147th Regiment NY Infantry Company I; transferred to 91st Infantry June 5, 1865.

9. Vanvilliez, Charles F., age 24. enlisted August 21, 1862, at Oswego, N.Y., to serve three years; mustered in as private 147th NY Company A; promoted sergeant; captured and paroled, no dates; absent at Annapolis, Maryland for muster-out of company.

10. Union Major General William T. Sherman had captured Atlanta, Georgia, on September 2, 1863, and had begun his March to the Sea, which would

reach Savannah by Christmas. Despite the rumors, there is no evidence of discussions at Army headquarters about sending troops from the Petersburg area to reinforce Sherman. In fact, Grant initially wanted Sherman to load up his men on ships and sail up to reinforce *him* in Petersburg.

11. December 15–16, Major General G.H. Thomas defeated Confederate General J.B. Hood in the decisive Battle of Nashville.

12. Major General George Stoneman's 1864 East Tennessee raid targeted the salt production facilities at Saltville, Virginia. Stoneman and Burbridge defeated the Confederates, under Major General John C. Breckenridge (former Vice President of the United States), at the Battle of Marion on December 17–18. Then, on December 20–21, the saltworks were captured and destroyed. The raid carried on through the Cumberland Gap to Kentucky and Tennessee.

AFTERMATH

There is a class of events which, by their very nature and despite any intrinsic interest that they may possess, are foredoomed to oblivion. They are merged in the general story of those greater events of which they are a part, as the thunder of a billow breaking on a distant beach is unnoted in the continuous roar.

—*Ambrose Bierce*

E VERYBODY knows how the Civil War officially ended. After ten months of siege, the lines protecting Richmond and Petersburg crumbled. Confederate troops escaped westward hoping to resupply near starving men and horses, but the Union Army played chase until Lee buckled and surrendered at the Appomattox Courthouse on April 9, 1865. Slavery was abolished (at least in a legal sense) and the states remained unified. Wars and battles end, but the victor is not always clear. Right, wrong, truth, and reason vary depending on perspective. The lens through which the world is viewed can make what is obvious and clear to one, seem distorted, backwards, and upside-down to another. Current counts estimate that one in ten men were lost to the war, either from death in battle or as a consequence of injury or illness. Consider now the number of survivors who returned home only to die shortly thereafter, those who endured long, but crippled lives, physically and emotionally, and the children never conceived. I agree with Charlie and the Duke of Wellington—next to a battle lost, the saddest thing is a battle won.

Despite the fact that Charlie used his gun effectively, I believe he meant what he said when he wrote that he was "a Quaker as far as war is concerned." The drive for survival plays out differently for everyone. One person shies away from danger by any contrivable method, whereas the next instinctively runs into battle, either unthinking and blind, or knowing full well that they simply would not survive their own conscience doing otherwise. After writing the last letter included in this book, Charlie was engaged in a few more battles and skirmishes, he took a furlough, and was again absent due to illness—I found only a handful of partial letters written by him about those final months of the war.

As he predicted, he returned safely home after being discharged on June 7, 1865. Charlie survived without reporting a single injury inflicted by enemy fire, yet he carried scars from the war for the rest of his life. From the hundreds of family letters, which I am still sorting through, it appears that shortly after the dust settled Charlie picked up a lifelong dependency on alcohol. Before becoming a soldier his family criticized him for being a slacker. After his return he was despised for being a drinker. It seems the best part of Charlie was developed and spent in the field. His daughter Emma's letters and journals give no indication that she, nor any of Charlie's family, knew anything about his military life, despite saving the letters. Charlie's life is marked by a weathered gravestone placed in the Macedon cemetery and by a legacy of freedom. He died on April 18, 1912.

Acknowledgments

I owe a lifetime of gratitude to my husband, Matt, and children, Sarah, A.J., Billy, and Anna, who made room for Charlie in their lives and never fail to give me their unconditional support and buckets of encouragement; they are the true definition of love. Thank you to my writing mentor, Fred Wilcox, for always pushing me and never letting me off the hook (even when I have such worthy excuses as "a dilapidated computer destroyed two years of work"). Charlie's letters and my understanding of them would have been shallow without the countless records, statistics, maps, and personal accounts, which are only available because of the diligent historians of all levels who devote their time to documentation, preservation, and interpretation. I owe more thanks than could ever be allotted by ink to historian and cartographer Hal Jespersen for giving me the guidance I needed to bring the project to this end. Thank you to the generous and skilled editors at Paramount Market Publishing in Ithaca, N.Y., who agreed to publish and polish my work. It is always my desire to "keep it local" and I feel lucky and grateful to have them in my backyard.

Above all, my deepest gratitude goes to those in uniform that risk their lives to protect the civil rights of others who too often go through life unrecognized, misunderstood, and underappreciated; to soldiers, thank you.

BIBLIOGRAPHY

Conover, George S., and Lewis Cass Aldridge. *History of Ontario County New York*, Chapter XXI, History of Farmington. Syracuse: D. Mason & Co. Publishers, 1893.

Davis, Jefferson. *The Rise and Fall of the Confederate Government.* New York: D. Appleton & Company, 1881.

Eicher, John H., and David J. Eicher. *Civil War High Commands.* Stanford, CA: Stanford University Press, 2001.

Evans, Jonathan. *A Journal of the Life Travels and Religious Labors of William Savery, A Minister of the Gospel of Christ, of the Society of Friends, Late of Philadelphia.* London: Richard Barret, Printer, 1844.

History of Macedon Academy 1841-1891. Fairport: Mail Stream Printing House, 1892.

McPherson, James M. *Battle Cry of Freedom: The Civil War Era.* New York: Ballantine Books, 1988.

Monuments Commission for the Battlefields of Gettysburg and Chattanooga. Final report on the Battlefield of Gettysburg. Albany: J.B. Lyon Company, Printers, 1900.

New York in the War of the Rebellion, 1861-1865. Albany: Lyon, c. 1912.

Perret, Geoffrey. *Personal Memoirs by Ulysses S. Grant.* p. 553. New York: C. L. Webster, 1885

Phisterer, Frederick. *New York in the War of the Rebellion.* 6 vols. 3rd ed. Albany: J. B. Lyon Co. 1912.

Report of the Adjutant-General. New York. Albany: Argus, 1895-1906

Shotwell, Ambrose Milton. *Annals of Our Colonial Ancestors and their Descendants.* Lancing: Robert Smith and Co. Printers and Binders, 1895.

The Union Army: A History of Military Affairs in the Loyal States, 1861–1865 — Records of the Regiments in the Union Army — Cyclopedia of Battles — Memoirs of Commanders and Soldiers, Volume II. Madison: Federal Publishing Company, 1908.

CHRONOLOGY OF LETTERS

INDEX

ABOUT THE AUTHOR

Katie Aldridge is a marathoner, elite class, and first-time author. She lives with her family on a historic farm in Upstate New York where she is still sorting through the box of letters and working on her next book. You may contact her at: *CFBiddlecom.gmail.com*